CONSPIRACY THEORY IN AMERICA

Discovering
AMERICA

Mark Crispin Miller, Series Editor

This series begins with a startling premise—that even now, more than two hundred years since its founding, America remains a largely undiscovered country with much of its amazing story yet to be told. In these books, some of America's foremost historians and cultural critics bring to light episodes in our nation's history that have never been explored. They offer fresh takes on events and people we thought we knew well and draw unexpected connections that deepen our understanding of our national character.

Lance deHaven-Smith

CONSPIRACY THEORY IN AMERICA

University of Texas Press

AUSTIN

First edition, 2013
Second paperback printing, 2016

Requests for permission to reproduce material from this work
should be sent to:
    Permissions
    University of Texas Press
    P.O. Box 7819
    Austin, TX 78713-7819
    utpress.utexas.edu/index.php/rp-form

♾ The paper used in this book meets the minimum requirements
of ANSI/NISO Z39.48-1992 (R1997) (Permanence of Paper).

LIBRARY OF CONGRESS CATALOGING-IN-PUBLICATION DATA

DeHaven-Smith, Lance.
    Conspiracy theory in America / by Lance deHaven-Smith. —
First edition.
        p.   cm. — (Discovering America)
    Includes bibliographical references and index.
    ISBN 978-0-292-74379-3 (cloth : alkaline paper)
    ISBN 978-0-292-75769-1 (pbk. : alkaline paper)
    1. United States—Politics and government—1945–1989.
2. United States—Politics and government—1989–   3. Conspiracies—
United States—History.   4. Conspiracy theories—United States—
History.   5. Political culture—United States—History—20th century.
6. Political culture—United States—History—21st century.   I. Title.
    E839.5.D44   2013
    364.10973—dc23   2012044739

doi:10.7560/743793

☰ CONTENTS ☰

≡ ILLUSTRATIONS AND TABLES ≡

Figures

Photos

Tables

≡ ACKNOWLEDGMENTS ≡

This book would not have been written without the encouragement of Mark Crispin Miller, a professor of media ecology at New York University. He convinced me to undertake the project and also helped me frame the analysis.

The book could not have been completed without considerable help from the great editorial team that is led by Theresa May at the University of Texas Press. I am a bit reluctant to single out any particular person on her staff because they work together so closely, but I would be remiss if I did not acknowledge the tremendous help I received from Sue Carter, who reviewed and edited the manuscript. No better feedback have I ever received on my writing.

In a more general way, my writing and research have benefited from ongoing correspondence with Aaron Good, a doctoral student in political science at Temple University. Aaron has an encyclopedic knowledge of American history and the vast literature on conspiracy theories. He has provided very helpful suggestions about manuscripts and has been an invaluable source of historical information.

My greatest debt intellectually is to Matthew T. Witt, a professor of public administration at LaVerne University.

He contacted me in 2006 after reading my article on elite political criminality ("When Political Crimes Are Inside Jobs"), and we have been collaborating on one project or another ever since. He has a wide knowledge of postmodern social theory and knows how to use it to gain insight into what he aptly describes as the holograph-like character of popular thinking and public discourse in modern society. I have learned much from him about cultural analysis, and it is reflected in the increasing attention I have been paying to the cultural implications of antidemocratic elite conspiracies.

I am also grateful to Matthew for bringing me into contact with Alex Kouzmin, a professor of public administration at Southern Cross University and the University of South Australia. The three of us collaborated on many projects. Regrettably, Alex passed away in 2011, but he lives on in our work, which still bears his influence.

CONSPIRACY THEORY IN AMERICA

≡ HIGH-CRIME BLIND ≡

G iven its title, you might think *Conspiracy Theory in America* is simply another addition to the long list of books criticizing conspiracy theories. You probably expect the book to blame the popularity of these theories on some flaw in American culture or character. No doubt, you have encountered this view many times, not just in books and magazines but also on radio and television.

The argument that conspiracy beliefs reflect cultural weaknesses that are peculiarly American was first made by political scientist Richard Hofstadter, who, in a 1964 essay in *Harper's Magazine*, said popular conspiracy theories stem from the "paranoid style in American politics." [1] This was a year after the assassination of President Kennedy, but Hofstadter was not talking about that. He was referring to right-wing fears of communism in the McCarthy era. Other authors over the years have traced conspiracy beliefs to, among other character defects, Americans' racial prejudices, hostility toward immigrants, distrust of intellectuals, and anxieties about social change, concentrated wealth, and secularization.

In short, if you are at all familiar with the commentary on

conspiracy theories—and it would be hard not to be, given the media attention conspiracy deniers and debunkers attract—you are surely wondering what more could possibly be said on the topic. Actually, however, the answer is, quite a lot.

This is because most of the criticism directed at conspiracy beliefs is based on sentimentality about America's political leaders and institutions rather than on unbiased reasoning and objective observation. Most authors who criticize conspiracy theories not only disagree with the theories' factual claims, they find the ideas offensive. Among the most common conspiracy theories are allegations of U.S. government complicity in terrible crimes against the American people, crimes that include the assassination of President Kennedy and the terrorist attacks of 9/11. For conspiracy deniers, such allegations constitute outlandish slurs against America's leaders and political institutions, slurs that damage the nation's reputation and may encourage violence against U.S. officials at home and abroad.

This visceral reaction to conspiracy theories is understandable. However, it often results in blanket dismissals that treat all conspiracy theories as equally ludicrous and insulting. In fact, conspiracy beliefs vary widely in terms of their supporting evidence and plausibility. Some conspiratorial suspicions make sense and warrant investigation, while others do not. For example, suspicions that elements of the U.S. government somehow facilitated the assassination of President Kennedy range from the theory that the murder was approved by the vice president and other top leaders to the view that the government just slipped up by failing to monitor Lee Harvey Oswald's activities during Kennedy's visit to Dallas and then concealed this from the Warren Commission to protect the FBI's reputation. [2] Although the first suspicion has only modest evidentiary support (but might still be true), the second allegation about the FBI's failure to keep track of Oswald and then covering this up has been fully confirmed. [3, 4] This does not necessarily mean the Kennedy assassination was an "inside job," but it does cast doubt on the official account of the assassination as a crime that could not have been prevented, and it raises the possibility that the FBI's culpability was more extensive than has thus far been admitted. In any event, a common mistake made by conspiracy deniers is to lump together a hodgepodge of speculations about government intrigue, declare them all "conspiracy theories," and then, on the basis of the most improbable claims among them, argue that any and all unsubstantiated suspicions of elite political crimes are far-fetched fantasies destructive of public trust.

The literature's hasty dismissal of antigovernment suspicions is not merely an incidental attitude, a bias in the balance of opinion for and against various contested claims. To the contrary, objective observation and analysis have been foreclosed by the very terms employed to frame and conceptualize the subject matter. Most important in this loaded language is the phrase "conspiracy theory" itself, or more specifically the meaning attached to it in use and application.

A Curious History

The term "conspiracy theory" did not exist as a phrase in everyday American conversation before 1964. The conspiracy-theory label entered the American lexicon of political speech as a catchall for criticisms of the Warren Commission's conclusion that President Kennedy was assassinated by a lone gunman with no assistance from, or foreknowledge by, any element of the United States government. Since then, the term's prevalence and range of application have exploded. In 1964, the year the Warren Commission issued its report, the *New York Times* published five stories in which "conspiracy theory" appeared. In recent years, the phrase has occurred in over 140 *New York Times* stories annually. A

Google search for the phrase (in 2012) yielded more than 21 million hits—triple the numbers for such common expressions as "abuse of power" and "war crime." On Amazon.com, the term is a book category that includes in excess of 1,300 titles. In addition to books on conspiracy theories of particular events, there are conspiracy-theory encyclopedias, photographic compendiums, website directories, and guides for researchers, skeptics, and debunkers.

Initially, conspiracy theories were not an object of ridicule and hostility. Today, however, the conspiracy-theory label is employed routinely to dismiss a wide range of antigovernment suspicions as symptoms of impaired thinking akin to superstition or mental illness. For example, in a massive book published in 2007 on the assassination of President Kennedy, former prosecutor Vincent Bugliosi says people who doubt the Warren Commission report are "as kooky as a three dollar bill in their beliefs and paranoia." [5 p. xv] Similarly, in his recently published book *Among the Truthers* (Harper's, 2011), Canadian journalist Jonathan Kay refers to 9/11 conspiracy theorists as "political paranoiacs" who have "lost their grip on the real world." [6 p. xix] Making a similar point, if more colorfully, in his popular book *Wingnuts*, journalist John Avlon refers to conspiracy believers as "moonbats," "Hatriots," "wingnuts," and the "Fright Wing." [7]

The same judgment is expressed in more measured terms by Cass Sunstein and Adrian Vermeule in a 2009 journal article on the "causes and cures" of conspiracy theories. [8] Sunstein is a Harvard law professor appointed by President Obama to head the Office of Information and Regulatory Affairs. He and Vermeule claim that once a person buys into them, conspiracy theories are resistant to debunking because they are "self-sealing." That is, because conspiracy theories attribute extraordinary powers to elites to orchestrate events, keep secrets, and avoid detection, the theories encourage their adherents to dismiss countervailing evidence as fabricated or planted.

In a book on technology and public opinion, Sunstein argues further that conspiracy-theory groups and networks are proliferating because the highly decentralized form of mass communication made possible by the Internet is altering the character of public discourse. Whereas television and radio provide platforms for debating competing viewpoints on matters of widely shared interest, the Internet tends to segment discussion into a multitude of small groups, each focusing on a separate and distinct topic. Sunstein argues that this splintering of discourse encourages extremism because it allows proponents of false or one-sided beliefs to locate others with similar views while at the same time avoiding interaction with competing perspectives. In Sunstein's words, "The Internet produces a process of spontaneous creation of groups of like-minded types, fueling group polarization. People who would otherwise be loners, or isolated in their objections and concerns, congregate into social networks." [9 pp. 82–83] Sunstein acknowledges that this consequence of the Internet is unavoidable, but he says polarization can and should be mitigated by a combination of government action and voluntarily adopted norms. The objective, he says, should be to ensure that those who hold conspiracy theories "are exposed to credible counterarguments and are not living in an echo chamber of their own design." [9]

In their law review article, Sunstein and Vermeule expand this idea and propose covert government action reminiscent of the FBI's efforts against the civil rights and antiwar movements in the 1960s. They consider a number of options for countering the influence of conspiracy theories, including public information campaigns, censorship, and fines for Internet service providers hosting conspiracy-theory websites. Ultimately rejecting those options as impractical because they would attract attention and reinforce antigovernment suspicions, they call for a program of "cognitive infiltration" in which groups and networks popularizing conspiracy theories would be infiltrated and "disrupted."

A Flawed and Un-American Label

As these examples illustrate, conspiracy deniers assume that what qualifies as a conspiracy theory is self-evident. In their view, the phrase "conspiracy theory" as it is conventionally understood simply names this objectively identifiable phenomenon. Conspiracy theories are easy to spot because they posit secret plots that are too wacky to be taken seriously. Indeed, the theories are deemed so far-fetched they require no reply or rejoinder; they are objects of derision, not ideas for discussion. In short, while analyzing the psychological appeal of conspiracy beliefs and bemoaning their corrosive effects on public trust, conspiracy deniers have taken the conspiracy-theory concept itself for granted.

This is remarkable, not to say shocking, because the concept is both fundamentally flawed and in direct conflict with American legal and political traditions. As a label for irrational political suspicions about secret plots by powerful people, the concept is obviously defective because political conspiracies in high office do, in fact, happen. Officials in the Nixon administration did conspire to steal the 1972 presidential election. [10] Officials in the Reagan White House did participate in a criminal scheme to sell arms to Iran and channel profits to the Contras, a rebel army in Nicaragua. [11] The Bush-Cheney administration did collude to mislead Congress and the public about the strength of its evidence for Iraqi weapons of mass destruction. [12] If some conspiracy theories are true, then it is nonsensical to dismiss all unsubstantiated suspicions of elite intrigue as false by definition.

This fatal defect in the conspiracy-theory concept makes

it all the more surprising that most scholars and journalists have failed to notice that their use of the term to ridicule suspicions of elite political criminality betrays the civic ethos inherited from the nation's Founders. From the nation's beginning, Americans were fearful of secret plots by political insiders to subvert constitutional governance. Those who now dismiss conspiracy theories as groundless paranoia have apparently forgotten that *the United States was founded on a conspiracy theory*. The Declaration of Independence claimed that "a history of repeated injuries and usurpations" by King George proved the king was plotting to establish "an absolute tyranny over these states." Today, most Americans are familiar only with the Declaration's opening paragraphs about self-evident truths and inalienable rights, but if they were to read the rest of the document, they would see that it is devoted to detailing the abuses evincing the king's tyrannical design. Among the complaints listed are onerous taxation, fomenting slave rebellions and Indian uprisings, taxation without representation, and indifference to the colonies' complaints. The document's signers claimed it was this "design to reduce them under absolute despotism," not any or all of the abuses themselves, that gave them the right and the duty "to throw off such government, and to provide new guards for their future security."

The Founders considered political power a corrupting influence that makes political conspiracies against the people's interests and liberties almost inevitable. They repeatedly and explicitly called for popular vigilance against antidemocratic schemes in high office. Educated in classical political philosophy, they understood that one of the most important questions in Western political thought is how to prevent top leaders from abusing their powers to impose arbitrary rule, which the Founders referred to, appropriately, as "tyranny." Whereas Great Britain relied on common law to define the powers and procedures of its government, the generation that established the American republic developed a written constitution to set clear limits on public officials. Nevertheless, they understood that all constitutions are vulnerable to subversion because ultimately they are interpreted and administered by public officials themselves. The Founders would view today's norms against conspiratorial suspicion as not only arrogant, but also dangerous and un-American.

The Founders would also be shocked that conspiracy deniers attack and ridicule *individuals* who voice conspiracy beliefs and yet ignore *institutional* purveyors of conspiratorial ideas even though the latter are the ideas that have proven truly dangerous in modern American history. Since at least the end of World War II, the citadel of theories alleging nefarious political conspiracies has been, not amateur investigators of the Kennedy assassination and other political crimes and tragedies, but the United States government. In the first three decades of the post–World War II era, U.S. officials asserted that communists were conspiring to take over the world, that the U.S. bureaucracy was riddled with Soviet spies, and that the civil rights and antiwar movements of the 1960s were creatures of Soviet influence. More recently, they have claimed that Iraq was complicit in 9/11, failed to dispose of its biological weapons, and attempted to purchase uranium in Niger so it could construct nuclear bombs. Although these ideas were untrue, they influenced millions of Americans, fomented social panic, fueled wars, and resulted in massive loss of life and destruction of property. If conspiracy deniers are so concerned about the dangers of conspiratorial suspicions in American politics and civic culture, why have they ignored the conspiracism of U.S. politicians?

Finally, there is something very hypocritical about those who want to fix people who do not share their opinions. Sunstein and Vermeule say conspiracy believers need to have their discussions disrupted, because they are dangerous. But what could be more dangerous than thinking it is acceptable to mess with someone else's thoughts? Sunstein and Vermeule's hypocrisy is breathtaking. They would have government conspiring against citizens who voice suspicions about government conspiracies, which is to say they would have government do precisely what they want citizens to stop saying the government does. How do Harvard law professors become snared in such Orwellian logic? One can only assume that there must be something bedeviling about the idea of conspiracy theory.

Naming the Taboo Topic

In what follows, I shall attempt to reorient analysis of the phenomenon that has been assigned the derisive label of "conspiracy theory." In a 2006 peer-reviewed journal article, I introduced the concept of State Crime against Democracy (SCAD) to displace the term "conspiracy theory." [13] I say *dis*place rather than *re*place because SCAD is not another name for conspiracy theory; it is a name for *the type of wrongdoing about which the conspiracy-theory label discourages us from speaking.* Basically, the term "conspiracy theory" is applied pejoratively to allegations of official wrongdoing that have not been substantiated by public officials themselves.

Deployed as a pejorative putdown, the label is a verbal defense mechanism used by political elites to suppress mass suspicions that inevitably arise when shocking political crimes benefit top leaders or play into their agendas, especially when those same officials are in control of agencies responsible for preventing the events in question or for investigating them after they have occurred. It is only natural to wonder about possible chicanery when a president and vice president bent on war in the Middle East are warned of impending terrorist attacks and yet fail to alert the American public or increase the readiness of the nation's armed forces. Why would Americans not expect answers when Arabs with poor piloting skills manage to hijack four planes, fly them across the eastern United States, somehow evade America's multilayered system of air defense, and then crash two of the planes into the Twin Towers in New York City and one into the Pentagon in Washington, DC? By the same token, it is only natural to question the motives of the president and vice president when they drag their feet on investigating this seemingly inexplicable defense failure and then, when the investigation is finally conducted, they insist on testifying together, in secret, and not under oath. Certainly, citizen distrust can be unwarranted and overwrought, but often citizen doubts make sense. Americans are not crazy to want answers when a president is assassinated by a lone gunman with mediocre shooting skills who manages to get off several lucky shots with an old bolt-action carbine that has a misaligned scope. Why would there not be doubts when an alleged assassin is apprehended, publicly claims he is just a patsy, is interrogated for two days but no one makes a recording or even takes notes, and he is then shot to death at point-blank range while in police custody *at police headquarters*?

Of course, some suspicions go too far. The idea that lizard-like aliens from space are secretly infiltrating top positions in government and business is ludicrous. However, the conspiracy-theory label makes fun of conspiratorial suspicions *in general*. Consequently, the label discourages Americans from registering doubts about their leaders' motives and actions *regardless of the circumstances*. Any suspicions that public officials conspired to cause a tragedy or allowed it to happen are dismissed without further discussion because, supposedly, public officials simply do not engage in conspiracies.

Communication scientists Ginna Husting and Martin Orr,

both of whom are professors at Boise State University, have studied the use of the conspiracy-theory label as a putdown. At the beginning of a peer-reviewed 2007 article on the subject, they point out how the label works rhetorically:

> If I call you a conspiracy theorist, it matters little whether you have actually claimed that a conspiracy exists or whether you have simply raised an issue that I would rather avoid . . . I twist the machinery of interaction so that you, not I, are now called to account. In fact, I have done even more. By labeling you, I strategically exclude you from the sphere where public speech, debate, and conflict occur. [14 p. 127]

Husting and Orr go on to explain that the accusation of conspiracy theory discredits any explanations offered for specific social or historical events "regardless of the quality or quantity of evidence." The label has this discrediting, end-of-argument effect because conspiracy theories have come to be seen as mere suspicions with no basis in fact, not as reasonable inferences from circumstances and evidence about matters of great importance.

In contrast, the SCAD construct does not refer to a type of *allegation* or *suspicion*; it refers to a special type of transgression: *an attack from within on the political system's organizing principles.* For these extremely grave crimes, America's Founders used the term "high crime" and included in this category treason and "conspiracies against the people's liberties." SCADs, high crimes, and antidemocratic conspiracies can also be called "elite political crimes" and "elite political criminality." The SCAD construct is intended, not to supersede traditional terminology or monopolize conceptualization of this phenomenon, but rather to add a descriptive term that captures, with some specificity, the long-recognized potential for representative democracy to be subverted by people on the inside—the very people who have been entrusted to uphold the constitutional order.

SCADs are defined as concerted actions or inactions by government insiders intended to manipulate democratic processes and undermine popular sovereignty. [13] Examples of SCADs that have been officially proven include the Watergate break-in and cover-up; [10, 15–17] the illegal arms sales and covert operations in Iran-Contra [11, 18]; and the effort to discredit Joseph Wilson by revealing his wife's status as an intelligence agent. [19, 20]

Many other political crimes in which involvement by high officials is reasonably suspected have gone uninvestigated or have been investigated only superficially. They are included in SCAD studies even when the evidence of state complicity is contested, because excluding them would mean accepting the judgment of individuals and institutions whose rectitude and culpability are at issue. The nature of the subject matter is such that official inquiries, if they are conducted at all, are usually compromised by conflicts of interest. Hence the evidence must be evaluated independently on its merits, and decisions must be made on a case-by-case basis about which events are most likely elite political crimes. Of course, as Husting and Orr point out, engaging the evidence is precisely what the pejorative conspiracy-theory putdown is deployed rhetorically to avoid.

SCADs constitute a special type of political criminality. Unlike bribery, kickbacks, bid-rigging, and other, more mundane forms of political corruption, which tend to be isolated and to affect only pockets of government activity, SCADs have the potential to subvert political institutions and entire governments or branches of government. Committed at the highest levels of public office, they are crimes that threaten democracy itself. Clearly, such crimes and the circumstances that allow or encourage them warrant scientific study, both to better understand elite politics and to identify institutional vulnerabilities that can be corrected to make antidemocratic conspiracies less likely and less likely to succeed. Hence, one would have expected elite political crime, like white-collar crime, hate crime, and racketeering, to have been singled out for research and theorizing by social scientists long ago.

However, because powerful norms discourage Americans from questioning the integrity of their top leaders, and because anyone who raises such questions is likely to be seen as a "conspiracy theorist" who may be mentally unbalanced, the topic has been almost completely ignored by scholars. Social scientists have studied various forms of state crime, but in almost every case the potential for public officials in liberal democracies to subvert democratic institutions has been disregarded. [21; for an exception, see 22] Political science research on Watergate, Iran-Contra, and other U.S. political scandals has sidestepped questions about state criminality by studying the use of congressional investigations and independent prosecutors as political tactics in partisan competition. [23]

Of course, a vast popular literature exists that presents a wide range of conspiracy theories of domestic assassinations and other high crimes, but the form of analysis employed, while careful and in many ways insightful, is not really scientific. Amateur investigators have uncovered important evidence overlooked by official inquiries, but, with only one or two exceptions, they have failed to investigate the general phenomenon of high criminality and instead have speculated about one suspicious incident at a time. There is a body of work on the assassination of President Kennedy, another on the events of 9/11, and still others on the 1980 October Surprise, the disputed 2000 presidential election, and the anthrax letter attacks. To be sure, we do learn a lot about each case; we learn a great deal, for example, about the assassination of President Kennedy and the assassination of Martin

Luther King, but we learn next to nothing about assassinations in general, such as their typical targets, tactics, and timing, nor do we learn much about differences and similarities between assassinations and false-flag terrorism as political tactics. [24] By the same token, since we learn little about the nature of elite political criminality in general, we gain little insight into the extent, nature, and role of elite crime and intrigue in American politics.

Perceptual Silos

The tendency to consider suspicious political events individually and in isolation rather than collectively and comparatively is not limited to the conspiracy-theory literature; it is built into the conspiracy-theory label and has become a pervasive predisposition in U.S. civic culture. For Americans, each assassination, each election breakdown, each defense failure, each war justified by "mistaken" claims is perceived as a unique event arising from its own special circumstances. While Americans in the present generation have personally witnessed many political crimes and tragedies, we see them as if through a fly's eye, situating each event in a separate compartment of memories and context. [For an exception, see 25.]

Even when obvious factors connect political crimes, the crimes are thought of as disparate and unrelated. For example, John Kennedy and Robert Kennedy were brothers; both were rivals of Richard Nixon and were hated by Lyndon Johnson; their murders occurred less than five years apart; both were killed while campaigning for the office of president; and both appeared likely to win the upcoming presidential election. Without their murders, neither Nixon nor Johnson would probably have ever become president. Nevertheless, the assassinations of John and Robert Kennedy are seen as entirely unrelated; parallels, if they are recognized at all, are dismissed as coincidences. It is seldom considered that the Kennedy assassinations might have been serial murders.

In fact, in speaking about the murders, Americans rarely use the plural, Kennedy assassina*tions*. In the lexicon, there is the Kennedy assassination (singular), which refers to the murder of *President* Kennedy, and there is the assassination of *Robert* Kennedy. Clearly, this quirk in the Kennedy assassination(s) lexicon reflects an unconscious effort by journalists, politicians, and millions of ordinary Americans to avoid thinking about the two assassinations together, despite the fact that the victims are connected in countless ways and that they also deserve better—they deserve to be remembered as brothers who stood for the same values and who were somehow struck down by forces still beyond our grasp. This clever feat of keeping the Kennedy assassinations singular and separate might be called linguistic "compartmentalization," for, by avoiding the plural of "assassination," we have unconsciously split and compartmentalized in our awareness significantly related events.

For another example, consider how we compartmentalize our perceptions of the disputed 2000 and 2004 presidential elections. The election breakdowns are not widely suspected of being repeat offenses by the same network of political operatives employing the same tactics and resources, even though both elections were plagued by very similar problems, including inadequately equipped and staffed polling places in heavily Democratic areas, computer anomalies in the tabulation of county and state totals, highly partisan Republicans in charge of election administration, aggregate vote tabulations benefiting George W. Bush, and exit polls indicating that the other candidate had won rather than Bush. [26] The two elections are seen as separate and without any forensically important parallels. No one called for statisticians to review both elections for similar problems or signs of election tampering. No one speaks of "the disputed Bush-Cheney elections," or of "the back-to-back election disputes," or even simply of the plural, "election breakdowns."

A slightly different example of this phenomenon of compartmentalization is offered by contemporary perceptions of, on the one hand, the hijacked-airplane attacks on September 11, 2001, and on the other hand, the anthrax letter attacks that began a few weeks later. Today, 9/11 and the anthrax mailings are cognitively dissociated even though initially they were thought to be closely connected. It made sense to think they were connected because they shared many characteristics: they occurred closely together in time; both were acts of terrorism; both targeted private individuals as well as government officials; and both exploited essential services (commercial air travel and the postal service). In fact, for the first few months, the anthrax letter attacks were blamed on the terrorist group that was assumed to have carried out the hijacked-airplane attacks on the Twin Towers and the Pentagon.

Soon, however, the FBI investigation reached the conclusion that the anthrax came from a strain developed by the U.S. military at the Army Medical Research Institute of Infectious Diseases at Fort Detrick, Maryland. This discovery should have caused investigators and the public to wonder if the events of 9/11 might likewise have been connected in some way to the U.S. military. Alarm bells should also have sounded when, shortly after the anthrax letter attacks were discovered, the FBI authorized the destruction of a rare collection of anthrax samples at Iowa State University. According to scientists, this made it much more difficult to trace the anthrax in the letters to domestic laboratories. [27] However, rather than look for connections between the anthrax case, the 9/11 hijackings, and what appears to have been an effort to prevent the domestic origins of the anthrax from being discovered, everyone just dropped the anthrax attacks from consideration as a terrorist threat. Talk of duct tape ended. In effect, the anthrax letter attacks were quickly sealed off cognitively, and awareness of their domestic origins did not have to be reconciled with what Americans later learned about 9/11—about the warnings President Bush received in his daily briefing in August 2001; about the war games that were scheduled on 9/11, some of which included hijacked airplanes and interfered with the response to the real hijackings; about the expedited flights of Osama bin Laden's relatives . . . The list could go on. The point is that the domestic origins of the anthrax became a side story, and yet, at the time the anthrax letters were being received and people were being infected, the anthrax attacks appeared to be an integral part of a war on America.

But once the anthrax was traced to Fort Detrick, the fear was relieved and the crime was mentally cordoned off. There were no calls for investigators to look for U.S. military personnel with multiple connections to air defense, war games, and germ warfare. There was never any effort to identify government officials who were involved in national defense policy and who owned or had recently purchased stock in pharmaceutical companies that manufactured medicines for preventing or treating anthrax infections. To the contrary, rather than look for people linking anthrax, 9/11, air defense, and biological weapons, the investigation was narrowed to lone microbiologists who were considered to be disgruntled, emotionally troubled, or opportunistic.

Causes and Consequences

It should be stressed that this way of thinking about elite political crimes—this very common tendency to view parallel crimes separately and to see them as disparate and unrelated—is *exactly opposite the way crimes committed by regular people are treated.* If a man marries a wealthy woman and she dies in a freak accident at home, people would be suspicious simply because she was wealthy and the accident was improbable. If this same man then marries another wealthy woman who dies in a freak accident at home, foul play would naturally be suspected, and the husband would be the leading suspect in the wives' demise. If the husband had taken out a life insurance policy on either wife a few weeks or months prior to the accidents, it would be considered circumstantial evidence of foreknowledge. If police failed to recognize the obvious similarities in the wives' deaths, they would be considered incompetent, negligent, or bought off.

It is routine police protocol to look for patterns in burglaries, bank robberies, car thefts, and other crimes, and to use any patterns that are discovered as clues to the perpetrators' identity and the vulnerabilities to crime that are being exploited. This method of crime analysis is shown repeatedly in crime shows on TV. It is Criminology 101. There is no excuse for most Americans, much less criminal investigators, journalists, and other professionals, to fail to apply this method to assassinations, election fiascos, defense failures, and other suspicious events that shape national political priorities.

Why do we compartmentalize crimes involving political elites while doing just the opposite with the crimes of ordinary people? At least two factors discourage us from connecting the dots in elite political criminality. One is the term "conspiracy theory," which is applied to crimes that have major political consequences but not to other crimes. The conspiracy-theory phrase encourages cognitive compartmentalization because the phrase is not meant to apply to interconnected crimes. In American public discourse, multiple crimes planned and committed by a single group are generally called "organized crime," not conspiracies. The term "conspiracy" is reserved for plots surrounding one major criminal objective and for the networks that come together for that purpose. The Mafia is not a conspiracy; it is an organization. A conspiracy theory about the assassination of President Kennedy is implicitly a theory about a temporary combination of plotters, not an enduring assassination squad or lethal criminal organization. Therefore, even if we think the assassination of John Kennedy was a conspiracy, and we think the assassination of Robert Kennedy was a conspiracy, we are nevertheless unlikely to see the two as connected, because the conspiracy concept envisions them as isolated, self-contained schemes.

The second factor impeding us from drawing connections between political crimes involving political elites is that looking for connections requires being suspicious to begin with, and yet being suspicious of political elites violates norms that are embodied in the pejorative connotations of the conspiracy-theory label. As shown by our speech habits and observation tendencies about assassinations, disputed elections, and terrorist attacks, we are averse to talking about such events as connected in any way.

This aversion is learned. Americans know that voicing suspicions about political elites will make them objects of hostility and derision. The verbal slaps vary, but they are difficult to counter because they usually abuse reason. For example, in using the conspiracy-theory label as a putdown, conspiracy deniers imply that *official accounts* of troubling events are something altogether much more solid than *conspiratorial suspicions*—as if official accounts are in some sense without speculation or presuppositions. In fact, however, conspiracy deniers and debunkers are relying on an unstated theory of their own—a very questionable theory. In the post-WWII era, official investigations have attributed assassinations, election fiascos, defense failures, and other suspicious events to such unpredictable, idiosyncratic forces as lone gunmen, antiquated voting equipment, bureaucratic bumbling, innocent mistakes, and, in the case of 9/11 (to quote the 9/11 Commission, p. 339), a "failure of imagination." In effect, official accounts of suspicious events have answered *conspiracy* theories with *coincidence* theories.

Far from being more factual and plausible than theories positing political crimes and intrigues, coincidence theories become less and less plausible as coincidences pile up, which they have been doing for decades in the U.S. It is like flipping a coin ten times and it always falls on heads. In general, as SCADs and suspected SCADs pile up, the odds of coincidence drop rapidly. The Bush-Cheney ticket winning in one or two states despite exit polls indicating they had lost could have been the result of random variations in exit poll samples. When the same thing happens in state after state; when the difference between exit polls and election returns almost always favors the same candidates, the odds of this being by chance alone are astronomically low. [26] This does not necessarily mean the elections were stolen, but it does mean something caused the election returns to differ from how voters said they voted.

The CIA's Conspiracy-Theory Conspiracy

If political conspiracies in high office do, in fact, happen; if it is therefore unreasonable to assume conspiracy theories are, by definition, harebrained and paranoid; if the Declaration of Independence is a conspiracy theory; if the United States was founded on a conspiracy theory that alleged King George was plotting to take away the colonists' rights; if the conspiracy-theory label makes it difficult to see connections between political crimes that, in fact, may be connected; if, because it ridicules suspicion, the conspiracy-theory label is inconsistent with the traditional American ethos of vigilance against conspiracies in high office; if, in summary, the conspiracy-theory label blinkers perceptions, silos thinking, and is un-American and unreasonable, *how did the label come to be used so widely to begin with?*

Most Americans will be shocked to learn that *the conspiracy-theory label was popularized as a pejorative term by the
Central Intelligence Agency (CIA) in a propaganda program
initiated in 1967.* [28] This program was directed at criticisms of the Warren Commission's report. The propaganda
campaign called on media corporations and journalists to
criticize "conspiracy theorists" and raise questions about
their motives and judgments. The CIA told its contacts that
"parts of the conspiracy talk appear to be deliberately generated by Communist propagandists." In the shadows of
McCarthyism and the Cold War, this warning about communist influence was delivered simultaneously to hundreds
of well-positioned members of the press in a global CIA propaganda network, infusing the conspiracy-theory label with
powerfully negative associations.

The Rest of the Book

Conspiracy Theory in America is about the transformation of
America's civic culture from the Founders' hard-nosed real-
ism about elite political intrigue to today's blanket condem-
nation of conspiracy beliefs as ludicrous by definition. This
cultural reversal did not occur spontaneously; it was planned
and orchestrated by the government itself. The impetus for
the change originated in obscure debates in political philosophy during World War II, and in the secret world of espionage
and intrigue that has become a permanent threat at the heart
of American government. The conspiracy-theory label intentionally suppresses discussion of the issue of where, if at all,
secrecy, domestic surveillance, and government propaganda
campaigns fit in American democracy.

The rest of the book is divided into six chapters, each of
which focuses on a particular aspect of, or premise about,
conspiracy belief that is particularly important to the res-
toration of our anti-tyranny sensibilities but has been

overlooked in the conspiracy-theory literature, public discourse, or both.

Chapter 1 highlights the decisive role played by unstated and untested conventional beliefs in determining what counts as a conspiracy theory in the pejorative sense of the term. It turns out that, in the hands of conspiracy deniers, what counts as a conspiracy theory depends, not, as the label suggests, on an allegation's form and subject matter as a hypothesis about a secret plot, but on its relation to conventional beliefs about the motives and integrity of political elites. Conspiracy theories about the Mafia in America or politicians in Russia are fine; the same theories directed at U.S. politicians are supposedly ludicrous and paranoid.

Chapter 2 challenges the widely shared view that representative democracy depends on public trust and civility, both of which conspiracy theories supposedly erode. The chapter focuses on the important role the Founders believed is played in representative democracy by distrust—citizen distrust of their elected officials, and officials' distrust of one another. The chapter examines the role of conspiratorial suspicions in the political science of the Founders and in the application of that science to the U.S. Constitution and to nineteenth- and twentieth-century political reforms. Suspicion is written into and energizes the constitutional system of checks and balances, which displays the Founders' method of dividing and separating powers, dispersing vetoes, and requiring cooperation for authoritative action. The chapter concludes with a discussion of how the legal concept of conspiracy was applied for the first time to governments and political organizations in the Nuremberg war crimes trials, which, in part, were intended to instruct the German people about their responsibility as citizens in a parliamentary democracy to be constantly vigilant against efforts in high office to expand, extend, and consolidate power.

Chapter 3 shows that the intellectual foundations for the

shift to conspiracy denial were laid during and shortly after World War II. In the early decades of the twentieth century, one of the nation's leading historians and political scientists was Charles Beard, who was famous for exposing elite schemes to sew advantages for the wealthy into the U.S. Constitution. In the shadow of the world war, however, two European political philosophers—Karl Popper and Leo Strauss—placed much of the blame for totalitarianism, World War II, and the Holocaust on forms of conspiratorial theorizing that fueled social prejudice and undermined respect for authority. As Popper and Strauss' ideas entered universities and influenced teaching and research, conspiracy theories of all kinds came to be lumped together and condemned, including plausible suspicions of crimes in high office.

Chapter 4 explicates the assumptions and implications of the CIA propaganda program that spread the terms "conspiracy theory" and "conspiracy theorist" and gave them pejorative connotations. The label's use and connotations are tracked in the *New York Times* and *Time* magazine. Evidence is presented that connects specific negative connotations of the conspiracy-theory label directly to the CIA program.

Chapter 5 turns to theory and research on State Crimes against Democracy (SCADs) in the United States. SCAD research is introduced alongside examples in the history of science where scientific discoveries have overcome mistaken but seemingly irrefutable perceptions, such as the perception that the earth is stationary rather than spinning on its axis. The analysis of SCADs highlights a number of commonalities in SCAD targets, timing, tactics, and policy consequences. These patterns were previously unrecognized because of compartmentalization in people's perceptions of high crime. The SCAD patterns point to military and military-industrial interests as likely suspects in SCADs that foment social panic, encourage militarism, and are associated with wars. SCAD timing, targets, and policy consequences also suggest that the capabilities of national security agencies are being drawn into U.S. domestic politics by the White House. The chapter concludes by applying lessons from SCAD research to 9/11 and the anthrax letter attacks, raising questions about possible U.S. foreknowledge, the language of the war on terror, and the connection between the name "9/11" and the U.S. telephone number for emergencies (9-1-1).

Chapter 6 considers the possibilities for strengthening popular sovereignty and the rule of law in American democracy. The proliferation of SCADs in the post–World War II era is attributed to several related factors, chief among them the political class's growing sense that both the Constitution and the people are impediments to policies needed to protect the nation in an age of weapons of mass destruction and ruthless enemies. Also important is the popular view, seldom acknowledged publicly but seemingly widely shared, that occasional government crimes are acceptable if they help keep America safe. These ideas are shown to be naïve and mistaken in assuming that liberty and democracy can endure when enjoyed partially. SCADs are not occasional deviations from popular sovereignty; they start wars, steal elections, shift the nation's direction, and foment fear and hatred. The chapter recommends statutory reforms to encourage aggressive investigations of high crimes and allow independent law enforcement professionals to do their jobs. In large part this is what goes missing when top leaders appoint blue ribbon panels and investigative commissions. When it comes to SCADs, the people who insist that the laws and rules be enforced are frontline personnel.

THE CONSPIRACY-THEORY LABEL

T he Rosetta Stone for understanding the origins and use of the conspiracy-theory label is the assassination of President John F. Kennedy. The conspiracy-theory label took form and gained meaning over a period of several years (or longer) in the context of efforts by the CIA, one of the world's leading experts in psychological warfare, to deflect accusations that officials at the highest levels of American government were complicit in Kennedy's murder. Although the Warren Commission did not use the exact phrase, it referred repeatedly to the "issue of conspiracy," "questions of conspiracy," and similar constructions, and it focused its inquiry on whether Lee Harvey Oswald had been acting on his own or instead had received help. The more compact phrasing, "conspiracy theory," gained currency as a name pushed by the CIA for any and all theories that rejected the official account that Kennedy had been killed by a "lone gunman."

The CIA's campaign to popularize the term "conspiracy theory" and make conspiracy belief a target of ridicule and hostility must be credited, unfortunately, with being one of the most successful propaganda initiatives of all time.

Although most Americans today reject the official (lone gunman) account of the Kennedy assassination, they also have doubts about conspiracy theories and those who believe them.

This means the CIA program was successful, for its aim was not to sell the Warren Commission, but to sow uncertainty about the commission's critics. Today, people are not only uncertain, they have given up ever learning the truth. [1 p. 502]

In 1967, when the CIA was starting its whisper campaign against critics of the Warren Commission, people were just coming out of the state of shock they had been in since learning of the president's assassination and then witnessing the fatal shooting of his alleged killer on live TV. Everyone remembered where they were when they heard that Kennedy was dead. [1 p. 500] They remembered because to some degree they were stuck there emotionally, trying to figure out what it meant. But by January 1967, a few books and newspaper articles had appeared with new ways of seeing the events, people had gained some perspective, and they were starting to question the official story. [2–4] As the CIA explained in a cable to its field operatives (see Chapter 4), increasing numbers of people were saying that the individual who was probably responsible for the assassination was President Lyndon Johnson. Their reasoning was that Johnson was the one person who had benefited; he had become president.

To their credit, the American people were beginning to ask the basic question of crime investigation: *Qui bono?* Who benefits? This is the question that should have been asked from Day One.

Perspectives on Conspiracy Beliefs

The term "conspiracy theory" is no ordinary phrase. It was deployed to have a certain connotation by CIA technocrats

who are trained to break people psychologically, destroy relationships, tear apart governments, stir up old hatreds. [5]
These are scientists who are part of an organization that has
overthrown powerful regimes and is partly responsible for
the collapse of the Soviet Union. The reach of these people
should never be underestimated. [6]

The conspiracy-theory concept is deceptive. It seems to
refer merely to speculation about a secret plot. But when it
is applied to elite political crimes, it destroys context, background, and perspective. It is the conceptual equivalent of
looking at an elephant through a microscope.

The conspiracy-theory label framed the debate about Kennedy's murder in a way that, to this day, straitjackets most
thinking about political assassinations and about elite political crimes in general. By focusing on the issue of conspiracy,
the conspiracy-theory label posited that the most important
question about the Kennedy assassination was *how many
people were involved*, and typically this was interpreted to
mean *how many shooters*. It did not matter which side of this
issue people were on. Whether they were conspiracy believers or conspiracy deniers, they had swallowed the premise that the number of shooters was the decisive issue. This
became the central question in investigations of the Kennedy
assassination by the government as well as by the government's critics. Indeed, it has been the focus of inquiries into
*almost all political assassinations and assassination attempts
since then*, including those of Martin Luther King, Robert Kennedy, George Wallace, Ronald Reagan, and the five
people killed and two U.S. senators targeted by the anthrax
letter attacks.

The constraints on insight imposed by the conspiracy-
theory framing of political crimes are difficult to see until the
Kennedy assassination is approached as a suspected SCAD,
that is, as a crime possibly committed by political insiders to
achieve political or ideological aims they could not accom-

plish within the confines of existing governance institutions. The SCAD framing of the Kennedy case widens the angle of inquiry, telescoping out from the shooting, rising above the scene of the crime, and bringing into view the larger context of elite rivalries, power struggles, groups with skills displayed in the murder, and perhaps other political crimes with similar characteristics.

Viewing President Kennedy's assassination as a SCAD and setting aside the details of the shooting, the circumstances of the president's assassination appear suspicious because of who was at the scene of the crime and what was going on politically at the time. Kennedy was killed while touring the home state of the vice president, who, of course, became president upon Kennedy's death. Moreover, it was rumored Johnson was going to be dropped from the president's ticket in Kennedy's upcoming bid for reelection. In a Senate investigation that had begun in August, Johnson had been linked to a bribery scandal centered on Senate Majority Secretary Bobby Baker. Baker had resigned in October, but there were still lingering questions about whether Baker had channeled kickbacks to Johnson. [7] In fact, in January 1964, two months after the assassination, Johnson admitted he had accepted an expensive phonograph from Baker as a gift, and he acknowledged wrongdoing to Congress, which, no longer wanting to pursue the case against him now that he was president, ended further inquiry into Johnson's role. [8] Before the assassination, however, Johnson was vulnerable to being both replaced and prosecuted. Kennedy had picked Johnson to be his running mate in 1960 to help gain support from voters in Texas and other states from the Old Confederacy. However, once Kennedy and Johnson took office, the president excluded Johnson from decision making and gave him no visible role in the administration. Hence as early as May 1962 journalists were asking if Kennedy was going to keep Johnson as his running mate if he decided to seek a second term. [9] Kennedy and his press people were always reassuring, but doubts were growing simply because the question would not go away. [10]

The morning of the assassination, the rumor about Johnson possibly being dumped from the Kennedy ticket appeared on the front page of the Dallas newspaper. The rumor came from none other than former vice president Richard Nixon, who happened to be in town on business and had been interviewed by the newspaper the day before. Nixon was a rival of President Kennedy, if not a blood enemy. [11] He had been defeated by Kennedy in 1960 in one of the closest presidential elections in American history.

In short, two of the nation's most powerful politicians hated Kennedy and had much to gain from his death, and both were in Dallas on the day he was killed. In any objective investigation of the assassination, they would be suspects, and their statements and behavior in relation to the killing would be scrutinized. Actually, both men did things that were suspicious. However, Johnson's actions were especially egregious. As we shall see, while still in Dallas, Johnson allowed if not directed Secret Service agents to hinder the investigation of Kennedy's murder in ways that violated Texas laws and resulted in the destruction of critically important evidence.

But there is more. The broader domain of inquiry entailed by the SCAD construct also includes, as indications of elite motives and strategic considerations, the statutory and constitutional reforms introduced in response to the assassination. The Twenty-Fifth Amendment to the U.S. Constitution, which authorizes a process by which the vice president can remove the president from office and take his place, was quietly moved through Congress in 1965 and endorsed by enough states to take effect in 1967.

The Assassination of President Kennedy

On November 22, 1963, President Kennedy was killed while riding in a motorcade in Dallas, Texas. He was touring the home state of the vice president, Lyndon Johnson. The latter was in the motorcade when the president was killed, but seven cars back. In addition to Kennedy, also wounded in the attack was Texas governor John Connally, who was in a "jump seat" in front of the president.

Unlike other assassinations and assassination attempts on presidents and presidential candidates before and after Kennedy's, all of which involved handguns fired at close range, Kennedy was killed and Connally was wounded by rifle shots fired from a distance. This is a skill of the military and should have been considered circumstantial evidence of involvement by military or paramilitary forces, especially given that the target was moving and only the upper body was exposed. Setting aside questions about how many shooters there were, the fact that neither of the women in the limo was hit suggests it was a highly precise operation by skilled professionals.

About ninety minutes after the assassination, Dallas police arrested Lee Harvey Oswald, a Texas School Book Depository employee who left the building shortly after the assassination. [12] Oswald maintained his innocence throughout his questioning and protested publicly that he was "just a patsy." Two days later, while being transferred from police headquarters to the county jail, he was shot once in the stomach at point-blank range by Jack Ruby, a local bar owner who had slipped into the police station. Oswald died in the ambulance on the way to the hospital. With Oswald's death, questions immediately arose about whether he and Ruby had been part of a conspiracy. The suspicion was that Ruby might have murdered Oswald to keep him from talking.

The official account of the Kennedy assassination came

from a blue ribbon commission appointed by President Johnson and chaired by Earl Warren, chief justice of the U.S. Supreme Court. The executive order establishing the Warren Commission was signed by Johnson one week after the assassination. The commission released its final report ten months later, in September 1964. The report stated that President Kennedy had been shot by Oswald and only Oswald, firing from the sixth floor of the Texas School Book Depository, and that no evidence had been found "of conspiracy, subversion, or disloyalty to the US government by any Federal, State, or local official" (p. 22). The commission also said there was "no direct or indirect relationship between Lee Harvey Oswald and Jack Ruby" and "no evidence that Jack Ruby acted with any other person" (p. 22). In other words, Kennedy had been killed by a lone gunman who in turn had been killed by a lone gunman.

The Single-Bullet (or Magic-Bullet) Theory

As soon as it was published, the Warren Commission report met with wide-ranging criticism. The criticism was prefigured by the question of conspiracy that had been raised shortly after the assassination. The critics went looking for evidence of a second assassin. They focused on observations directly related to the shooting: the wounds to Kennedy and Connolly, an 8-millimeter movie taken of the shooting by Abraham Zapruder, and the rifle that had been found on the sixth floor of the Texas School Book Depository. The Warren Commission's own evidence, conspiracy believers argued, contradicted its conclusion that the shots that killed Kennedy came exclusively from six floors above and behind him to his right.

The lone-gunman hypothesis appeared to be contradicted by, among other things, the locations of the holes in Kennedy's shirt and corresponding wounds from the first bullet that hit him. The facts in evidence were that the hole in the front of the president's shirt was less than 1 inch below the collar button, while the hole in the shirt's back was 5 ¾ inches below the top of the collar. This meant the hole in back was slightly lower than the hole in front. Clearly, however, if Kennedy had been shot in the back from six floors up, the bullet's trajectory would have been downward, and the hole in the back of his shirt would have been higher than the hole in front. The location of the holes strongly indicated that the shot that wounded Kennedy in the neck had come from a location in front of the president and slightly above street level.

In 1997, more than thirty years later, the *New York Times* (July 3, p. 48) reported that recently declassified documents revealed that Gerald Ford had been instrumental in having the Warren Commission's description of the bullet wound in Kennedy's back changed to say the wound was not in his back but was at the "base of the back of his neck." [13 p. 3] Ford was a member of the Warren Commission. Critics of the Commission's report argue that this change intentionally distorted the medical evidence to bring it into line with the single-bullet theory. [7, pp. 472, 487] The Warren Commission also tried to explain away the shirt-hole evidence by assuming, contrary to the photographic record, that the president had been leaning steeply forward when he was struck.

In any case, there were still more questions about this bullet's trajectory. The bullet that caused the wound in the president's throat was the subject of the single-bullet (or magic-bullet) theory. After supposedly exiting Kennedy's throat, this bullet was assumed by the Warren Commission to have hit Governor Connally in the back, exited Connally's chest, gone through his right wrist, and ended up in his left thigh, only to later fall out of his thigh onto the stretcher at the hospital, where it was found.

The single-bullet theory was necessary for two reasons. First, the three shell casings found with the carbine at the

*The so-called magic bullet that struck President Kennedy
and Governor Connally. (Source: National Archives)*

Texas School Book Depository meant only three shots had
been fired. One shot was known to have missed because a
stray bullet chipped the curb in front of the motorcade and
sent concrete flying that cut the cheek of a man in the crowd.
Another shot had hit the president in the head. This left only
one bullet to cause the president's neck/back wound and the
wounds to Connally's back, chest, wrist, and thigh. Second,
the rifle found in the Texas School Book Depository could
not be fired rapidly enough to produce two shots in the time
between the visible indications (in the Zapruder film) of
Kennedy and Connally having been hit, so the Warren Commission decided the president and the governor had been
hit simultaneously, but the latter had reacted more slowly.
Connally, meanwhile, insisted his wounds were caused by a
separate shot, a claim supported by the photographic record.
The Warren Commission report noted this discrepancy but
asserted that the whole issue was irrelevant:

Although it is not necessary to any essential findings of the Commission to determine just which shot hit Governor Connally, there is very persuasive evidence from the experts to indicate that the same bullet which pierced the President's throat also caused Governor Connally's wounds. However, Governor Connally's testimony and certain other factors have given rise to some differences of opinion as to this probability but there is no question in the mind of any member of the Commission that all shots which caused the President's and Governor Connally's wounds were fired from the sixth floor window of the Texas School Book Depository. [13 p. 19]

The report did not explain why the commission continued to assert that all the shots came from the Texas School Book Depository when the number of wounds, as well as the trajectory and timing of the shots, indicated otherwise.

The Assumption Someone Would Talk

This is as far as discussions about the facts of the case usually go, because it is hard to defend the Warren Commission's findings when the evidence for the single-bullet theory is examined. Discussion usually shifts at this point to questions about the plausibility of conspiracy theories in general. The most common question is what to make of the fact that government conspiracies do, in fact, happen. Conspiracy believers think this shows that conspiracy deniers are obviously wrong to dismiss all conspiracy theories as harebrained. But of course those who use the conspiracy-theory label as a putdown to dismiss suspicions of political skullduggery know that political conspiracies sometimes do occur. They are aware of Watergate, Iran-Contra, and Iraq-gate, but they argue that official exposure of these scandals proves that secrets in the United States cannot be kept and plots in high

office will always be found out. [14] They say this is especially true of the kinds of crimes alleged by conspiracy theories, including the assassination of President Kennedy and
facilitation of the terrorist attacks of 9/11. In their view, if
the crimes of Watergate and other scandals were uncovered,
then, surely, so would offenses that are much more egregious.
By implication, theories that remain unsubstantiated by the
government must be untrue.

This argument warrants close examination, because it is
the reason why conspiracy theories are widely seen as outlandish. Actually, this view is another example of an assertion without evidence based on a romantic view of American government. Public officials are quite capable of keeping
secrets. An example is the U.S. government's construction
of the atomic bomb during WWII. The Manhattan Project
took several years and involved tens of thousands of people,
but it did not become known to outsiders, either in the public or inside the government, until the first atomic bombs
were dropped. Even President Truman did not learn of the
project until he had been president for a week. [15 pp. 376–
379] Similarly, secrecy was maintained throughout World
War II about America's success in breaking German and
Japanese encryption systems. Clearly, when the U.S. government wants to keep its capabilities secret, it can do so
even when the secret must be harbored by many people and
multiple agencies.

America's experience with political conspiracies in high
office also challenges the premise that conspiracies are
inexorably exposed because someone talks. Most of the conspiracies that have been officially confirmed came to light
fortuitously. Before the Watergate burglars were caught, they
had already successfully broken into the Democratic Party
headquarters on a previous occasion and planted wiretaps on
two telephones. The night of their arrest was several weeks
later, when they were returning to repair a wiretap that

had stopped working. [16, 17] They were apprehended only because one of the operatives failed to remove a strip of tape that had been placed on a door to prevent it from relocking after the lock had been picked. Similarly, the Iran-Contra conspiracy was exposed only because a plane carrying a CIA agent crashed in the jungles of Nicaragua and the agent was captured alive. Apparently, when it comes to conspiracies in high office, no one talks until someone is caught, and apprehension usually depends on missteps by the perpetrators, not established mechanisms of detection.

Those who dismiss conspiracy theories as implausible overlook evidence like this because they rely almost entirely on speculation and supposition. They also accept, uncritically, sanguine beliefs and prejudices about American politics and government. Sunstein and Vermeule, for example, refer casually to "abundant evidence that in open societies government action does not usually remain secret for very long." [14 pp. 208–209] The "abundant evidence" they cite is the exposure of warrantless wiretapping in 2005, and of secret CIA prisons in 2007. In both cases, the news came too late for voters to consider in the very close and disputed 2004 presidential election. Moreover, the warrantless wiretapping was exposed in 2005 only because James Risen, the *New York Times* reporter who uncovered this illegal program, was about to have a book published in late summer 2005 revealing the program. Some conspiracies may come to light, but if it takes years or decades, conspiracy theories go condemned and disbelieved until the truth no longer matters, and then we learn they were true all along.

Flawed Definitions

Despite their criticism of conspiracy theories as deranged and pernicious, conspiracy deniers have been unable to formulate a definition of the term that would allow observers to accurately differentiate irrational conspiratorial suspicions from reasonable beliefs. This failure has dangerous implications, for the term "conspiracy theory" has become a mechanism of social control, a label with normative implications backed by force. It equates those who voice suspicions of crimes in high places with the enemies of reason, civility, and democracy. Those who indulge in speculating about possible political conspiracies are subjected to ridicule, may lose their jobs, and risk being singled out by government agencies for surveillance and restricted mobility.

Richard Hofstadter said he was referring to belief systems that were conspiratorial and paranoid, but such thinking is not always inaccurate. Obvious examples include belief in the existence of the Mafia and the Ku Klux Klan. Both of these groups are large and well organized, and are engaged in sinister conspiracies that attack the way of life of law-abiding Americans.

Since the 1960s, many more definitions of conspiracy theory have been offered, but most of them have been in the mold set by Hofstadter and have carried over its defects. Examples of other, more recent definitions include the following:

- A theory "that traces important events to a secretive, nefarious, cabal." [18 p. 21]
- "Fears of nonexistent conspiracies." [19 p. 1]
- An "explanation of important events as a result of coordinated scheming by mysterious forces that try to control worldly affairs." [20 p. 2]
- "The conviction that a secret, omnipotent individual or group controls the political and social order or some part thereof." [21 p. 1]
- "The belief that an organization made up of individuals or groups was or is acting covertly to achieve some malevolent end." [22 p. 3]
- An "effort to explain some event or practice by reference

to the machinations of powerful people, who attempt to conceal their role (at least until their aims are accomplished)." [14 p. 205]

All of these definitions suffer from the same problem as the characterization offered by Hofstadter. That is, each would count, as unreasonable "conspiracy theories," some beliefs that are known to be true, such as belief in the influence of organized crime, underground terrorist organizations, and covert operations by intelligence agencies.

Critics of conspiracy theorizing continue to arrive at unworkable definitions because they are trying to identify a way of thinking about political intrigue that is irrational per se, whereas in reality there is nothing inherently irrational about suspicion directed at powerful persons. It all depends on the nature of the allegation, the evidence for and against it, the context supporting suspicion or trust, and so on. Consequently, there is no alternative but to engage each conspiracy theory on its merits.

A few authors have recognized this problem, but rather than reconsider the pejorative connotations of the conspiracy-theory concept, they have tried to stipulate away these connotations. For example, acknowledging that some conspiracy theories are true, Sunstein and Vermeule say their criticisms of conspiracy theory are directed only at conspiracy theories that are false. Unfortunately, they go on to argue that all conspiracy theories can and should be assumed to be false unless they have been verified by official (government) inquiries. By this reasoning, we would ignore such well-documented SCADs as President Johnson's misrepresentation to Congress of the Gulf of Tonkin incident [23] and the Bush-Cheney administration's skewing of intelligence about Iraqi weapons of mass destruction. [24] Neither of these SCADs is mentioned by Sunstein and Vermeule, who say, "Our focus throughout is on demonstrably false conspiracy theories, such as the various 9/11 conspiracy theories, not ones that are true or whose truth is undetermined." [14 p. 206] For that matter, despite the existence of evidence that U.S. public officials had some foreknowledge of the 9/11 attacks, Sunstein and Vermeule do not present any evidence that 9/11 conspiracy theories are false.

Another effort to deal with the problem of true conspiracy theories is journalist David Aaronovitch's suggestion that conspiracy theories in the pejorative sense of the term are beliefs that are unnecessarily complicated and sinister. Aaronovitch defines conspiracy theory as "the attribution of secret action to one party that might far more reasonably be explained as the less covert and less complicated action of another" [25 p. 6]. The problem with this definition is that it arbitrarily privileges those accounts of contested events that are parsimonious and trusting even though the nature of political conspiracies is that they are complex and concealed. Using Aaronovitch's definition, we would dismiss as an unreasonable "conspiracy theory" the suspicion that the Watergate break-in was an act of political espionage rather than merely a bungled burglary.

The only author on conspiracy theory to have faced this issue squarely is historian Kathryn Olmsted. In her words, "A conspiracy occurs when two or more people collude to abuse power or break the law. A conspiracy theory is a proposal about a conspiracy that may or may not be true; it has not yet been proven" [26 p. 3]. This definition is not only clear and simple, it acknowledges that conspiracy theories can be true. However, it also ignores the accepted meaning of "conspiracy theory" as beliefs that are considered to be irrational and pernicious. By Olmsted's definition, the official account of 9/11 is a conspiracy theory because the role of Osama bin Laden has not been proven. The evidence that bin Laden masterminded the attacks is based on confessions obtained through torture and on a videotape of dubious authenticity.

The Term's Meaning in Practice

Struggling to define the underlying (flawed) logic of the set of political beliefs they have designated as "conspiracy theories," conspiracy deniers end up with definitions that fail in application. This is because what they actually have in mind are suspicions that simply deviate from conventional opinion about the norms and integrity of U.S. officials. In practice, it is not the form or the object of conspiracy theories, or even the absence of official confirmation, that differentiates them from other (acceptable) beliefs; it is their nonconformity with prevailing opinion. In Arnold's words, "Conspiracy theory is sometimes used as a pejorative label for ideas that other people think are outlandish." [20 p. 4] This arbitrariness in the term's meaning can also be seen in its application. Conspiracy theories about the Mafia are considered to be fine; conspiracy theories about the president and the CIA are thought to be ludicrous and paranoid. This is why the conspiracy-theory label is so dangerous as a principle for regulating political speech; it equates intellectual nonconformity with irrationality and seeks to enforce conformity in the name of reason, civility, and democracy.

On the surface, as Olmsted points out, the term "conspiracy theory" would seem to refer to a suspicion that some troubling event was the result of a secret plot. The term's usage, however, implies something quite different. Not every theory that alleges a secret plot qualifies as a conspiracy theory in the current sense of the term. The official account of 9/11 claims that the Twin Towers were brought down by a team of Muslims who conspired to hijack planes and fly them into buildings. The theory posits a conspiracy, but the theory is not what most people would call a "conspiracy theory." Conspiracy theories of 9/11 claim more than that the attacks were secretly planned and executed by an organized team. Most conspiracy theories of 9/11 allege that the U.S. government itself carried out the attacks, or that officials knew the attacks were coming and allowed them to succeed. [27]

Still, a conspiracy theory is not simply a theory about a government plot. Conspiracy theories in the pejorative sense of the term are *counter*-theories: that is, they are posed in opposition to official accounts of suspicious events. Today's most popular conspiracy theories involve the assassinations of John Kennedy, Robert Kennedy, and Martin Luther King; the October Surprise of 1980; the defense failures on 9/11; and the anthrax letter attacks in 2001. Conspiracy theorists argue that official accounts of these events ignore important evidence, contain anomalies and inconsistencies, and are tendentious in their exoneration of public officials.

Thus, the conspiracy-theory label, as it is applied in public discourse, does not disparage conspiratorial thinking or analysis in general, even though this is what the term suggests. Rather, the broad-brush "conspiracy theory" disparages inquiry and questioning that challenge official accounts of troubling political events in which public officials themselves may have had a hand. A conspiracy theory directs suspicion at officials who benefit from political crimes and tragedies. The theories are considered dangerous not because they are obviously false, but because, viewed objectively and without deference to U.S. political officials and institutions, they are often quite plausible.

A SCAD Hypothesis

What gets lost in all these issues about definitions, plausibility, and the psychological basis for conspiracy belief and denial are the empirical questions about the events at issue, events that are gravely important and about which people everywhere want to know the truth. The question about whether President Kennedy was killed by a lone gunman or multiple shooters is a red herring. The real issue is whether the assassination was a SCAD, a conspiracy among political insiders to get rid of Kennedy and disguise the coup as a random murder.

If we stop focusing on the shooting and look instead at the elites, we will see that the behavior of Vice President Johnson suggests he and possibly agents of the Secret Service were part of the assassination. In the immediate aftermath of the shooting, Johnson quickly took charge, and Secret Service agents under his direction removed President Kennedy's body from Parkland Hospital and returned to DC with the corpse. The problem was that they violated Texas law in not first allowing an autopsy to be performed by a Dallas medical examiner. They were informed of the law, and they violated it willfully and over the strenuous objections of local authorities.

The inclination of patriotic Americans is to look for an innocent explanation, and at first there seems to be one. The Secret Service agents appear to have been motivated by the belief that Kennedy would receive more competent treatment in DC, and that his status and the dignity of his office would have been insulted by relinquishing his corpse to a city hospital. At one point in the confrontation between the Parkland Hospital officials and Secret Service agents (and some of Kennedy's staff), one of the Secret Service officers shouted out words to the effect that "this is the president of the United States of America, and we are taking him with us, back to the nation's capital."

Still, there is a less generous and more compelling interpretation of these actions that must be considered. The bottom line was that the agents prevented an independent autopsy from being conducted. Arguably, this was the aim and is why the Secret Service behaved so desperately. A simple jurisdictional issue could have been resolved pragmatically by having the Dallas medical examiner accompany federal officials to Washington and handling the autopsy

42

there in the presence of military doctors. Or conversely, Kennedy's physician, who had accompanied the president to Texas, could have been allowed to participate in the autopsy in Dallas. Innocent explanations of the Secret Service agents' behavior—for example, that the agents were upset because of the assassination—are brought into doubt as soon as we consider the potential implications of an independent autopsy. Given what we now know about the location of bullet wounds in Kennedy's throat, back, and head, namely, that the throat and back wounds, and probably also the head wound, strongly indicated that the president was shot from the front, the Secret Service agents' adamant and threatening posture takes on a different light. The behavior may not prove, but it certainly gives some support to, the suspicion that the agents had an ulterior motive, which was to prevent anyone from autopsying the president's body except handpicked military doctors in Washington who would be under the control of command authority and bound by secrecy agreements that override even sworn testimony. Anyone who was part of the conspiracy to murder President Kennedy had good reason to be concerned that the doctors at Parkland Hospital might cast doubt on the official account of the assassination as the crime of a lone gunman shooting from six floors up and behind the president. For the Parkland physicians who worked on Kennedy's throat said from the beginning that they thought the hole beneath Kennedy's larynx was an entry wound because it had to be expanded to make room for a tracheotomy.

There is an understandable reluctance to face what, frankly, are rather obvious implications once we stop being sentimental, stop feeling sorry for the Secret Service agents, and stand back to consider the full situation. What gets forgotten in the effort to excuse the Secret Service agents' behavior is that the agents were disregarding Texas laws. Yes, they may have been upset, but people get upset all the time and we do not allow them to commit felonies. The Secret Service took custody of the corpse of an assassinated president. The agents were not only breaking the Texas law requiring autopsies, they were obstructing justice, stealing evidence, breaking the chain of custody of evidence, and circumventing other procedures designed to protect the integrity of investigations. If Lee Harvey Oswald had not been killed but instead had been tried in Dallas for murder, the Secret Service agents' actions would have cast doubt on the government's case because a trial would have raised questions about evidence tampering. Consider, too, that doubts about the autopsy evidence and custodial control of the president's body are partly responsible for the uncertainties that to this day haunt Americans about the assassination of their president. The Secret Service agents did not merely violate protocol, act irresponsibly, and break the law, they robbed Americans of confidence in the investigation of the assassination and hence also in their political institutions and leaders.

By law, the autopsy of President Kennedy should have been performed by Dallas medical examiners, because legally, the crime was a murder under Texas law. (It was not a federal crime in 1963 to assassinate a president.) While Kennedy's body was still at Parkland Hospital, local officials informed the federal officials who were present that the latter could not take possession of Kennedy's body until the autopsy had been completed by a Dallas medical examiner who was already at the hospital. Nevertheless, at the vice president's instruction, Secret Service agents had a casket delivered, took control of Kennedy's body (some reports say at gunpoint [28]) as Parkland Hospital doctors and staff tried to block their way, put the body inside the casket, placed it in an ambulance, and had the ambulance take it to the airport. In his extensive study of the assassination, Phillip Nelson attributes the decisions for these actions to the vice president. [7 p. 561] At approximately 2:15 p.m., less than two hours after the shooting, the casket was lugged up the stairs of Air Force One, squeezed

President Kennedy's casket being loaded onto Air Force One with Jacqueline Kennedy a few steps behind. (Source: National Archives)

Lyndon Johnson being sworn in as president aboard Air Force One while Mrs. Kennedy stands beside him. (Source: Library of Congress)

through the narrow airplane door, and set down in the rear of the presidential plane, where seats had been removed to make room. Vice President Johnson boarded immediately afterward, but, even though Jacqueline Kennedy was on board, he delayed the plane's departure for almost an hour, until a federal judge could get there whom he had selected to administer the oath of office. He then insisted that Mrs. Kennedy come out of the plane's bedroom and stand beside him as he was sworn in and photos were taken.

Moreover, the vice president's disregard for the law did not end with the removal of the president's body from Parkland Hospital before an autopsy could be conducted. The federal entourage destroyed critically important evidence by having the president's limousine washed, all the blood cleaned from the limo's seats and carpets, and the bullet-pocked windshield and interior chrome replaced. [29] The bullet marks and blood spatter were essential for determining the direction and number of shots fired. Presumably, the fact that Kennedy had been shot from the front would have been clearly indicated by the large amount of blood, hair, and skull fragments covering the limo's trunk. The washing started in public and in broad daylight while the limo was still at Parkland Hospital. [30] At 8:00 p.m. on the evening of the assassination, the limo was flown by cargo plane to Washington, DC. The limo was kept under guard, but not to protect the evidence; the car had already been washed. Johnson's involvement could be construed as circumstantial evidence of guilt since it suggested knowledge of a frontal shooting; it also amounted to obstruction of justice and destruction of evidence in a capital crime.

Johnson's actions in having the limo washed and repaired rather than taken into evidence were illegal, but for the most part, they went unnoticed, and it may not have been simply because he was the new president. People may have ignored the limo being washed because they unconsciously wanted to wipe away the events of that day. An aide to Governor Connally took the governor's bloody suit to the cleaners and had it processed quickly so he could turn it in that night as evidence. Clearly, washing the suit was a bad idea, since it was needed for tracing the trajectory of the bullet and investigating how many times Connolly had been hit. It may be that the events of the day created a profound sense of instability and loss, and may have triggered a need to take control by cleaning up the site, disposing of debris, and generally setting things right. Still, this would not be expected to override training and established protocols for crime scene processing. At most it might account for the failure of people to speak out when the limo was being washed at Parkland Hospital, and when the casket with the president's corpse was being manhandled onto Air Force One.

Also indicating, in a different way, some awareness of this compulsion to clean up and set right, Jacqueline Kennedy responded not by yielding to the impulse but by pushing back against it. She would not wash herself or change clothes despite having splotches of blood in her hair and on her shoes and skirt. Urged by the White House physician to wipe the blood off her clohes, she angrily replied, "No, let them see what they have done." [31 p. 13] In the photo of her going up the steps of Air Force One, she is about five feet behind the men who are muscling the coffin containing her husband toward the airplane door. No one seems aware of her presence. She is no longer the First Lady. She is like a ghost.

The Warren Commission report contains only a brief, one-paragraph section on the key events. The heading for the paragraph is, "The Removal of the President's Body." Although it reports the actions at Parkland, it fails to comment on their illegality. It says:

A casket was obtained and the President's body was prepared for removal. Before the body could be taken from the hospital, two Dallas officials informed members of the President's staff that the body could not be removed from the city until an autopsy was performed. Despite the protests of these officials, the casket was wheeled out of the hospital, placed in an ambulance, and transported to the airport shortly after 2 p.m. At approximately 2:15 p.m. the casket was loaded, with some difficulty because of the narrow airplane door, onto the rear of the presidential plane where seats had been removed to make room. Concerned that local officials might try to prevent the plane's departure, [presidential aid Kenneth] O'Donnell asked the pilot to take off immediately. He was informed that takeoff would be delayed until Vice President Johnson was sworn in. [13 p. 58]

By implication, this description of the events reveals two important facts. First, those involved in "removing the body" were fully aware they were violating the law, for they feared local officials might prevent their departure. Second, the person who was in charge of these decisions was Vice President Johnson, for it was Johnson who decided to wait to be sworn in before taking off for Washington.

Reforms after President Kennedy's Assassination

In response to the Kennedy assassination, two main reforms were adopted. Both speak volumes about what elites thought about the president's assassination. First, a federal law was enacted in 1965 and signed by President Johnson making it a federal crime to assassinate a president or vice president. This had been recommended by the Warren Commission, which in its report had said in reference to the law in 1963 that the lack of federal jurisdiction in the investigation of President Kennedy's murder was "anomalous." Thus, for the

Warren Commission, the vice president's crimes in comman-
deering Kennedy's body and preventing a legally required
autopsy had no bearing on the question of who might have
been behind the assassination. Indeed, federalizing the investigation of assassinations would ensure that if the same thing
ever happened again and the vice president needed to take
control of the president's corpse and spirit it away from public officials not under his or her control, he or she would not
have to break the law. Furthermore, the change intensified a
moral hazard that was already problematic, for the vice president becomes president if the president is killed. Placing in
this same person's hands control over the subsequent investigation is like making your doctor the heir to your estate.

The second reform was to greatly strengthen the office of
the vice president through the Twenty-Fifth Amendment to
the United States Constitution. Among other provisions, this
amendment specifies that the vice president becomes president if the office of the president becomes vacant; requires
the president to nominate a vice president if the office of the
vice president becomes vacant; states that the vice presidential nominee in such cases takes office when confirmed by a
majority vote of both Houses of Congress; and, in the most
significant change, establishes procedures for the vice president to remove and take the place of the president by peace-
ful means. This last provision is contained in Section 4 of the
amendment. It states that the vice president immediately
assumes the office of acting president upon sending a letter
to the president pro tempore of the Senate and the Speaker
of the House of Representatives, with the support of "half of
the principal officers of the executive departments," declaring "that the President is unable to discharge the powers and
duties of his office." The president can initiate a process to
regain the office by sending a letter declaring his competency,
but the vice president remains acting president and has four
days to make the claim again that the president cannot carry

out his or her duties, at which point Congress must assemble and decide the issue. The president can then be removed by two-thirds vote of both Houses.

Adding this provision to the Constitution suggests that the problem in 1963 was that the vice president and others in the government believed President Kennedy was incapacitated in some sense, but the Constitution included no provision for removing him by constitutional or legal means other than impeachment, which is a lengthy and time-consuming process and leaves the president in office until he or she is convicted by the Senate. This hypothesis is supported by evidence in Nina Burleigh's well-reviewed biography of presidential mistress Mary Meyer that Kennedy was heavily sedated for his back pain, was a sex addict, and was allegedly experimenting with marijuana and LSD in the White House with his sexual partners, one of whom was the girlfriend of a Mafia boss and another the ex-wife of a high-ranking CIA officer [32]. The president backed down from military confrontations with the Soviets during both the Bay of Pigs invasion and the Cuban missile crisis. It is conceivable, and perhaps even likely, that his decisions in these instances were interpreted by General Curtis LeMay and others, not as prudence, but as an inability to maintain resolve when confronted by Soviet belligerence. [33 pp. 354–355] LeMay was head of the Air Force and one of the nation's highest military commanders. In fact, LeMay had accused Kennedy of "appeasement" in a meeting where other administration officials were present. In the context of World War II, this accusation was an insult of the highest order and bordered on insubordination. [31 pp. 164–165]

Thus, when the focus is shifted from the shooting and the question of whether Lee Harvey Oswald had accomplices; when the scope of inquiry is expanded to include the larger context of conflicts and issues among top leaders; when the actions of likely suspects on the day of the assassination are considered; and when subsequent reforms are taken into account, it appears the Kennedy assassination may have been an extralegal but orderly action by top officials to remove the president, replace him with the vice president, and then establish procedures so that in the future such actions could be taken without bloodshed. In oligarchic systems of government, such actions are referred to as "coups" and "purges."

To be sure, the conclusions reached by broadening the scope of inquiry are merely speculations and conjectures. But, even so, they point to long-overlooked evidence that helps make sense of a presidential murder that most Americans still consider unresolved. At a minimum, the exercise of using the SCAD construct as a framework for investigating the Kennedy assassination highlights the extent to which the conspiracy-theory label limits our imagination and therefore hobbles high-crime investigations. Once the assassination is viewed, so to speak, from above and at a distance; once the focus is taken off the shooting itself; once all the questions about how many shots were fired and from where are set aside and the spotlight is placed on the people in power, the broad outlines of a very different account of why the assassination occurred and what individuals and interests were behind it emerge simply from observing elite behavior.

The hypothesis that President Kennedy's assassination was a coup or purge tailored to the U.S. constitutional order is supported by comments later made by Richard Nixon in an unguarded moment. [34] In 1965, the former vice president was visiting a university in Moscow and was asked by a professor, in reference to the Kennedy assassination, what he, the professor, should tell his students when they asked how a president could be killed in a "freedom loving country." Nixon replied sarcastically that "evidently the US is not perfect," and he then threw the question back at the Muscovite. "We could ask in turn," Nixon continued, "what happened to Beria? Why was he killed? Trotsky, what happened to him?"

Beria and Trotsky had been leaders in the communist revolution in Russia and had later held important positions in the Soviet government. Beria was head of the government's intelligence agency. Although the circumstances of their deaths were different, both Beria and Trotsky were killed in a political purge. Thus, Nixon's comment seemed to suggest that Kennedy was likewise killed because his loyalty and judgment had become suspect at the highest levels.

THE AMERICAN TRADITION
OF CONSPIRACY BELIEF

D ismissing suspicions of elite political criminality as harebrained "conspiracy theories" is an alarming development in modern American history. For it not only signals a shift in American civic culture away from the nation's traditional distrust of power, but also may mark the end of America's historic reliance on the political science of the nation's Founders when confronting new challenges in democratic governance. During the first decades of the republic, the leaders of the Revolution drafted the United States Constitution to replace the Articles of Confederation, secured the Constitution's ratification by the states, added the Bill of Rights to restrict the national government's powers, put the new government in place operationally and paid off the debts from the Revolutionary War, resolved a disputed presidential election (the election of 1800), vastly expanded the nation's frontiers by purchasing the Louisiana territories, and fought a second war with Great Britain more or less to a draw. In the process of designing, erecting, and periodically reforming the national government, the Founders worked out a new political science that was not an abstract disquisition about the nature of government, but instead a set of working principles, subject to revision on the basis of experience, for engineering self-balancing, cross-checking elements of representative government and nested hierarchies of federal authority.

Over the course of American history up to the Cold War, the political science of the Founders was applied successfully to new forms of corruption, division, and collusion that emerged both domestically and in international relations as the United States expanded geographically, industrialized, and became increasingly engaged in global trade and international affairs. Domestically, the Founders' science was employed to deal with the rise of national political parties, the spoils system, giant corporations, and more. In each instance, reform followed their basic model for republican government, which was to divide power into separate offices, require agreement between offices to make authoritative decisions, and give each office veto powers over certain issues in some situations. In this way, the natural tendency for each office to extend its powers would be restrained by the same tendencies of the others.

Internationally, the most striking example of the application of the American science of politics was in prosecuting the Nazi leadership after World War II. American officials convinced the Allied powers, which favored summary executions of most officials and large segments of the officer corps, to instead conduct trials of Germany's top political and military officials to show the German people and the world that liberal democracies are vulnerable to antidemocratic conspiracies, and to show the world that national leaders can and should be held accountable by applying the legal concept of conspiracy to political leaders and political organizations. [1]

The Political Science of the Founders

America's Founders had no choice but to develop a new science of politics because the nation's circumstances and opportunities were historically unique. James Madison pointed out that the United States was an emergent form of political organization never before seen: a "large commercial republic." The republics of old had been martial city-states that lived off conquest and plunder. They were small, aggressive, and self-sufficient. On the other hand, empires, both ancient and modern, were oligarchies backed by large standing armies that supported trade for the wealthy at the expense of liberty and political equality for the masses. Great Britain was an empire and viewed the colonies, not as equals and partners, but as subordinate units of consumption and production within the imperial enterprise. The British imposed the unpopular tea tax in an effort to make the colonies pay the expenses incurred by the Crown for the use of its armies in the French and Indian War.

The Founders assumed that political authority flows from the consent of the governed and that therefore governing institutions should include elections and other mechanisms for securing popular support. But they also thought representative democracy was vulnerable to, in their language, "conspiracies against the people's liberties" by "perfidious public officials," and to "tyrannical designs" by "oppressive factions." The political science of the Founders called for pitting one office against another, making the exercise of authority contingent on cooperation between rivals, binding officials to their offices with oaths and the threat of impeachment, and in other ways harnessing to good purposes the selfish and tyrannical tendencies that flow from human nature. Moreover, political innovations were judged by their fruits. The practical aims of the new political science were to preserve the union of states long enough for the nation to grow into an organic whole, provide the national government with sufficient authority and financial resources to maintain "domestic tranquility," suppress insurrections and "provide for the common defense," arrange the duties and offices of the national government so as to prevent power from becoming concentrated and enlarged, bring new states and territories into the union, and ensure that all states in the union had a republican form of government.

Conspiracy Theories of the Founders

The political science of the Founders grew from the soil of experience with a manipulative and tyrannical king fully schooled in the ways of power, advised by a large staff of ministers, and supported by one of the world's most powerful armies. The Declaration of Independence cited a series of abuses by King George as proof he was plotting to subject the colonies to "an absolute tyranny." The leaders of the Revolution knew better than to wait to stand up for their rights until they were impoverished by taxes and surrounded by troops quartered in their own homes. The elected legislators of the state governments announced their decision and pledged their lives, their property, and their sacred honor to the cause of revolution.

The revolutionaries were not alone in their suspicions of the Crown's intentions. The conspiracy theory articulated in the nation's founding document reflected the thinking of most colonists. In the decades leading up to the American Revolution, as Bailyn shows, [2 pp. 151–159] the colonists grew increasingly convinced that the British government was pursuing a deliberate conspiracy to destroy the balance of the Constitution and eliminate their freedom. [2, 3] John Dickinson, a militia officer during the Revolution and a delegate to the U.S. Constitutional Convention of 1778, explained in one of his letters to friends in Parliament that, as wrongs against the colonies accumulated, Americans began to connect the dots and recognize ulterior motives in the pattern of Great Britain's actions. "Acts that might, by themselves, be excused," began to be regarded "as parts of a system of

oppression." [4] This is the essence of conspiratorial suspicion, which reconstructs hidden motives from confluent consequences in scattered actions.

This logic is not paranoid; it is a laudable effort to make
sense of political developments in a degenerating constitutional order. Constitutional government seldom becomes
tyrannical overnight. Freedom dies from a multitude of small
cuts. First, a right may be infringed for an unpopular group;
then an exception may be made to a minor procedural safeguard; then a dissenter may be banished or imprisoned. The
principles at stake are concealed by their infringement in
small increments. This is the meaning of Martin Niemoller's
famous sermon about how he remained silent when the
Nazis came for communists, and then for the social democrats, and then for the trade unionists, so that when they
finally came for him, there was no one left to speak out. [5]
Political awakenings in the context of creeping tyranny
depend on recognizing the large implications of small but
accumulating abuses.

Political awakenings also pose either-or choices. As hos-
tilities began in the 1760s, revolutionaries throughout the
colonies organized "Committees of Safety," which by the
mid-1770s were demanding that the undecided either swear
an oath to the revolutionary authorities or leave the country
[6]. Those colonists who were deemed to be Loyalists or even
just inadequately committed to the Revolution were lashed,
tarred, and feathered, had their houses and crops burned, and
in some instances were hanged or lynched. According to Wil-
liam Polk, a historian at the University of Chicago, by the end
of the Revolutionary War more than one hundred thousand
colonists had fled. This number amounted to one in every
twenty residents [7 p. 14].

After the war, when the colonists turned to strengthening
their own national government, they brought with them their
deep fear of conspiracies, treason, and constitutional corrup-

tion. The United States Constitution was designed with the expectation that public officials are likely to conspire to abuse their powers and undermine popular control of government. The framers of the Constitution saw their central problem to be establishing a national government strong enough to protect national security and maintain domestic order, and yet sufficiently constrained to adhere to the spirit of popular government and the rule of law. In the words of James Madison (Federalist 51), "you must first enable the government to control the governed; and in the next place oblige it to control itself." [8] In Madison's view, the greatest threat to the constitutional order comes from "factions," that is (per Federalist 10), "a number of citizens, whether amounting to a majority or a minority of the whole, who are united and actuated by some common impulse of passion, or of interest, adverse to the rights of other citizens, or to the permanent and aggregate interests of the community." To the extent that a faction has a hidden agenda or an unannounced plan for gaining and exercising power, it is a political conspiracy.

The Constitution was designed to deal with factions and conspiracies in a number of ways: separation of powers, checks and balances between branches, large congressional districts, oaths of office, and provisions for impeachment for treason and other high crimes and misdemeanors. Freedom of speech was protected by the First Amendment as well as by limiting treason to "overt acts" in support of enemies (Article III, Section 3). The Founders pitted the branches of government against one another, so that each would guard against abuses by the others. They expected factions to plot to subvert the constitutional order because they considered human beings prone to collusion for financial gain and power. If tyranny came, Madison warned, it would be in the form of a consolidation of legislative, executive, and judicial powers in the hands of a single individual or group.

The Founders worried most about the potential for power

to become concentrated in the executive because of real or pretended threats to national security. Hence the Constitution includes numerous provisions designed to restrain the executive from entangling the nation in international conflicts. The Founders wanted a permanent or standing navy so they could, in Hamilton's words, secure access to ports on good terms, but they opposed standing armies and intended for the national government to have to call upon the state militias to engage in wars and suppress rebellions. They made the president commander-in-chief only when the nation's armed forces were assembled, and the armed forces were to be assembled only for limited periods. To further restrain the executive's martial ambitions, they vested the power to declare war in the Congress; they authorized Congress to appropriate funding for warfare for only two years at a time; they prohibited the president from entering into treaties without the approval of two-thirds of the Senate; and they required the president to swear an oath to protect, preserve, and defend, not the nation, but the Constitution. (The oath of all other officers of the government is only to "support" the Constitution.)

The Founders would be surprised by how leaders today deal with what the Founders referred to as "oppressive factions" and "high crimes." Today, factions include not only religious movements (e.g., the Christian Right), sectional interests (e.g., the South), and various "causes" (e.g., environmentalism), but also interest blocks with structural power by virtue of their control over key political and economic resources: the military-industrial complex, the intelligence community, the banking system, and so on. A quick read of the reports of the Warren Commission, the 9/11 Commission, and other investigative bodies shows they pay little attention to factions unless the factions are directly involved in the events in question, such as the airlines in 9/11. When commissions investigate government failures like the Kennedy assassination and 9/11, they invariably focus on threats external to the political system and leave questions about the motives and possible machinations of factions unasked. Discouraging "conspiracy theories" means ignoring internal threats from factions, because conspiracy theories are essentially "faction theories." Suspect factions in the assassination of President Kennedy, that is, factions that should have been suspect, included the intelligence community plus Cuban expatriates, organized labor in connection with organized crime, and the military-industrial complex.

The Sedition Act of 1798 and the "Burr Conspiracy"

In the late 1790s, the Founders confronted mass suspicions similar to those faced by political leaders today who see conspiracy theories as paranoid and pernicious. The Founders' response is instructive and, when compared to contemporary derision of conspiracy belief, a sad indication of how far the quality of American leadership and journalism has fallen. Although the Founders became polarized over foreign policy and flirted with censorship and suppression of dissent, they quickly came to the conclusion that freedom of speech must be protected even if, or especially if, it maligns the government or insults the integrity of public officials.

As the constitutional order took form in the first decade after the U.S. Constitution became effective in 1789, questions arose about whether limits should be placed on antigovernment speech inciting sedition or rebellion against the new political system. British common law designated "seditious libel"—statements critical of the government or its officials—as a crime subject to severe punishments, with the truth of such statements inadmissible as a defense. During medieval times, trials for seditious libel were conducted in the notorious Star Chamber, in which proceedings were secret, defendants could be compelled to testify against themselves, and defendants could not confront and cross-examine their accusers. A number of rights codified in the U.S. Constitution were included precisely to prevent such practices in America: the right against self-incrimination (Amendment 5), the guarantee of trial by jury (Amendments 6 and 7), and the right to confront one's accusers (Amendment 6). Further protection for political speech was afforded by limiting treason to an "overt act."

Nonetheless, the Washington and Adams administrations, dominated by Federalists who saw themselves as the originators and authors of the new political order, feared sedition and civil disorder, and tried to impose a weaker version of the British law. After President Washington put down the Whiskey Rebellion in Pennsylvania, he asked Congress to consider enacting a law against political clubs like those that had fomented resistance to the federal tax on whisky. He viewed the right of assembly to allow only spontaneous and temporary protests, not enduring organizations of antigovernment agitators. [9] Congress demurred, and, to his credit, Washington let the matter drop. But when John Adams took office and found himself and his administration the brunt of popular ridicule and unsubstantiated rumors, he persuaded the Federalists in Congress to enact the Sedition Act of 1798. While drawing on the British concept of seditious libel, the act departed from British law in allowing truth as grounds for acquittal. [9]

Vice President Thomas Jefferson strongly opposed the Sedition Act, mainly because in his view the power to regulate antigovernment speech was reserved to the states by the U.S. Constitution, which, in the First Amendment, prohibited Congress from enacting laws "abridging the freedom of expression, or of the press." The historical record is unclear on Jefferson's views at the time about the legitimacy of state laws against seditious libel, but his opposition to the Sedition

Act became normative in American civic culture both federally and in the states. Jefferson was so hostile to the Sedition Act that he left the nation's capital and spent the rest of his vice presidential term at his home in Virginia.

Jefferson also formed a new political party and defeated Adams in the presidential election of 1800. In his first inaugural address, Jefferson articulated the principle, now widely cherished as a birthright, that Americans are allowed by the Constitution to "think freely and to speak and to write what they think." He made it clear that in his view this was true even for speech advocating the overthrow of the government. In Jefferson's words, "If there be any among us who would wish to dissolve this Union or to change its republican form, let them stand undisturbed as monuments of the safety with which error of opinion may be tolerated where reason is left free to combat it." Congress let the Sedition Act expire in 1801.

Jefferson was also influential in establishing the precedent for investigating and prosecuting suspicions of anti-democratic conspiracies by top leaders. As president, he advocated the prosecution of Aaron Burr for treason in what came to be called the "Burr conspiracy." The latter is described below; suffice it to say now that Burr had been Jefferson's running mate in the election of 1800, but this did not deter Jefferson from urging the federal courts to hold Burr accountable for crimes he may have committed after leaving office.

The Twenty-Fifth Amendment to the Constitution, which, as discussed in the preceding chapter, was adopted after the assassination of President Kennedy, is only the latest in a series of efforts to work out a salubrious role for the vice president in the constitutional framework of divided powers. Under the original design of the Constitution, the president and the vice president were to be rivals and antagonists. Electors in the electoral college cast two votes, one each for different persons, but in the Constitution that took effect in 1789, the votes were not assigned, as they are now, one to the presidency and one to the vice presidency. The expectation was that the most popular presidential candidate would receive a plurality or majority of votes, and the second most popular candidate would become vice president and would preside over the Senate as president of the Senate.

Thus the plan was for the vice president and the president to have different sources of political support and somewhat different political priorities, and for their priorities to be reconciled through the legislative process. The role of the vice president as president of the Senate was reinforced by the Senate's veto power over many of the executive's appointments and all treaties, and the Senate president's authority to break tie votes. This rivalry between the two offices indeed emerged in 1796, when John Adams was elected president and Jefferson vice president. However, the rivalry led not to a healthy give-and-take, but to near dissolution of the union.

The idea of running mates was one of several early efforts of the generation of the Founders to use political parties to circumvent elements of the Constitution's design for divided powers. However, in 1800 it led to a tie vote in the Electoral College as Democratic-Republicans cast one of their electoral votes for Jefferson and one for Burr. When Jefferson and Burr ended up with equal numbers of votes in the Electoral College, the election went to the House of Representatives for a decision, with each state having a single vote. Burr remained silent as the states repeatedly cast a tie vote. Eventually, Jefferson won after Alexander Hamilton, not a member of Congress but influential in the Federalist Party, called on his fellow partisans in the House to support Jefferson over Burr. As the number-two vote getter, Burr became vice president, as intended by Jefferson to begin with. To prevent this problem in the future, the Twelfth Amendment to the U.S. Constitution was adopted; it required votes in the Electoral

College to be specifically designated, one for the office of the president and one for vice president.

In subsequent years Hamilton implied in a variety of statements that Burr had betrayed Jefferson by conspiring with members of the Federalist Party to secure the presidency for himself. When Jefferson made it clear he was going to drop Burr from the Democratic-Republican ticket in the 1804 election, Burr ran for governor of New York, and Hamilton campaigned against him. Burr lost the gubernatorial election, which was held in April. In July of 1804, Burr challenged Hamilton to a duel in which Hamilton was killed.

During his second term as president, Jefferson voiced his belief that Burr was leading a conspiracy to form a separate nation by breaking away western lands from U.S. control. Fortunately for the nation's future, Jefferson was not dismissed as a harebrained lunatic. This was long before political elites and pundits tried to convince Americans that conspiracy theories are a form of flawed reasoning akin to superstition.

Jefferson's suspicion was based on reports that Burr had approached several friends, one of whom was a high-ranking officer in the U.S. Army, with a scheme to establish an independent nation in the west. Jefferson urged federal prosecutors to take action, and Burr was tried for treason. Burr was acquitted on the basis that he had not committed an overt act to aid America's enemies—the test for treason in the Constitution—but the trial vindicated Hamilton's allegations that Burr was dangerously ambitious and untrustworthy, and Burr's reputation was ruined.

For the next hundred years, American statesmen regularly voiced suspicions regarding antidemocratic conspiracies when circumstantial evidence suggested hidden intrigue. Nineteenth-century conspiracy theories included, among others, Andrew Jackson's allegations of a "corrupt bargain" between John Quincy Adams and Henry Clay to give the presidency to Adams in 1824; Abraham Lincoln's charge, made on the floor of the House of Representatives, that President Polk had fabricated a reason to initiate the Mexican-American War; claims by the chief prosecutor that the assassination of President Lincoln had been organized and financed by top leaders of the Confederacy; [10] the theory that the Fourteenth Amendment to the U.S. Constitution was intentionally drafted by railroad-connected Congressmen to precipitate court rulings granting the rights of individuals to corporations; [11] and suspicions that, contrary to the government's claims in launching the Spanish-American War, the U.S. battleship *Maine* had not been sunk by a Spanish mine but had been deliberately sunk by U.S. or Cuban operatives to precipitate the war. [12, 13]

The Dialectic of Corruption and Reform

The conspiracy-theory literature overlooks not only the conspiracism of the Founders, but also America's history of innovation and reform to deal with new and changing forms of political corruption. As explained in more detail elsewhere, [14] political corruption in the U.S. has taken two principal forms: [15] misuse of office for personal material gain, as in graft, nepotism, embezzlement, and kickbacks; and antidemocratic corruption, where democratic processes for arriving at collectively binding decisions are subverted, usually to benefit a ruling faction or class, or to violate the rights of minority factions or individuals. The latter form of corruption is captured in large part by the SCAD construct. Examples here include election tampering, assassination, malicious prosecution, voter disenfranchisement, and unlawful incarceration. These two forms of corruption are not mutually exclusive, but they are sufficiently distinct to permit analysis of corrupt behavior in terms of its origins and aims.

Over the course of American history, political corruption has shifted back and forth between these two forms, and the organization of corruption has changed too, thus necessitating significant new reforms to counter the new threats as they have emerged. The main eras of corruption and subsequent reform are listed and described in Table 2.1 (page 204). Because reforms have never been totally effective, vulnerabilities from earlier eras continue to be problematic even though they have been mitigated. In this sense, the form and scope of political corruption have expanded over time. Because of the rise of political-economic complexes, SCADs are becoming far more complicated and sophisticated and are combining antidemocratic and pecuniary motives of an extreme nature.

The new forms of counter-constitutional organization and/or outright corruption include political parties, political machines, iron triangles and subgovernments, and political-economic complexes.

POLITICAL PARTIES

As the framers themselves soon recognized, the system of checks and balances was vulnerable to manipulation by elite conspiracies that established alliances between officials in the different offices and branches of government. The archetype of multibranch alliances is the political party. The two-party system was in place by 1800, and each party was already trying to tyrannize the other. Over the next several decades, the parties developed rules and procedures to regulate the majority and protect the minority's ability to be heard.

POLITICAL MACHINES

Officials in the executive branch of government at all levels began to use the powers of their offices to entrench themselves and their parties throughout the political system. Their main objective was to capture and distribute gov-

ernment jobs and other resources. Political machines pro-
liferated until, toward the end of the nineteenth century,
public administration scholars and practitioners profes-
sionalized American government by instituting professional
civil service requirements, prohibiting the use of government
resources in political campaigns, and moving to the council-
manager system in local government.

Political machines represented the first time that a large
part of the political class formed what the Founders had
called a faction. The Founders had expected political leaders
to be divided because they came from and represented distinct constituencies or factions and therefore would have difficulty uniting.

IRON TRIANGLES AND SUBGOVERNMENTS

The reforms of the Progressive Era brought organizational
changes that weakened the system of checks and balances
in new ways. A new instrument of government, the independent regulatory commission, was introduced, which combined legislative, executive, and judicial powers in a single
unit. By creating what became in effect self-contained mini-
governments, such commissions opened the door to a car-
telization of the political system, whereby public power
and resources were divvied up and distributed to various economic, social, and geographic constituencies. [16]
This pattern was repeated with the vast expansion of federal grants-in-aid to states and localities under the New
Deal and the Great Society. Policymaking and administration were fragmented into a plethora of separate and distinct arenas where public and private "stakeholders" could
work out mutually acceptable compromises more or less
independent of the larger political process. The resulting
political-economic conglomerates have been described vari-
ously as "iron triangles," "whirlpools," "subsystems," and
"subgovernments." [17, 18]

The proliferation of iron triangles was accompanied by a new type of pecuniary corruption in which stakeholders in a given policy arena colluded to manipulate legal and procedural technicalities for the benefit of special interests. Frequently, the stakeholders in question were corporations and industrial interests—especially railroads, electric utilities, and oil companies—that were suspected of bribing, hoodwinking, or otherwise influencing policymakers to gain legal and financial advantages at the public's expense. Eventually, concerns about the growing potential for these kinds of special-interest abuses in America's increasingly fragmented and technical system of government were addressed with restrictions on campaign contributions and lobbying, financial disclosure requirements for public officials, public records and open meeting laws, and other reforms to reduce improper influences in policymaking and administration.

POLITICAL-ECONOMIC COMPLEXES

The most recent corruption-related development in American government has been the rise of political-economic complexes with the ability to affect the political priorities of the political system as a whole. For the first half of the twentieth century, American government's increasing fragmentation was seen by scholars and practitioners as a positive development that allowed popular participation in policymaking while at the same time preventing majority tyranny. [19] In keeping with James Madison's theory of faction, with each policy arena dominated by different factions, no faction or combination of factions would be able to control the government as a whole, and national priorities would have to emerge incrementally from "partisan mutual adjustment" among diverse power blocks.

By mid-century, however, scholars and practitioners began to realize that not all policy arenas and stakeholders are equal. As President Eisenhower warned in his farewell address: military leaders and armament manufacturers had become a "military-industrial complex" capable of influencing the entire direction of American government. [20] Since Eisenhower's day, the military-industrial complex has expanded while other, related complexes have formed around energy, finance, and pharmaceutical interests. Complexes differ from iron triangles in their command over resources that affect overall societal conditions, mass perceptions, and political priorities. Falling energy prices can help save a presidency, as they did in 2004. Unlike iron triangles, which typically involve narrow economic interests and mid-level policymakers, complexes pose moral hazards for the highest offices of government because their assets can be used to wield dominant control over the national political agenda.

With advantageous and profitable connections proliferating between government and business in political-economic complexes and therefore between individuals who can be of mutual service to one another, the political class is becoming increasingly cohesive as a group aware of itself and motivated by this awareness to increase its cohesion and influence. It is comprised of the officials, lobbyists, technocrats, think tanks, and other individuals and organizations who participate in the nation's governing processes. The Founders do not appear to have anticipated the mobilization of political officials and insiders as a unified force. Otherwise they surely would have tried to devise institutional arrangements to insert checks and balances between various parts of the organism. The political class as a whole appears to be on its way to forming into a cohesive, self-serving faction of its own, independent of both the distinct constituencies its various components may represent and the branch or significant structural unit in which it may be located. Class consciousness and cohesion are increasing in part because officials are indeed becoming a separate and distinct group, even independent of government, rotating in and out of the private sector, taking up positions in nonprofit corporations where they work with both the executive and legislative branches, so that political functionaries as a group are somewhat independent of the governmental apparatus and the people who in theory send them to Washington. Another way of thinking of this development is that the political class is becoming a sort of super-faction, a transcendent faction with interests that are higher, more general, and, to those in the class, more important than the interests of the lesser factions that legislators, lobbyists, and other political elements are supposed to serve.

ANTICORRUPTION POLICIES

Although they need to be strengthened and better enforced, policies for preventing pecuniary corruption are already in place. In recent years, the main threats from these forms of corruption have come from innovative schemes to circumvent existing controls. A good example is how the savings and loan industry was looted in the 1980s. [21, 22] This special-interest corruption in the finance and banking industry was repeated little more than a decade later, when Enron evaded controls on energy pricing and asset accounting. [23] The collapse of Enron and other financial conglomerates led policymakers to strengthen regulations for monitoring corporate accounting and holding corporate officers responsible for their companies' actions.

These examples suggest that once particular types of vulnerabilities have been recognized, the system of checks and balances will eventually be activated if schemes are devised to attack the same weak points in a new way. However, the political system's vulnerability to a deadly new form of anti-democratic corruption—conspiracies in high office to undermine popular sovereignty, often by manipulating national circumstances or priorities—has yet to be widely recognized, much less targeted for corrective action.

Conspiracy Charges at Nuremberg

Just as Americans have forgotten that the United States was founded on a conspiracy theory, they have also apparently forgotten that the Nuremberg war crimes trials after World War II were based on what was essentially a conspiracy theory. Nuremberg marked the first application of the legal concept of conspiracy to crimes of the state and of political organizations. [24] The International Military Tribunal (IMT) was authorized by its charter to try the Nazi defendants for "participating in the formulation or execution of a Common Plan or Conspiracy" to wage aggressive war. [25] Adopting the legal concept of conspiracy, the tribunal's charter stipulated that everyone who had been a party to the plan or conspiracy was responsible for all crimes committed in the plan's execution. The military tribunal was also empowered to designate entire groups as "criminal organizations" (Article 9). Anyone who had belonged to one of these groups was automatically judged guilty of any crimes committed by any of the group's members. [26 p. 396]

The IMT did not use the term "state crimes" or "crimes against democracy," but its jurisdiction and judgments prefigured the SCAD construct. [1] The indictment said the defendants intended to use false-flag terrorism, faked invasions, and similar tactics to turn democratic Germany into a police state by fomenting social panic and mobilizing mass support for authoritarian government and war. [25–28] Out of the twenty-two members of the Nazi Party leadership indicted on the conspiracy charge, eight were convicted, and four organizations in which one or more of these individuals had been members were designated as criminal.

It is important to understand that the Nazis did not come to power democratically. Before Germany's democratic institutions were eviscerated by Hitler and his supporters, the Nazis were unable to win control of Parliament through the electoral process. In the 1932 elections, when they reached their peak legitimately, they received only 37 percent of the total vote and gained only 230 of 608 seats. [24] The Nazis acquired control of Parliament by committing a number of SCADs in 1933 after President Hindenburg selected Hitler to head the cabinet as Chancellor of the Reich. Among other terrorist actions, Nazi conspirators set fire to the Parliament's headquarters (the Reichstag) and pinned the blame on a feeble-minded communist whom they had planted at the scene. [27, 24 pp. 45–46, 29 pp. 191–193] Claiming that a communist revolution was imminent, Hitler convinced Hindenburg to sign a decree suspending those sections of the Constitution that protected civil liberties [29 p. 194]. Then, using this decree, Hitler outlawed the Communist Party and arrested its leaders, thus giving the Nazis control of Parliament. [24, 29] Hitler then pushed through legislation that delegated legislative powers to himself and his cabinet. [29 p. 194]

By 1939, Germany had moved into Austria and Czechoslovakia in swift actions that Britain, France, and others protested but did not contest militarily. Hitler turned next to Poland, ordering false-flag attacks on several German towns near the Polish border. [24] Germans who had been condemned to a concentration camp were dressed in Polish military uniforms, drugged, and taken to the scene of the staged attack, where they were shot and killed. When Hitler invaded Poland, he defended the invasion as a counter-attack.

To the charge of conspiracy to wage aggressive war, only one of the Nazi conspirators tried by the IMT (Albert Speer) confessed guilt; all of the other defendants vigorously defended their actions. [26 pp. 376–379, 28 pp. 441–442] They argued that power needed to be given to a strong leader to maintain order in a nation with terrible economic conditions and threatened by communist revolutionaries; they said that at the time, they had believed the invasion of Poland was in fact a legitimate response to aggression; they denied knowledge of the Holocaust and war crimes against prisoners; and they presented evidence showing that Nazi policies had been formally developed and approved through legally mandated procedures. Despite the defendants' arguments and claims, the tribunal found them guilty.

The lesson that Americans, Germans, and others should have drawn from the evidence presented at Nuremberg is that modern liberal democracies are vulnerable to being hijacked by authoritarian leaders willing to carry out ruthless conspiracies. When leaders claim to need extraordinary powers to deal with threats, citizens should look carefully at the threats and consider the possibility that the threats are contrived. This is the time to be very strict in the application of all procedural requirements, from crime scene control and crime investigation to requirements related to legislative procedures and testifying truthfully to legislative and juridical forums as required by law. Violations of the law should be swiftly and aggressively prosecuted. Public officials are inclined to do just the opposite: to conduct a cursory investigation of the Reichstag fire or to let Lyndon Johnson abscond with President Kennedy's body. These are precisely the circumstances under which rigid conformity to the law should be practiced.

How Conspiracy Deniers Misread History

How did the existing literature on conspiracy theories, not to mention the many public officials and pundits who deploy the conspiracy-theory label in public discourse, manage to overlook the conspiratorial suspicions of the nation's Founders, especially when the Founders' fears of antidemocratic plots were stated in the Declaration of Independence, elaborated in the Federalist Papers, and written into the U.S. Constitution? How could the literature fail to notice that the Allied powers after World War II prosecuted and convicted Nazi leaders for conspiring to subvert representative democracy in Germany and wage wars of aggression? The literature attacking conspiracy theories has been blind to all this because most conspiracy deniers have accepted the conspiracy-theory label and its pejorative connotations uncritically. It would probably be too much to expect greater awareness of the CIA's conspiracy-theory propaganda program, even though it was made public in 1976, but many scholars and journalists still deserve criticism for failing to ask when and under what conditions norms against conspiracy belief emerged in elite discourse. Instead, generally they have embraced these norms and have simply assumed that conspiracy theories are patently irrational and pernicious. This has led journalists and scholars alike to search for the historical roots, not of contemporary elite norms against conspiracy theorizing, but of the supposedly delusional, conspiratorial mind-set.

As previously stated, Hofstadter traced the "paranoid style" in American politics to mass fears in the eighteenth and nineteenth centuries of Catholics, immigrants, the Illuminati, Masons, and anarchists. He argued that these loosely defined groups had been replaced in the popular imagination by specific individuals because of the influence of mass media. However, to pull the rabbit of modern conspiracy theories out of the hat of earlier social prejudices, Hofstadter had to omit from his list nineteenth-century conspiracy theories that, like those of concern today, pointed to specific individuals, as with the conspiracy theories involving King George, Aaron Burr, Henry Clay, John Quincy Adams, James Polk, Jefferson Davis, and others. In Hofstadter's analysis, the vigilant civic culture of the Founders disappeared behind a collage of mass fears directed at groups, organizations, and political ideologies.

In actuality, conspiracy beliefs about public officials constitute a separate and distinct category of political thought that has been part of American public discourse throughout its history. Their status as a subject matter governed by discursive norms was widely recognized at least by the late 1840s. Consider Lincoln's claim that President Polk misled the nation into the Mexican-American War. Lincoln carefully parsed President Polk's own words to show that Polk had spoken carefully because he intended to deceive. At times, Lincoln said, Polk attempted "to prove, by telling the truth, what he could not prove by telling the whole truth." Lincoln's analysis presupposed that speech by public officials in the context of deliberations about war is governed by recognized norms. Presidents are expected to speak plainly, and accusations of prevarication are not to be made without firm evidence.

In short, the post-WWII literature disparaging the popularity of "conspiracy theories" and linking them to nineteenth-century ethnocentrism and bigotry is simply an inaccurate and misleading account of American history.

3

CONSPIRACY DENIAL IN THE SOCIAL SCIENCES

An obvious question arises: how could a nation wary of power and founded on a conspiracy theory, a nation that divides and cross-checks government powers because it expects antidemocratic intrigues in high office, come to dismiss and disparage all manner of conspiratorial suspicions? Surely, a CIA propaganda program, no matter how cleverly contrived, would not be able to persuade such a nation that suspicions of elite political conspiracies are ludicrous. There must have been more to cause such a dramatic cultural shift.

Indeed there was, although the impact of the CIA should not be underestimated. Before conspiracy theories began to be ridiculed in the civic culture, they came into question in philosophy and social science in the early years of the Cold War. The rise of authoritarian social movements and totalitarianism in Europe in the first decades of the twentieth century were clearly fueled by ideologies that blamed war, economic upheaval, and other large-scale societal problems on economic classes, races, ethnic groups, and the like. These ideologies were a far cry from suspicions about the assassination of President Kennedy, nor were they comparable to historical studies of how political agreements are negotiated among powerful people. Nevertheless, about fifteen years before Kennedy's murder the notion of a generic conspiratorial worldview gained currency in philosophy and social science, and this, along with some related developments discussed below, led to a new blueprint for the conduct of social inquiry that excluded conspiracy theories of all kinds.

Understanding these intellectual developments and their significance requires drilling down from the broad sweep of history that we have been discussing to focus on roughly the first decade after World War II and the competing ideas of three scholars of that era. Before the war, much research in history and political science looked for behind-the-scenes decisions. After the war, the new method, referred to as "behavioralism," examined individual behavior in contained settings (such as voting behavior, administrative behavior, consumer choice, etc.) and sought to identify principles and strategies underlying behavioral patterns.

At about the same time that behavioralism was coming into vogue, another movement in philosophy and social science was taking hold in the study of ancient and modern political philosophy. Politically conservative, scholars in this movement advocated elite political intrigue in modern representative democracies to shore up mass patriotism and foster popular support for a vigorous confrontation with authoritarian rival nations. There is more than irony in the fact that scholars in one field were actively discouraging mass suspicions of elite political intrigue while scholars in another field were teaching elites that such intrigue is necessary. These unfortunately complementary movements in the academy, when combined in the larger society, may have made America preternaturally vulnerable to elite political conspiracies.

The Transformation of U.S. Social Science

The intellectual basis for abandoning the conspiratorial concerns of the Founders was developed in the 1940s and 1950s by two European philosophers: Karl Popper and Leo Strauss. It would be only a modest exaggeration to say that Popper and to some extent Strauss blamed conspiracy theory for totalitarianism in Europe, World War II, and the Holocaust. Popper is largely responsible for the mistaken idea that conspiracy theories are modern variants of ancient superstitions and nineteenth-century social prejudices, and that, thus rooted in irrationality and paranoia, are the seeds of authoritarian political movements [1 pp. 94–97]. For his part, Strauss did not use the term "conspiracy theory," but he advocated state political propaganda and covert actions to protect a society's traditional beliefs and ongoing illusions about its origins and virtues from unrestrained inquiries or, in other words, conspiratorial theorizing [2 pp. 146–173]. Strauss' thinking differed from much of Popper's analysis but saw scientific criticism of official accounts of important historical events as a precursor to totalitarianism because it undermines respect for the nation's laws and traditional beliefs; it ushers in, with philosophy and science, the view that nothing is true; and it unleashes tyrannical impulses in the political class as top leaders compete for popular support. [3] Although Popper and Strauss arrived by different routes, they agreed that conspiracy theories can fuel totalitarian political movements that threaten respect for human dignity, popular sovereignty, and the rule of law. [4]

Before these European ideas came to America in the aftermath of World War II, U.S. social science was thoroughly American, and concerns about oppressive factions and antidemocratic intrigues were central to the study of American politics and government. One of the nation's leading scholars was Charles Beard, who was famous for tracing features of the U.S. Constitution to the financial interests of the Constitution's framers. In his last book, which appeared shortly before his death in 1947, Beard made a strong case that President Franklin Roosevelt provoked the Japanese attack on Pearl Harbor and withheld from military commanders in the Pacific intelligence about when and where the attack would occur. [5] In the shadow of the Nuremberg war crimes trials and the execution of Nazi leaders for conspiring to wage wars of aggression, Beard's conspiratorial accusations took on grave significance, and yet America's political class assigned them little importance, having concluded, in the wake of the Allies' victory, that Roosevelt's tactics may have been deceptive but his policy had been vindicated. Similarly, although Beard's allegations held up well to subsequent academic scrutiny, they were nevertheless brushed aside by a new generation of historians and political scientists who, under the influence especially of Popper, turned away from studying prospects and impediments to democratic governance and took up research, instead, on the behavior of citizens and mid-level public officials in various mundane forms, including voting and program administration.

Today, Popper and Strauss are familiar to most scholars, but in the 1940s, they were obscure figures in Europe and more or less entirely unknown in America. In the early stages of their careers, when World War II began, both men were studying classical political philosophy and modern political theory in an effort to understand the genesis of modern totalitarian government within a culture committed to reason and freedom of expression. Both suggested that modern liberal democracies were vulnerable to totalitarianism because of societal tensions caused by scientific erosion of traditional beliefs that otherwise reinforced established laws and norms.

Popper and Strauss' ideas quickly proved influential in the academy for at least two reasons. One was that U.S. scholars in political science, the oldest social science, were divided between, on the one hand, traditionalists who studied political philosophy, law, political economy, and the like, and on the other hand a new generation of "behavioralists" committed to "value-free," quantitative studies of voting behavior, public opinion, legislative roll-call voting, and other narrow subject matters approached with "mid-range" theories. Popper's ideas appealed to the new generation and swept through the social sciences as young scholars rose and many traditionalists retired or died.

The shift within U.S. social science to mid-range theory and behavioralism was propelled not only by demographics and Popper's influence in political philosophy but also by McCarthyism and associated hostility toward what were referred to at the time as "political economy" and "comprehensive political theory," both of which compared capitalist and communist systems and suggested that each had important strengths and weaknesses. Not surprisingly, the agenda for social scientific theory and research during the Cold War, especially during the 1940s, 1950s, and 1960s, raised very few questions about the rectitude of public officials and the democratic character of U.S. political institutions. Social scientists assumed that, to repeat an often-used phrase from the period, political leaders in the United States "obeyed the rules of the game." By 1964, when the Warren Commission presented its dubious account of the assassination of President Kennedy to a stunned nation, U.S. mainstream social science, with its Popperian devotion to mid-range theory and behavioral research, lacked conceptual resources to recognize a possible coup or purge. Hence American scholars, unlike their European counterparts, voiced no criticisms of the Warren Commission's report. This left American public opinion subject to the influence of a lopsided competition of ideas as the pejorative conspiracy-theory label was deployed by the CIA to cast doubt on the Warren Commission's critics.

For his part, Strauss rallied the small band of scholars who remained committed to classical political philosophy, and they launched a successful rearguard action to hold a small piece of social scientific territory dedicated to the study of esoteric teachings in philosophical texts revered within Western civilization. Today, "Straussians," as they are called, generally have limited influence inside the academy, which remains predominately behavioral and quantitative, but they are a major presence in political philosophy and through the latter exert considerable influence outside the academy. Indeed, Straussians are largely responsible for the rise of what is known as "neoconservatism" in U.S. foreign policy. [6, 7] When President Reagan referred to the Soviet Union as the "evil empire," his use of moral language was attributed to the emphasis of Straussians on standing up for democracy against tyranny both abroad and at home. Not all neoconservatives are Straussians, and vice versa, but there is much overlap between the two groups, and neoconservatives have determined or at least have significantly affected the course of U.S. foreign policy since the 1980s. [7, 8]

Popper and Strauss were influential also because their ideas were original, timely, and highly relevant to the Anglo-American alliance of World War II and the Cold War. These obscure philosophers offered novel insights into revered texts in the canon of classical and modern philosophy, located the roots of World War II and the Cold War in the philosophical foundations of Western culture, and suggested that liberal democracies could protect themselves from totalitarian tendencies by placing normative restrictions on social scientific theory and research [1 pp. 172–177, 9, 10].

Ironically, however, Popper and Strauss' analyses were on most points in fundamental disagreement with each other, including the implications of social scientific conspiracy theories, such as some variants of Marxism, the theory of the "power elite," and other positions in sociology and political science that attributed undesirable events to secret plots among powerful people [11]. Both Popper and Strauss suggested that candor about such matters could unleash distrust, intolerance, and authoritarianism in liberal societies, but Popper said this was because such theories are always *false*, while Strauss suggested it was because they are often *true*. This issue was never addressed, much less resolved, and yet conspiracy belief was nonetheless condemned by both camps and, because of this and other factors (demography, the postwar expansion of the universities, McCarthyism), it rapidly became unpopular in the American academy.

Philosophical Perspectives on Conspiracy Theory

In addition to weakening the nation's reliance on the Founders' political science, the stigmatization of conspiracy theory in U.S. social science involved a radical change in the nation's progressive vision of history. The generation of the American Revolution was imbued with the ethos of the Enlightenment, which expected freedom of speech and inquiry to fuel gradual but steady progress in knowledge, technology, tolerance, and civility. The Founders assumed that the constitutional framework of divided powers and checks and balances would facilitate orderly historical progress so long as political institutions did not become rigged or subverted by the untoward influence of an oppressive faction. This was also the view of history embraced by Charles Beard as he sought to expose antidemocratic intrigues in American politics and inherited advantages for dominant classes in U.S. political institutions.

However, the rise of totalitarianism in Europe, World War II, and the Cold War challenged this optimistic vision of history and led to major reformulations of both liberal and conservative political philosophies. In this endeavor, Karl Popper became one of the founding voices of what is today called

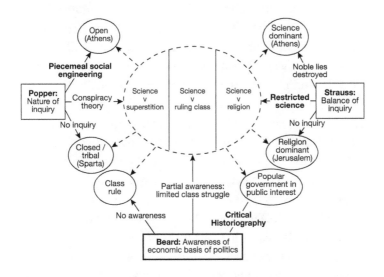

Figure 3.1. Political alternatives delineated by Beard, Popper, and Strauss.

"neoliberalism," while Leo Strauss more or less singlehand-edly founded "neoconservatism" (or so some scholars claim). Figure 3.1 sketches Beard's, Popper's, and Strauss' politico-historical theories and situates their take on modern indus-trial democracies in the context of their different accounts of the origins, trajectory, and options for those systems. To reflect their relative positioning on a left-right continuum of modern political ideologies, Popper's theory is on the left, Strauss' theory is on the right, and Beard's theory is in the middle. As discussed in more detail below, each theory can be reconstructed for the sake of analysis as delineating three alternative forms of society and positing a political factor that, hypothetically, determines where a society is positioned in the spectrum of societal possibilities. In each theory, mod-ern representative democracies (depicted by the large circle in the center of the figure) are seen as residing between two alternative political formations and therefore as liable to move in either direction. The large circle articulates three different "tensions" because Popper, Beard, and Strauss all discussed modern liberal democracies in general and American democracy specifically, but they conceptualized it differently depending on their account of the options. The levers of change posited by all three theories are related to principles governing the scope and nature of inquiry into the society's history, traditions, and political institutions.

One of the reasons for explicating the three theories in such detail is to highlight the theoretical premises needed to support positions on the existence of elite conspiracies and the implications of popular beliefs (theories) about such conspiracies. Today, as we have seen, the pejorative connotations of the conspiracy-theory label have the effect of dismissing conspiratorial suspicions out of hand with no discussion whatsoever, when in fact the issues at stake are quite complex and also vitally important. Each of these conceptualizations of the societal possibilities and levers of societal change is like a transparency that can be superimposed on American politics and civic culture to locate crucial aspects of social theory and inquiry, including conspiracy theory, and trace their hypothesized effects on the overall society. Table 3.1 (page 206) lists the views of Beard, Popper, and Strauss on conspiracy and conspiracy theorizing in modern representative democracies. The table is a companion to Figure 3.1.

Significantly, although we speak of conspiracy theory as if it were an objective reality understood similarly by everyone who uses the term, its meaning varies from one theoretical context to another. Consequently, people are often talking past each other when they differ on the issue. When speaking of conspiracy theories, Beard, for example, means hypotheses about specific actions by identifiable persons or groups that result in identifiable advantages for these groups in law or political institutions. In contrast, Popper usually means a superstition-like belief that large societal calamities, such as wars, financial crises, famines, and the like, were caused by such amorphous categories of people as economic classes, races, ethnic groups, and so on. Strauss does not use the term "conspiracy" at all, but speaks instead of "noble lies," so for him a conspiracy theory would be an ill-considered speculation, probably by a non-elite and perhaps partially or fully true, casting doubt on a noble lie. Thus for Strauss we might say a conspiracy theory is a "dastardly truth."

Underlying these different accounts of society and of conspiracy theories are different assumptions about the basic components of societies, what holds societies together, what possible forms they can take, and more. Nevertheless, these frameworks are sufficiently commensurable to allow comparisons and empirical evaluation. All of the theories stress that traditional religious beliefs and accounts of the society's founding and values cannot withstand scientific scrutiny, but they differ on where conspiracy theory fits into such inquiry and whether unbridled inquiry in general leads to democracy or totalitarian tyranny. With respect to this last factor—the conduct of social inquiry and historical studies—the three theories pose stark choices.

In this reconstruction of Beard's theory, societies are assumed to move sequentially from tyranny by a propertied class to a limited democracy like the U.S., and then eventually to full democracy as the privileges of property are stripped out of governing institutions. However, Beard recognizes that modern democracies can regress into authoritarianism, as happened when the Nazis took control of Germany and as was occurring in America in Beard's lifetime as presidents (Wilson [5 p. 5] and Roosevelt [5 pp. 573–598]) increasingly misled the nation into wars of aggression. In his view, this danger springs from the conspiratorial, antidemocratic tendencies of political and economic elites. Therefore, the survival of democracy and continued progress in history depend on what Beard refers to as "critical historiography" to expose elite manipulation of democratic processes [5 p. 574, note 1]. Beard's economic interpretation of the Constitution, his conspiracy theory of the Fourteenth Amendment, and his critical account of America's entry into World War II exemplify this type of inquiry.

Popper argues that societies vary in the extent to which they allow freedom of speech and conscience [12 pp. 169–201]. In the early stages of their history, all societies are "closed," and their customs, religious beliefs, and values are taken for granted as natural. Contact with other societies that have different customs and beliefs leads all societies to become more "open" as myths are questioned and arbitrary restrictions on speech, lifestyles, and participation in making collective decisions are eliminated. However, this breakdown of tradition causes strain and discomfort for everyone, and it threatens classes that benefited from inherited beliefs. These threatened classes appeal to superstition, fear, and ethnic prejudices to divide the masses and generate support for authoritarian government and a return to traditional lifestyles. For Popper, conspiracy theories are a secular form of superstition and serve this antidemocratic agenda. This is why Popper, even though he is an advocate of the "open society," seeks to stifle conspiracy theorizing in the social sciences by arguing that conspiracy theory is unscientific (and irrational).

Strauss' vision of history is similar to Popper's with one important exception. [7, 8] Strauss agrees with Popper that societies start out with customs supported by a mythos and that, as they encounter societies with different beliefs, this mythos comes into question. But Strauss argues that if philosophy and science are allowed to utterly discredit the society's claims about its origins and about the value of its institutions and way of life, ruling elites will lose their respect for law and will abuse their powers as they compete with one another for popular support and glory. Strauss assumes that all but the most primitive societies are stratified into an elite and mass; that the elites are simply smarter, stronger, braver, and better than are the masses; and that the decisive factor in social organization is how the elites are controlled and managed. For the most part, he thinks the latter depends on the elites' reverence, or lack thereof, for the established laws and traditions. Elites who revere their societies' values and norms will be magnanimous, restrained, and caring. When traditional beliefs erode, the elites become gangsters and eventually one gangster rises through guile and brutality to the top, thus establishing tyranny. Therefore, whereas Popper envisions as the endpoint of societal development a totally open society without superstition, Strauss says such a society is not possible in the long run because it would eventually become totalitarian or, in Strauss' terms, "tyrannical." Democracy and respect for human dignity depend on "salutary myths" and "noble lies" that must be propagated by a special class of philosophical elites who are dedicated to guarding the society's values and traditions.

Strauss never defines what he means by "noble lies" beyond referring to Plato's *The Republic*, which is where the term originates. But this was certainly no oversight on Strauss' part, for it leaves the matter open, which is to say, unlimited. For Plato, noble lies included myths and stories about the society's origins, rigged lotteries for choosing marriage partners, infanticide, and other actions to create a strong people willing and able to defend themselves in a hostile world. This short list would seem to imply support for many antidemocratic elite conspiracies, including assassinating political leaders, framing dissidents, fomenting mass fear, demonizing rival societies, and letting enemy attacks succeed so that the masses are galvanized to deal with a gathering threat. [3] The upshot for modern democracies is that political leaders must conspire to manipulate mass opinion and reinforce patriotism, reverence for the Founders, religious faith and piety, and generally "love of one's own." Like science and philosophy, conspiracy theories (or "dastardly truths") are corrosive of political cohesion and the rule of (traditional) law because they undermine authority and raise doubts about foundational stories extolling the societies' founders and rules. Thus, from a Straussian perspective, conspiracy theories pose an existential threat to the social order, not because they are mistaken, but because they are likely to be true, and of course, being true, difficult to refute.

Clearly, all three of these theories of history and related accounts of conspiracy theories cannot be valid on all points, but the disagreements between them are subtle and complex. Such is the nature of differences between divergent philosophical perspectives. It is therefore incumbent on those who engage the topic of conspiracy beliefs to be theoretically self-aware and open to discourse about the implications of competing premises. Journalists, public officials, and scholars who ignore the lessons of Charles Beard, who do not remain on guard against potential intrigue by dominant classes to preserve their political power by rigging the system while they still can, and who dismiss conspiracy beliefs as outlandish and pernicious are actually embracing Popper's theory unawares, assuming that elite conspiracies cannot succeed or be kept secret and failing to consider whether, for example, there is any empirical evidence to recommend this theory over, say, the theories of Beard and Strauss. They may also wish to consider that the theory they are embracing— the conspiracy-denying theory of Karl Popper—is blind to the possibility that a segment of U.S. political elites, perhaps under the influence of Leo Strauss or a living Straussian, is conspiring to manipulate American democracy to make it more authoritarian for the sake of preserving a remnant of American democracy in a hostile world.

The Conspiracy Theories of Charles Beard

Charles Beard argued throughout his career that American democracy had been repeatedly manipulated by political insiders for personal gain or to serve hidden agendas. He put forward three major theories alleging elite intrigue to rig political institutions. In 1913 he became famous among academics, and infamous among political and economic elites, with the publication of *An Economic Interpretation of the Constitution of the United States*. In it, he applied Marxian class theory to American government by tracing key features of the U.S. Constitution to the framers' economic backgrounds and personal financial interests. [13]

Second, in 1927 Beard and his wife Mary put forward a theory of how political insiders had rigged the Constitution to benefit corporations. Within the academy, the theory came to be called the "conspiracy theory of the Fourteenth Amendment." The Beards claimed that railroad interests manipulated the amendment's drafting to open the way for the courts to say it granted the rights of individuals to corporations. [14 pp. 112–113]

Third, the allegations that Roosevelt lied to the public and manipulated the United States into World War II were presented by Charles Beard in *President Roosevelt and the Coming of the War, 1941: Appearances and Realities*. [5] The book says President Roosevelt withheld intelligence about the impending attack from U.S. commanders in the Pacific until it was too late for them to act, and then set an investigation in motion that blamed the commanders for being unprepared while it absolved the president and other officials in Washington of any responsibility.

Beard was fully aware that his conspiracy theories were often criticized, in his view incorrectly, for appealing to mass suspicions rather than reason and evidence. In 1936, he wrote *The Devil Theory of War*, which sought to differenti-

*Charles Beard. (Source: George Grantham
Bain Collection, Library of Congress)*

ate scholarly inquiries into the causes of war from propagation of unsubstantiated rumors that maligned financiers and armaments producers. [15] In the book, he denounced popular speculations that wars were caused by behind-the-scenes manipulations by people who stood to gain financially. He called his own research "critical historiography" because it started, not from ambiguous suspicions, but from the government's official account of events, drawing on official records to check the official account's validity.

Beard believed that presidential actions leading to America's entry into World War I and World War II jeopardized the constitutional separation of powers and brought the United States close to Caesarism. Unless Roosevelt and his administration were held accountable for their abuses of power and manipulation of democratic processes, Beard concluded, the precedents set by Roosevelt would allow future presidents to completely ignore their moral and constitutional obligations to keep Congress well informed and to defer to Congress' role in deciding whether to take the nation to war. [5 pp. 582–584]

Popper's Critique of the "Conspiracy Theory of Society"

Karl Popper was not the first scholar to employ the term "conspiracy theory," but he was the first scholar who defined and used the term much as it is understood today. As discussed above, scholars writing in the 1930s had referred to Charles and Mary Beard's "conspiracy theory of the Fourteenth Amendment." However, they did not intend the label to be a pejorative designation. It was simply used to distinguish the Beards' theory from the thesis that the wording of the Fourteenth Amendment reflected no hidden agenda.

Popper attached a pejorative connotation to the term "conspiracy theory" in the second volume of *The Open Society and Its Enemies*, which was first published during World

Karl Popper. (Source: Wikipedia)

War II and offered a full-throated philosophical defense of the Anglo-American cause, which in Popper's view was to preserve democracy and freedom against totalitarianism. Popper claimed to be concerned with conspiratorial explanations of isolated events only in relation to the "conspiracy theory of society." He defined this theory as "the view that an explanation of a social phenomenon consists in the discovery of the men or groups who are interested in the occurrence of this phenomenon (sometimes it is a hidden interest which has first to be revealed), and who have planned and conspired to bring it about." [1 p. 95] Popper said he was critiquing the conspiracy theory of society as a "view of the aims of the social sciences." [1 p. 95]

Popper assumed that the conspiracy theory of society is nonsense. He said the theory was widely held and very old, and was "a typical result of the secularization of a religious superstition." Ancient religions attributed wars to scheming by the gods. The (modern) conspiracy theory of society replaced the gods with "powerful men or groups—sinister pressure groups whose wickedness is responsible for all the evils we suffer from—such as the learned Elders of Zion,

or the monopolists, or the capitalists, or the imperialists."
[1 p. 95]

Popper recognized that conspiracies occur, but he claimed
that conspiracy theories are misguided because most plans
in social life rarely succeed, conspiracy or no conspiracy.
"Social life is not only a trial of strength between opposing
groups: it is action within a more or less resilient or brittle
framework of institutions and traditions, and it creates—
apart from any conscious counteraction—many unforeseen
reactions in this framework, some of them perhaps even
unforeseeable." [1 p. 95] By "brittle," Popper appears to mean
that institutions counteract the efforts of the people within
them. As an example, Popper cites the case of a man who
wants to buy a house; the man does not intend to cause a rise
in house prices, "but the very fact that he appears on the market as a buyer will tend to raise market prices." [1 p. 96] From
this, Popper concludes the conspiracy theory of society cannot be true because the theory amounts to the assertion that
all results are what people intended. Popper seems confused
on this point and has been criticized for it, [16] but the statement makes sense if we assume that what Popper is talking
about is the conspiracy theory of society as a basic strategy
of social scientific explanation. In principle, although probably not in practice, conspiracy-minded social scientists
would, upon encountering an event, seek to determine if it
could be accounted for by some collusion among powerful
people or groups.

So, to reiterate: the conspiracy theory of society is a strategy of explanation and inquiry in the social sciences that
assumes, counterfactually for the sake of research, that all
events were planned by powerful people who benefited from
them. However, the theory cannot be true in general, that is,
the conspiracy theory of society cannot be true, because, in
Popper's words "it amounts to the assertion that all results,
even those which at first sight do not appear to be intended

by anybody, are the intended results of the actions of people who are interested in these results." [1 p. 96] Clearly, though, there are plenty of examples where conspiracies (plans) fail and events are caused by something else.

The problem is that Popper takes this conclusion to apply to all conspiracy theories, not just the conspiracy theory of society, which is, so to speak, a "unified conspiracy theory." He says, incorrectly, that anyone who believes an event has been caused by a secret plot must believe in the conspiracy theory of society, that is, that all events have been caused by secret plots. In actuality, however, there is no reason why someone who believes some event is the result of a plot must believe *all* events are the result of plots. Popper is simply confused. [16] The claim that would be true is the reverse: if someone believes all events have been caused by secret plots, then this person must believe that any single event has been caused by a plot.

Popper mistakenly conflates all conspiracy theories with the conspiracy theory of society because he wants to reorient the social sciences from studying history and changes in the overall structure of society, and turn them toward piecemeal social engineering. Popper sees the conspiracy theory of society as a variation on "historicism" and indeed as the primitive prototype of "historicist thinking." Historicism, he explains, is the theory that history has a definite goal or endpoint. For Popper, conspiracy theory stands between the magical beliefs of tribal societies and the full-blown historical prophecies of Plato in the ancient era, and of Marxists, Nazis, and fascists in the modern era. In Popper's mind, this is why conspiracy theories are so dangerous: they are a simple version of the historicist theory that mobilizes totalitarian political movements.

In making this claim, Popper was assuming that conspiracy beliefs are what we would today refer to as "scalar," or "scalable," that is, they can vary in size or scope while retaining the same basic design. For example, on computer screens, letters are scalar; the font size or the screen magnification can be increased or reduced, and the letters grow larger or smaller while retaining their exact form. What Popper had in mind was that conspiracy beliefs could range from very narrowly focused suspicions to grand theories of history and they would still embody the same framework, produce the same motivational structure, and cause the same patterns of social action. Furthermore, while he did not say it in exactly these terms, Popper assumed that once the conspiracy-theory frame took hold in someone's mind, that person's thoughts would, so to speak, levitate from mundane suspicions to high-flying, grandiose philosophies of history.

The "scalability premise" is what drives contemporary critics of conspiracy theory to search for a definition of conspiracy theory that is universal and does not depend on conventional beliefs. Despite their best efforts, they quickly become tangled in the fact that some conspiracy theories are true. This means the flaw is not in the basic conspiratorial structure of the theory. Unfortunately, rather than admitting that this means conspiracy accusations must be evaluated on their merits and cannot simply be ridiculed and pooh-poohed because they allege crimes in high places, they do what they say they hate about conspiracy theorists: they jump to conclusions, refuse to consider all the evidence, and so on.

Popper also assumes that historical events or patterns are scalable. He sees direct parallels between World War II and the Peloponnesian War, between Sparta and Athens. Sparta represents the closed society that is using authoritarian governance to turn back the process of shedding archaic beliefs or superstitions and rationalizing social institutions. Athens is the open society, but it is threatened by internal oligarchs who want to follow the Spartan model and impose tyranny. On Popper's account, Plato is the oligarchs' intellectual spokesman. In the modern era, Sparta is played by communist Russia, Nazi Germany, and fascist Italy. They are closed societies trying to turn back the secularizing process of history.

Athens is played by the liberal democracies, especially the United Kingdom and the United States. Within the U.S., Popper believes, social sciences are voices for the conspiracy theory of society, and, as such, they play into totalitarian tendencies. Conspiracy believers are dangerous fools because they assume that history or major historical events have underlying causes, such as class consciousness, various "interests," dialectical materialism, and so on. This explanatory framework leads to totalitarian political movements directed at major historical goals and targeting classes, groups, races, and others who, according to the ideology propagated by oligarchs, are in the background scheming.

Popper argues that social scientists should have nothing to do with historicism or with the kind of grand theorizing it represents. They should examine individual actions in circumscribed institutional settings and track the effects of such actions on the reactions of others in the same settings. In Popper's words, "the main task of the social sciences" should be "to try to analyze these reactions and to perceive them as far as possible." [1 p. 94] Stated a little differently, the social sciences should "analyze the unintended social repercussions of intentional human actions." The focus should be on explicating what Popper called "the logic of the situation." [1 p. 97] Insight into what people are trying to achieve and how existing institutions are frustrating their intentions would serve as a basis for "piecemeal social engineering" to find more effective institutional arrangements. [1 p. 95]

Strauss on "Noble Lies" and "Salutary Myths"

Leo Strauss did not address conspiracy theory directly, but he did write about and endorse the propagation of "noble lies" and "salutary myths." The term "noble lies" was drawn from Plato's *The Republic*, along with the ideas that philosophers must be guardians of the state and must have as their first priority maintaining the political conditions necessary for philosophy to exist. On the basis of his study of classical political philosophy and the politics of ancient democracy, oligarchy, and tyranny, Strauss concluded that modern representative democracies could not survive domestic turmoil or wars with authoritarian foreign powers unless elites contrived to shore up patriotism, martial values, militaristic tendencies, and a certain degree of belligerence in international relations. [3] He drew this idea from Plato's dialogues but adapted it to the modern era. In effect, Strauss believed state political crimes, insofar as they reinforce the society's values and myths, are necessary and beneficial because without them, liberal democracies are doomed to become totalitarian or to be conquered by totalitarian regimes. The challenge in Strauss' view was to keep political intrigues within certain bounds and maintain some liberty and free speech while staying strong and well defended. Equating modern science with classical philosophy, he discovered in philosophy lessons for modern science about keeping some of its knowledge secret, respecting established religions, and inculcating in future leaders values conducive to respect for law and human dignity. [17]

Strauss' account of the initial stage of civilization is virtually identical to Popper's. All societies start out believing that their gods are the true gods and their conventions are the true and best way of life. When they encounter other societies they have only two options. They can hold to the primacy of their own values and assert that their culture is the one founded in truth, or the one with the only true God, or they can abstract away from existing societies to identify and live by the laws that are required by human existence in general. Strauss said that Jerusalem took the first path while Athens took the second. Modern liberal democracies, on the other hand, are the heirs of a Greco-Roman and Judeo-Christian civilization that incorporated both philosophy and religion into their systems of government and law. Western civilization is vibrant because philosophy and religion are in constant tension. In liberal democracies, this tension is institutionalized in the twin freedoms of religion and speech. If left unchecked, religion would prohibit impious speech, and science would prohibit laws to enforce piety.

On the basis of an innovative analysis of classical political philosophy, Strauss challenged modern belief in the civilizing effect of science. He concluded that the ancient philosophers had realized that a society based on philosophy alone eventually transformed into tyranny. [3] The truth discovered by philosophy is that there are no gods, the universe is eternal rather than created, and life according to nature is for the strong to rule the weak. If this truth is shared with people who are not philosophers, social order will be destroyed because non-philosophers will no longer revere their society as unique and exemplary and will become lawless and politically opportunistic. Elites will abandon restraint in their competition with each other, and the masses will turn to elite demagogues who promise them equality of power, wealth, and status. The result will be rule by the will of the tyrant rather than by the laws of the land.

Strauss argued that totalitarianism had arisen in Western civilization in the 1930s because modern philosophers had failed to conceal their dangerous truths from ordinary men. In Strauss' account, the positions of both Beard and Popper reflected the Enlightenment philosophy that discovering and spreading the truth will lead to technological and social progress. In Strauss' view, however, science had destroyed belief in God and in the laws of religion, and this led to totalitarianism and to what Strauss called "the crisis of the West." [4]

The political ideology of the representative democracies

was liberalism, which said that no lifestyle was better than another and that all lifestyles were allowed so long as political authority was obeyed. The problem with this philosophy, Strauss taught, was that it was too tolerant. It implied that there were no values worth fighting for, a belief that left modern democracies unable to mobilize the martial zeal necessary to wage war against an enemy fighting to prove its strength and valor, and unconstrained by traditional respect for the rules of war, human dignity, and so on.

Strauss saw little possibility for religious faith to be renewed spontaneously in the face of scientific reasoning. He agreed with Nietzsche and Weber, his immediate predecessors in German philosophy, that Western morality was erected on an increasingly untenable religious foundation. But he seems to have believed that religion could be salvaged by philosophers if the latter would only recognize the need to do so for philosophy's sake. Totalitarianism prohibited free speech and brought an end to true philosophy and science. Strauss concluded that Western culture could be preserved only by somehow insulating biblical beliefs from scientific criticism.

For Strauss, the only strategy likely to succeed in preserving liberal democracy and the philosophical way of life it allowed was to prop up confidence in Western values and the democratic system of government. He believed this necessitated noble lies and salutary myths, which would include an account of history showing that the democracy in question was fair in war and generous in peace, and that its founders were unmatched in courage, honesty, and overall greatness. Strauss said there is a natural tendency to revere ancient authority, but this human inclination must be reinforced with tales of heroism. Presumably, civic culture would also need to be buttressed by calculated acts of hypocrisy by the nation's leaders—for example, President Roosevelt maneuvering Japan to attack the United States; the victorious Allies trying and executing Japanese and German leaders for war crimes the Allies had also committed; and harping about the threat of global communism during the Cold War when much of the "expansionism" the U.S. decried was coming from the U.S. itself. Strauss did not speak openly of all that would be condoned by his point of view, but SCADs to shore up hatred against the enemy would seem to be acceptable. The key consideration would be the ability to avoid detection. Just about anything would be allowed if it could be kept secret.

Dirty tricks would also be justified for discrediting scientists, historians, journalists, independent investigators, and others who formulated conspiracy theories that discredited or cast doubt on beliefs important to the democratic society's existence in a hostile world, a world in which liberal democracies are faced with powerful, totalitarian enemies. In this context, formulating and popularizing conspiracy theories that undermine popular confidence in the nation's leaders, institutions, and traditions would border on treason. Hence the state could reasonably resort to targeting domestic conspiracy-theory groups and networks with Sunstein and Vermeule's program of "cognitive infiltration."

American Neoconservatism

The plans of Popper and Strauss for bringing liberal democracy through the era of totalitarianism appear to have succeeded. The only questions are, whose methods were employed to deal with the threat of totalitarianism domestically, and what effects did they have on America's democratic governance institutions and civic culture? The answers to these questions have important implications for the prospects and character of American democracy today.

The Allied victory over totalitarianism is apparent in at least two respects. Of course, one is the end of the Cold War. The dissolution of the Soviet Union was unexpected and was due in part to doubts harbored by Russia's political class about the ability and willingness of Soviet intelligence agencies to adapt to democratic institutions and the rule of law. However, the Soviet collapse also stemmed from the Allies' policy of containment, which was adopted at the beginning of the Cold War and was adhered to carefully in the conflicts over Korea, Cuba, Berlin, Vietnam, and Afghanistan, to name only the major hotspots.

America's success in managing the confrontation with totalitarianism is also evident, and may have been made possible, by the hard-line, militaristic political culture called for by Popper and especially by Strauss. Scholars of all persuasions generally agree that the range of ideas considered in American politics is very limited and is slanted in ways benefiting political, military, and/or business elites. No serious student of American politics would expect any new president to be able to recast or break free of this circumscribed consensus and take U.S. policy in a radically different direction. American politics is generally conservative and militaristic, and its policy agenda in international affairs is characterized by stability and firmness in the face of external pressures. For better or for worse, the United States stands its ground and defends its interests around the world. In the slightly more than six decades that have elapsed since the death of Franklin Roosevelt, America has been led by twelve different presidents, six of whom were Republicans and six Democrats. Despite all of this change in leadership, the nation's military posture and policies have remained remarkably stable.

The question, though, is how this stability across the post-WWII era was achieved. All of the major theories in the social sciences assume, perhaps naïvely, that the limited range of variation in U.S. public policy stems from natural and legitimate factors in American politics. The theories are rational choice liberalism, pluralism, elitism, critical theory, and postmodernism. While these theories vary widely, all of them trace American militarism to such natural processes as, respectively, collective action problems in mobilizing individuals to address issues of broad concerns as opposed to special and distinct concern; the political advantages of affluent classes and organizations; the unified perspective of elites who circulate between business and government; [11] capitalist principles of organization that restrict government interventions into the economy; [18] and the imperatives of population management or "governmentality" embedded in the modern bureaucratic state. [19, 20]

Like the social scientists who came after them, Beard and Popper assumed that the conservative, militarily aggressive priorities and policies in American politics were a genuine reflection of political processes that are more or less democratic. Of course, in comparison to mainstream theories, their theories allowed for a high degree of oligarchy and intrigue, but they saw this as a publicly acknowledged and accepted part of the system. For example, Beard would agree that the conspirators who drafted the Fourteenth Amendment were not violating a criminal statute, and Popper would argue that the drafters of the Fourteenth Amendment, even if the conspiracy had been criminal, probably achieved few of their goals. Beard would attribute the conservatism of American politics to upper-class bias built into America's political institutions. Popper would cite the brittleness of all institutions.

However, the possibility remains that American militarism has been maintained by SCADs, or more generally the policies advocated by Strauss. If the system followed the Platonic model of guardians, the requisite actions would be assigned to covert operatives by an inner circle of national security elites. The operatives would have developed their skills in covert operations overseas. The tactics might include, for example, political assassination, false-flag terrorism, election theft, military provocation, and contrived economic crises. [21, 22] In theory, national security elites would stage, facilitate, or execute events that discipline politics and policy by changing either the lineup of top policymakers or the perceived constellation of major problems and threats facing the social order. Their objectives would be to foster social panic and militarism in the American mass public and belligerency in U.S. foreign policy. [21]

Of course, the source of American neoconservative militarism in the post-WWII era is an empirical question that poses serious difficulties for observation because of extensive government secrecy. There is also the potential for the object of inquiry to turn on its observers and not simply elude detection but deploy violence or other forms of force. Nevertheless, experience shows that at least some access to this milieu occasionally opens up, as it did with the Watergate hearings, Nixon's audiotapes, the Church Committee, and other inquiries. Consequently, the failure of all major research and theoretical traditions in U.S. social science to investigate the possibility of strategic interventions by national security elites and covert operatives into U.S. domestic politics can be reasonably attributed to powerful norms in academia, as in the broader society, against speculating about possible mischief in high office. Indeed, it is likely that the CIA propaganda program to instantiate the conspiracy-theory concept in America's civic culture was directed as much toward intellectuals as ordinary citizens. Of course, there is no reason to believe that the CIA program that was discovered by a Freedom of Information Act request is the only such CIA program that has been, or is, shaping U.S. culture.

This would explain the counterintuitive direction of U.S. social scientific research in the face of massive growth in U.S. military and intelligence resources, and in numerous indications that national security elites do at times become actively engaged in domestic politics. It would seem that Charles Beard served as an example that discouraged other scholars from inquiring into the rectitude of America's top leaders. For despite Watergate, Iran-Contra, Plame-gate, and other scandals involving SCADs and the politicization of national security policy and personnel, scholars in the postwar era have paid little attention to the dangers posed to modern representative democracy by the class of political elites who are responsible for guarding state secrets, gathering intelligence, identifying foreign and domestic enemies, and conducting covert operations against them.

Today in the United States, intelligence agencies are generally prohibited from carrying out covert actions against American citizens, but this prohibition is not always honored. When violations of the prohibition come to light, as with the warrantless wiretaps of the Bush-Cheney administration, they are dismissed as isolated mistakes of judgment by overzealous officials. In actuality, however, U.S. military and intelligence elites actively manipulate domestic affairs *as a matter of policy*. America's national security elites have long declared that U.S. public opinion must be molded and managed to maintain popular support for the nation's military actions and foreign policies. A well-known example of such thinking is NSC-68, a report authored in 1950 by the National Security Council. While advocating covert operations to subvert communist regimes overseas, NSC-68 called for a public relations strategy at home to strengthen America's resolve in the Cold War. [23] For decades, presidents and other top officials have been routinely misleading the public about the nation's foreign policies, tactics, and capabilities, and about the actions and capabilities of America's enemies. American involvement in various coups and assassinations has been denied; American provocations of military conflict have been concealed; U.S. citizens have been secretly and illegally wiretapped and monitored—all in the name of national security. To the extent that national security elites are influencing national political priorities by manipulating the constellation of issues confronting the nation, all of the theories in the social sciences and their associated research programs are studying downstream phenomena while the real explanation of events resides earlier in time and higher in America's authoritative hierarchy. In other words, it is quite possible that the social sciences are studying shadows and that the people making the shadows are designing them for effect. Of course, this was how Plato described the situation of the citizens, except that in his story, which we must assume was a noble lie, the philosophers were helping citizens understand the shadows, not using the shadows for social control.

THE CONSPIRACY-THEORY CONSPIRACY

T o this day, the U.S. political class remains firmly united in support of the Warren Commission's conclusion that President Kennedy was murdered by Lee Harvey Oswald shooting from the sixth floor of the Texas School Book Depository. The unwavering unity of America's political elite behind this account of one of the most shocking events in modern American history is both remarkable and telling. It is remarkable because the Warren Commission's account has for so long been discredited. It is telling because the political class has no choice; to admit the truth that the official account is untrue, that the one-bullet theory is impossible, means the Warren Commission covered up evidence of multiple shooters and therefore, legally, was an accomplice after the fact, making the commission guilty of the crime itself, of a presidential assassination. Therefore, the unity of the political class is remarkable and telling but not surprising. Although reports have occasionally appeared that at least a few U.S. officials harbor serious doubts that they have shared privately with other government insiders, virtually no one who is part of the national political elite—not even one of the Kennedys—has openly challenged the Warren Commission's findings. [1]

Nonetheless, the Warren Commission report is a noble lie that has been unable to withstand objective scrutiny. In fact, its credibility lasted less than two years. Newspaper articles and books appeared in 1965 and 1966 pointing out evidence in the Warren Commission report itself that contradicted the single-bullet and lone-gunman theories, [2–4] and by 1966 public opinion polls were beginning to indicate that a plurality of Americans rejected the findings of the Warren Commission as incomplete at best. [2, 5] As doubts about the official account mounted, people also started to question, first, the objectivity of the Warren Commission, and then the integrity of American democracy. It was at this point that the CIA launched its propaganda campaign.

This chapter examines the substance of the CIA's campaign and presents some evidence on its effects on speech and beliefs. The CIA document that laid out and launched the program to stigmatize conspiracy theorizing is critically important for understanding the agency's thinking about not only the assassination of President Kennedy but also popular suspicions that the CIA had committed the crime. The propaganda program was initiated in January 1967 by a "dispatch" that was numbered 1035-960. [6 p. 32] The heading included the notation "PSYCH" and instructions to "destroy when no longer needed."

Dispatch 1035-960 was sent by the CIA's top administrators to its system of "stations," or local offices. Presumably because the CIA's mission is primarily to gather intelligence and secondarily to carry out covert operations overseas, almost all of these locations are in foreign lands. (The CIA has had at least one station in the U.S.: MWAVE in Miami during the 1960s.) The dispatch was obtained through a Freedom of Information Act request nine years later (in 1976). A typed copy of the dispatch is included in the appendix. The

New York Times reported that the program was clearly geared to a domestic audience, which violated the agency's charter. [6] Essentially, Dispatch 1035-960 instructed CIA agents to contact journalists and opinion leaders in their locales about critics of the Warren Commission; ask for their assistance in countering the influence of "conspiracy theorists" who were publishing "conspiracy theories" that blamed top leaders in the U.S. for Kennedy's death; and urge their media contacts to criticize such theories and those who embrace them for aiding communists in the Cold War, trying to get attention, seeking to profit financially from the Kennedy tragedy, and refusing to consider all the facts.

Subtle Speech

CIA Dispatch 1035-960 appears to be a straightforward memo with clear language and reasonable motives, but it is actually a subtle document, conveying many of its messages by indirection and implication. To grasp the nuances in the text requires a very careful reading. Some sections of the dispatch clearly have a surface meaning for ordinary readers, and a deeper, less obvious meaning for readers who are listening for, as it were, a second frequency, a hidden meaning.

Multiple levels of meaning occur in various forms of speech. [7] Consider sarcasm and irony, for example. In both of these dual-channel speech forms, what is being said explicitly is belied by what is being implied, and the implied message is highlighted by a certain tone of voice, as when gaiety conceals a snide putdown. "What a lovely outfit; a sale at Wal-Mart, perhaps?"

Leo Strauss was famous in intellectual circles for discovering, or rediscovering, that the Platonic dialogues contained hidden messages. [8] He pointed out that in studying the dialogues, careful readers will notice that Socrates, the lead character in most of the books, expresses different views about the same topic to different characters, and to the same characters in different settings. This is because Plato has Socrates shade his answers differently depending on who is present. To figure out what Socrates actually believes requires that the dialogues be studied together and his comments compared from one situation to another.

CIA Dispatch 1035-960 is not a Platonic dialogue (although its authors may have been exposed to Strauss), [9] but it is a document written by spies for other spies, and spies know that, as a written document, it could fall into the wrong hands, as, in fact, it did because of the Freedom of Information Act request. So we should assume that the dispatch may contain some veiled meanings.

Take, for example, the dispatch number. This is probably unimportant, but the number could have at least two meanings. Most people would assume "1035-960" is a number in a numbering and filing system. However, 1035-960 can also be read as, "1035 *minus* 960." Who is to say the dash is just a dash and not a mathematical operator? Thus 1035-960 could mean "75," which might refer to the seventy-fifth day of the year or something else.

Decoding the Dispatch

Several points in the dispatch hint at tensions between the CIA and other elements of the national government or among the other elements themselves, and some of the instructions appear to have been intended to exploit these tensions and create problems for particular officials, including, especially, Robert Kennedy.

POSSIBLE FORMS OF THE CONSPIRACY

In the dispatch, the CIA notes that from the day the president was killed, there was speculation about "the responsibility for his murder." At first blush, this phrasing—"the responsibility for his murder"—seems a bit awkward but otherwise innocuous. And yet it actually frames the question about Kennedy's assassination very differently from the way it is framed in the Warren Commission report, and the CIA's framing brings uncertainty and room to speculate about intrigue surrounding the events in question. The Warren Commission asked if there was more than one shooter and if Oswald and Ruby had any prior connections. The Warren panel was looking for a conspiracy of *shooters*.

In contrast, the CIA dispatch does not ask if there was another shooter besides Oswald. The ambiguous wording the CIA chose when raising the issue of who was responsible for the assassination allows for Oswald to have been the lone gunman, or for there to have been one or more shooters in addition to Oswald or *instead* of Oswald. When the question is "who was responsible," the questions everyone had been asking about the identity of the shooters are no longer central. Someone other than the shooter(s) could have been responsible for the murder, that is, someone else could have organized and financed it but played no role in the hands-on operation. In fact, as suggested by the dispatch's comments later about how a wealthy person could easily arrange such a murder, it is highly unlikely that the principal in the killing would have any involvement at all in the execution. In short, the CIA dispatch is subtly suggesting that the official account of the assassination could be wrong about literally everything. The CIA is raising the possibility of a far-flung conspiracy backed by unspecified "responsible parties" who are in the shadows. Dispatch 1035-960 does not say this out loud, but it conveys this message between the lines simply by using the who-was-responsible language.

In using this language the CIA is also displaying a certain temerity. The CIA is willing to raise the specter of a web of intrigue extending beyond Oswald and Ruby to include (as discussed below) top officials in the U.S. government.

The dispatch also talks about the nature of the conspiracy in similarly ambiguous ways that move the inquiry outward and beyond the Warren Commission's focus, which was on a very small, gunman-centered type of conspiracy. After noting that a "new wave of books and articles" has been published criticizing the Warren Commission's findings with new evidence, the dispatch says most of the critics speculate about "some kind of conspiracy." This phrasing, too, leaves open the possibility of a conspiracy much more extensive and complex than Oswald and Ruby and perhaps one or two additional riflemen. "Some kind of conspiracy" can be *any* kind of conspiracy. In contrast, the Warren Commission's approach suggested that the only kinds of conspiracies to take seriously as possibilities were those centered on Oswald and Ruby, not those that might extend to government agencies or top officials.

THE MOST LIKELY SUSPECTS

Another place in the dispatch indicative of the CIA's temerity—its willingness to acknowledge organizational interests and rivalries—occurs when it presents the main conspiracy theories that (according to the CIA) have been proposed by the Warren Commission's critics. Three possible principals for "some kind of conspiracy" are mentioned. The first is the Warren Commission itself. Second is President Johnson. And third is "our organization," that is, the CIA. Significantly, of the three suspect principals, an argument supporting the accusation of guilt is presented for only one: President Johnson. In the dispatch's words, there is "an increasing tendency to hint that President Johnson himself, as the one person who might be said to have benefited, was in some way responsible for the assassination." No evidence is offered to support this contention about an "increasing tendency," nor is the locus of the alleged tendency identified. Is the tendency seen in the press, observed in elite "small talk," captured in public opinion polls, expressed in literature and films, or what? And of course the dispatch is almost silent about Oswald and says nothing about whether the CIA had been remiss in failing to monitor or keep track of a former U.S. Marine who had defected to the Soviet Union in 1959 and returned to the United States three years later. Conveniently selective, CIA Dispatch 1035-960 deflects suspicion of assassination-related CIA incompetence or collusion by subtly pointing the finger at President Johnson. Moreover, the CIA demonstrates it is such an artful communicator it can do this even though the agency reports directly to the president.

SIGNS OF A BAD CONSCIENCE

The dispatch is quite smooth and knowledgeable—even helpful—when it comes to talking about who might be suspected in the Kennedy assassination and why. Later in the dispatch there is a discussion about why the CIA or any knowledgeable assassin would have set up the murder differently. Comments are made about how a wealthy person could easily organize a presidential assassination. Apparently, all it takes is money. But the dispatch says experts in assassination would have done many things differently. They would have found somebody better than Oswald as a co-conspirator. He was a troubled loner; he was unpredictable and undependable. They would have picked a better location with easier escape routes. They would have carried it out in a closed setting so they would not have been dependent on the weather and other uncontrollable factors.

Of course there is a flaw in this argument, at least insofar as it is intended to suggest that Lee Harvey Oswald was truly the assassin and that the crime was not committed by an organization skilled in assassination and psychological warfare. The argument fails to consider how an agency like the CIA might plan and carry out a presidential assassination. It is highly unlikely that the agency would want to display the skills of assassination experts. In fact, the agency would probably make the assassination appear exactly as it did in Dallas. First, the agency would need a patsy to take the blame. Otherwise, there would be a nationwide manhunt that might sweep up some of the assassination team members. Second, agency experts would want the president shot from a distance so that no one would be able to tell exactly where the shots came from and who fired them, but the distance would have to be short enough for the patsy to make the shot. Third, the patsy would need to have a background that gave him a credible motivation for the crime and some experience with rifles. And fourth, ideally, the agency would want the patsy killed before he could be tried. If a trial could be avoided, there would never be a forum in which evidence in defense of the patsy could be presented. That the CIA dispatch overlooks this scenario is almost laughable, given that the CIA is constantly involved in operations that are designed to make its actions appear other than what they are. In the Bay of Pigs invasion, for example, great efforts were taken to make the invading force seem like an autonomous body of expatriate soldiers, not a surrogate army trained and equipped by the United States. In short, the assassination of President Kennedy actually had the hallmarks of true expertise, which is the ability to apply expert knowledge and skills while appearing amateurish.

In contrast to the dispatch's ease with discussing practical considerations in killing national leaders, the dispatch falls almost into gibberish near the center of Section 2. The part that is verbally mangled involves only two sentences, and they deal with people's suspicions about the CIA's involvement in the Kennedy assassination. The sentences are preceded by the first full paragraph of Section 2, plus one more sentence. This paragraph and sentence express anger and alarm about the damage the Warren Commission's critics and the people hinting at President Johnson's guilt are causing the "U.S. government, including our organization." The dispatch becomes almost hysterical when it says that the critics, in impugning the "Commission's rectitude and wisdom," have brought into question "the whole reputation of American government" and the "whole leadership of American society."

After making these rather extravagant claims, the dispatch then speaks for the CIA and presumably is trying to explain specifically how the agency has been hurt. It is here that the dispatch becomes almost incoherent. It says, "Our organization itself is directly involved: among other facts, we contributed information to the investigation."

The CIA is directly involved in *what*? The referent is ambiguous. It is almost as if the dispatch is saying the CIA is directly involved in the *assassination*?

The question also arises as to what is meant by "among other facts." Is one fact that the agency submitted information to the investigation? If so, what are the other facts? Or is the dispatch saying the CIA contributed to the investigation information plus some facts? If so, what is the difference between facts and information? Is information intelligence, secrets, speculation?

The next sentence is not much better: "Conspiracy theories have frequently thrown suspicion on our organization, for example by falsely alleging that Lee Harvey Oswald worked for us." Setting aside for the moment the many other relationships the CIA could have had with Oswald besides him being an employee, there is something almost surreal about this complaint. The dispatch is implying that the only reason popular suspicion has been directed at the CIA is because critics of the Warren Commission have put forward these conspiracy theories. Apparently, the dispatch means the CIA would not have come under suspicion simply because its director had been fired by Kennedy; Kennedy had threatened to destroy the agency; the CIA has been involved in assassinations and assassination attempts overseas; compartmentalization of information in the agency increases the potential for rogue operations; and, of course, many people would assume that the CIA would have been monitoring Oswald because he defected to the Soviet Union and returned to the United States. It is difficult to believe an agency like the CIA, which is able to reason so coldly about how a president would best be assassinated, is so naïve as to think Americans do not view it with some suspicion to begin with.

Mark Crispin Miller, a professor of media ecology at New York University, has pointed out that when people have trouble talking about a topic and yet are quite smooth when addressing other matters, something about the topic bothers them deeply. [10] The CIA has a problem talking about the assassination of President Kennedy, not in all contexts, but only when discussing people's suspicions that the agency itself might have been involved. The agency analysts and administrators who wrote this dispatch feel very awkward about their relationship with the American people. Presumably, they want to be trusted and are hurt to think they are not. Such an attitude seems naïve, if not, well, immature or romantic—certainly odd for an agency that practices treachery and betrayal. But in fact autobiographies of Daniel Ellsberg, [11] E. Howard Hunt, [12] and G. Gordon Liddy [13] reveal a deep-seated need to be appreciated as a dashing, adventurous man doing good things in a dangerous world. Notice that Hunt and Liddy model themselves on J. Edgar Hoover by using their initials and middle names, as in "E. Howard" and "G. Gordon." The CIA wants to be loved by the people it protects, but when asked by these people why a liar and a killer should be trusted, the agency does not have a good answer, so it stammers about "other facts" and "conspiracy theories."

CHARACTERIZING THE CRITICS
AND THEIR CRITICISMS

The CIA dispatch instructed agents to contact "propaganda assets" and "friendly elite contacts (especially politicians and editors)" and explain to them how best to respond to the Warren Commission's critics. A detailed set of what today are called "talking points" was included. The media assets were to be encouraged to address the subject only when and if it surfaced independently in a news story or editorial, or when a new book was published on the topic. Otherwise, they should not bring attention to the issue. When a story or book did appear, the CIA memo called for the agency's media voices to say that all critics of the lone-gunman scenario were implying that there had been a conspiracy and to raise questions about the conspiracy theorists' motives and competence, suggesting, for example, that they were just trying to sell books or attract attention, or that they had "fallen in love" with their theories and refused to entertain counter-evidence.

The dispatch says little directly about labeling the critics as conspiracy theorists, but it models the communication necessary to construct this identity without explaining how the verbal manipulation works, which would raise the listeners' defenses. The dispatch uses the terms "conspiracy theories" and "conspiracy theorists" only one time each, but it uses variations on the root term nine times. The dispatch constructs the image of the group and of their beliefs by indirection, that is, by contrasting them with other groups, speculating on their motives, identifying groups with which they are distant or close, and so on. As the group is given a place among other groups in the listener's belief system, it becomes, in effect, alive and endowed with personality in the observer's imagination.

Giving the group a single name and conveying its characteristics indirectly rather than frontally reflected the best social science available, then and now, on how mass publics think about politics and political issues. Research on the nature of belief systems in mass publics has determined that most people use group identities as a sort of shorthand for gathering and transmitting information about political issues. [14] A person interested in politics knows that if a political candidate is "a conservative," he or she is likely to line up in a predictable fashion across a wide range of issues. Because political positions are associated with particular groups, pointing to a group is like pointing to a whole block of issues, positions on those issues, groups with opposing views, and so on. In effect, the language used in political communication is groups. People are categorized: Liberals. Conservatives. Leftists. Hippies. Fascists. Socialists. Libertarians. Feminists. Environmentalists. These and similar labels are used by voters to sort out political candidates, convey information about new issues, and generally indicate where candidates stand and where new issues are located in the ideological terrain of group interests. If I am a socialist and am told a given political candidate is a conservative, I know that I should vote against the candidate without having to learn the details of his or her background and political positions.

The CIA propaganda program was designed to interject a new group into the pantheon of political groups Americans employ to pigeonhole political candidates, issues, movements, and so on. In this case, the group was called "conspiracy theorists," and its beliefs were described abstractly as "conspiracy theories" about the assassination of President Kennedy. However, like other group labels in American politics, the conspiracy-theory label was (and is) sufficiently vague and general to be applied to many other events, issues, and individuals in addition to the assassination of President Kennedy. The subject of the designated theories could be just about any incident that is politically important, but especially assassinations, wars, election breakdowns, and other surprising events of uncertain origin that affect national political priorities. In fact, as we shall see presently, the label's application rapidly spread not only to other assassinations, and not only to political events in addition to assassinations, but also to events that are entirely unrelated to politics.

The CIA instructions themselves specified where in the context of established group interests the new group—conspiracy theorists—was located. The political alignment of a group is easily conveyed by associating the new group with other groups that have already been defined. In the case of the CIA dispatch, the CIA agents were urged to warn the agency's media voices that "parts of the conspiracy talk appear to be deliberately generated by Communist propagandists." In the shadows of McCarthyism and the Cold War, this warning was delivered simultaneously to hundreds if not thousands of well-positioned members of the press in a global CIA propaganda network, infusing the conspiracy-theory label with powerfully negative associations.

PRESSURE DIRECTED AT ROBERT KENNEDY

Robert Kennedy left the White House and ran successfully for the United States Senate in 1964, several years before the CIA dispatch was distributed. As soon as he was elected to the Senate, open speculation appeared in the media that he might run for president in 1968, which would mean Kennedy challenging President Johnson for the Democratic Party nomination. Dispatch 1035-960 said CIA agents should point out to their media assets that any evidence of an assassination conspiracy would have been made public by Robert Kennedy while he was U.S. attorney general. In the dispatch's words: "Note that Robert Kennedy, Attorney General at the time and John F. Kennedy's brother, would be the last man to overlook or conceal any conspiracy."

In this case, the CIA dispatch is implying that Robert Kennedy's thinking on these matters can be inferred directly from his kinship relation to the deceased. But surely an agency with the temerity and cold logic of the CIA would have recognized that the situation for RFK would have been very complicated. Robert Kennedy would have seen the Zapruder film, read the Warren Commission report with its preposterous single-bullet theory about the wounds of Governor Connolly and President Kennedy, and known that the assassination involved at least two shooters and that this had been covered up by the FBI, the Warren Commission, and others participating in the investigation. Clearly, by including this talking point about Robert Kennedy in CIA Dispatch 1035-960, the agency's top management was intentionally misleading the CIA's own agents in hopes they would spread this false inference about Kennedy's beliefs concerning his brother's death.

In fact, a book by David Talbot was published recently that addresses this very question. [15] Talbot interviewed RFK's friends and family members, concluding that Robert Kennedy believed that his brother had been assassinated by a right-wing element within the government. RFK's plan was to run for president and, once elected, reopen the investigation into his brother's assassination. [15 pp. 356–359]

By planting the idea that the silence of Robert Kennedy was absolute proof that the Warren Commission had not been a cover-up, the CIA dispatch appears to have been designed to put RFK on the spot. This makes sense in light of what was happening at the time in politics at the highest levels of government. Democratic leaders were lining up to run against Johnson in the Democratic primaries. Although Robert Kennedy did not announce until the spring of 1968, he was rumored to be interested in running, and a theory began to circulate to the effect that the peace candidate, Eugene McCarthy, was a stalking horse for Senator Kennedy and planned to step aside when Kennedy declared his candidacy. Incidentally, observers noted that this was a "conspiracy theory," but the term was not yet pejorative, so its conspiratorial character did not taint its plausibility. The hope of many Democratic activists was that Senator Kennedy could unify the party, which was deeply and intensely divided over the Vietnam War. For his part, President Johnson could not shake suspicions about his possible role in President Kennedy's assassination. Senator Kennedy could have dispelled these doubts about Johnson by speaking out in strong support of the Warren Commission report and against conspiracy theories, but publicly Kennedy had never given more than perfunctory support for the official account of his brother's murder. As more time passed, Senator Kennedy's near-silence on the matter seemed to grow loud and damning. In any case, this particular point in the CIA dispatch appears to have been designed to generate newspaper stories that would push Robert Kennedy into the spotlight and cause journalists around the world to cite his tacit acceptance of the Warren Commission report as unequivocal proof that conspiracy theories of the assassination were unfounded.

CIA "Collaborator" John P. Roche

It is difficult to trace many of the pejorative connotations now attached to the conspiracy-theory label to Dispatch 1035-960, but a search of *Time* magazine and *New York Times* archives for language and arguments used in the dispatch did reveal an important connection. In January 1968, a letter from John P. Roche was published in the *London Times Literary Supplement* that was clearly following the directions contained in CIA Dispatch 1035-960 and was putting Robert Kennedy on the spot. The letter was widely covered in the U.S. press. It was about a *London Times* review of a new book on the assassination of President Kennedy.

Roche was a special assistant to President Johnson and a

political scientist who focused on American politics. January 1968 was about a year after the CIA dispatch had been received by the CIA "stations." Robert Kennedy had not yet announced his bid for the Democratic Party nomination for president, and it was also a few months before President Johnson would announce that he was not going to run for reelection. It was a time, in other words, when the tension between Johnson and Robert Kennedy was intense.

Roche's letter is an example of how a CIA propaganda initiative ostensibly directed at overseas targets can, like a "bank shot" in pool, immediately bounce off the foreign press and return to influence opinion in the United States. *Time* magazine wrote an entire story on Roche's letter, as if the letter was news from London and not a statement from the White House defending the Warren Commission with a new argument that involved one of the brothers of the slain president—the brother who was rumored to be preparing to challenge Lyndon Johnson for the presidency. [16]

The article in *Time* magazine starts by making clear that Roche supports the Warren Commission's account of President Kennedy's assassination. The article quotes what Roche immodestly calls "Roche's Law"—which appears to be adapted from Popper's critique of the conspiracy theory of society. Popper said conspiracies never succeed because social reality is too complex and "brittle." Roche says something similar, but with a much more dismissive, condescending attitude than Popper's. "Those who can conspire haven't got the time; those who do conspire haven't got the talent." As with Popper's critique of conspiracy theory, the implication of Roche's Law is that there are no successful conspiracies. In making this case, Roche seems unconcerned with the gravity of the issues at stake. He also displays no knowledge of the facts of the assassination, apparently having decided that Robert Kennedy's silence settles the conspiracy issue once and for all.

Roche is careful to follow the CIA script closely. He repeats the language in the CIA memo almost verbatim, except that he is more effusive and emotional. The dispatch suggested pointing out that "Kennedy would be the last man to overlook or conceal any conspiracy." Roche made this idea the theme of his letter:

> Every one of the plot theories must necessarily rely on the inconceivable connivance of one key man: Robert F. Kennedy, then Attorney General of the U.S. Any fair analysis of Senator Robert Kennedy's abilities, his character, and of the resources at his disposal, would indicate that if there was a conspiracy, he would have pursued its protagonists to the ends of the earth.

The *Time* article concludes by spouting some putdowns that are quoted widely overseas and in the U.S. "Though the conspiracy theory may be gospel to 'a priesthood of marginal paranoids,' said Roche, it is also 'an assault on the sanity of American society, and I believe in its fundamental sanity.' He concludes: 'I don't mind people being paranoiac, but don't make me carry their luggage.'"

Interestingly, these concluding comments themselves sound somewhat paranoid. Certainly, they convey anger, and if Roche sees in his fellow citizens who question the Warren Commission a "priesthood of marginal paranoids," his judgment appears to lack empathy, and he also seems rather indifferent to norms of civility. Moreover, there are clear signs that Roche feels persecuted. Who is making him carry their luggage? Why is questioning the official account of the assassination of President Kennedy an "assault on the sanity of American society"? Most people would not find suspicions about the Kennedy assassination threatening to their emotional stability because, as public opinion polls reveal, they share those suspicions. [5] About the best interpretation that can be attached to Roche's fear of conspiracy theories is that he may think free speech and open discussion are incapable of correcting errors of opinion, and yet this raises the question of why he would write a letter to the newspaper in an attempt to correct the views of readers who adhere to conspiracy theories.

Together with CIA Dispatch 1035-960, John Roche's letter is demonstrable evidence that the CIA manipulated the press to popularize the term "conspiracy theory," to associate it with deranged thinking, and to encourage bullying attacks on Americans who express doubts about the official story of President Kennedy's murder. Roche's letter is the first publication linking paranoia, marginality, and religiosity ("a priesthood of marginal paranoids") to the conspiracy-theory label. Although it is not the first publication to suggest that conspiracy theories are dangerous or pernicious, it is the first to say this while modeling an attitude of condescension and loathing. Roche is treated as an authority; the media present his views without seeking comments or counterarguments. He is said to have made a remarkable discovery that everyone else has overlooked, that he has realized that Robert Kennedy's silence proves there was no conspiracy. The overall effect of Roche's letter is to suggest that conspiracy theory, as a form of political speech and analysis, is pernicious and stupid, that it is espoused only by dangerous fools, and that therefore it deserves, at the very least, to be ridiculed to the point that it becomes stigmatized and people will watch what they say.

Popularization, Association, Connotation

The term "conspiracy theory" had only a very brief history before Roche and others carrying out the CIA propaganda program boosted the term's use and caused or contributed to its association with flawed thinking. Figure 4.1 is a line graph displaying the annual number of articles in *Time*, from 1913 (the magazine's beginning year) through 2011, that mention "conspiracy theory" or any of its variations. The figure also shows the number of such articles that appeared in the *New York Times* from 1875 through 2011. [17, 18]

Time first mentions the term "conspiracy theory" in 1965. It is in a cover story on Arthur M. Schlesinger, who served as a special advisor to President Kennedy. From his comments he appears to have been familiar with Popper's critique of the "conspiracy theory of society." The story says,

> Schlesinger believes in the "confusion theory" of history as opposed to the "conspiracy theory." According to Political Scientist James MacGregor Burns, the conspiracy theory holds that "if something happened, somebody planned it." Schlesinger, on the other hand, believes in "the role of chance and contingency, the sheer intricacy of situations, the murk of battle." Schlesinger is also scornful of the "prophetic" historians—Marx, Spengler, Toynbee— who use "one big hypothesis to explain a variety of small things." Says he: "They" have reduced the chaos of history to a single order of explanation, which can infallibly penetrate the mysteries of the past and predict the developments of the future.

Note that Schlesinger is repeating the mistake made by Popper, which is to claim that the "conspiracy theory [of history]" holds that everything that happens is the result of a conspiracy.

From 1964, when the Warren Commission report was released, through the 1970s, the connotation attached to "conspiracy theory" is in flux but gradually becomes associated with foolish speculation and mental impairment as comments like Schlesinger's are followed by harsher language like Roche's. Which words are planted and which

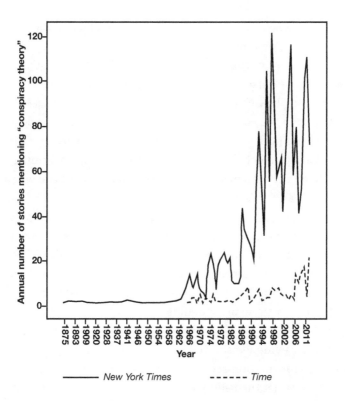

Figure 4.1. Annual number of stories mentioning "conspiracy theory," New York Times, *1875–2011, and* Time *magazine, 1913–2011.*

appear spontaneously is at this point difficult or perhaps impossible to determine.

Several events reinforced the argument for antigovernment suspicion. In 1968, District Attorney Jim Garrison in New Orleans prosecuted businessman Clay Shaw for participating in the conspiracy to assassinate President Kennedy. The events surrounding the case were the subject of the 1991 movie *JFK*, directed by Oliver Stone. Although Shaw was acquitted, the trial nevertheless kept alive the controversy surrounding the official account of the Kennedy assassination. Likewise, public confidence in public officials was further eroded by publication of the Pentagon Papers in 1971. [19] A history of the Vietnam War compiled by the Department of Defense, the Pentagon Papers confirmed many conspiracy beliefs about the government's real motives for engaging in the conflict, the dismal prognosis issued repeatedly to top policymakers for the war's outcome by the CIA, and perhaps most important, proof that the U.S. government had lied to the American people repeatedly about the war's rationale and prospects. [20]

Next, in 1973, came exposure of the crimes of Watergate, which had been committed in 1972, and release of transcripts from audiotapes of conversations in the Nixon White House. These confirmations of conspiracy beliefs were doubly problematic for the legitimacy of the political class. Falsification of their prior claims cast doubt on their candor generally. Also, the Nixon tapes, confessions by operatives, and other evidence showed the president not simply trying to keep information secret, but actually plotting to commit crimes against the people's liberties, to steal the 1972 presidential election, and paying what Nixon himself called "hush money" to the Watergate co-conspirators after their arrest. The president was quoted saying he could raise a million dollars in cash for payoffs and, after the *New York Times* published the Pentagon Papers, issue an order for the Internal Revenue Service to audit the tax returns of every *New York Times* employee.

Use of the term "conspiracy theory" by the *New York Times* ratcheted upward over the years. By the mid-1970s the label was appearing in twenty to thirty stories each year. The term's usage increased in part because its application spread quickly beyond politics to entertainment and business. These were areas of society where, as in politics and government, insiders have a recognized ability to exert considerable influence on events without being easily detected. In 1966 the

Watergate security guard log book for June 17, 1972, showing entry about unlocked door. This discovery led to arrest of the Watergate burglars. (Source: National Archives)

conspiracy-theory label was used for the first time in sports. *Today, roughly 25 percent of all New York Times stories that mention "conspiracy theory" appear in the sports pages.* [21] The 1966 story described suspicions about difficulties Cassius Clay was encountering in his search for a venue for a boxing match. Soon, the concept was picked up and applied in other sports and in other areas of society to refer to theories of collusion for nefarious purposes. In sports, it went from boxing to other sports and then to other positions in matches and on teams, such as coaches and referees. In economic arenas, it was used to explain fashion trends, gas shortages, and gas prices. The rapid spread of the conspiracy-theory label to sports and business suggests that suspicion of elite intrigue is normal when things that are subject to control and manipulation change in ways that benefit those who are in positions to control and manipulate them.

The conspiracy-theory label acquired the pejorative connotations it possess today by repeated characterizations that attached negative associations to this new group on the political landscape: the conspiracy theorists. CIA Dispatch 1035-960 suggested associating the conspiracy theorists with greed, yearning for attention, and succumbing to the influence of Soviet propagandists. Perhaps drawing from Hofstadter, Roche implied that the mind-set of conspiracy theorists is a dangerous mix of mental problems, superstition, and extremism. Over time, the conspiracy-theory label came to be associated in the *New York Times* with a variety of pejorative terms as editorial writers, letter writers, and occasionally reporters (quoting others) attacked the competence, objectivity, motives, and other characteristics of conspiracy believers.

The connection between conspiracy theories and various pejorative terms can be tracked with queries in the archives of the *New York Times*. The following list shows the most frequently used pejoratives in order of the year in which they first showed up in a story mentioning conspiracy theory. Numbers in parentheses indicate the total number of times the pejorative word appeared in a conspiracy-theory story during the time period under analysis (1875–2011).

1968 paranoid (20), radical (20)
1973 crackpot (3)

1975 left-wing (2)
1978 cult (16)
1979 obsession (7)
1984 psychotic (13)
1986 freak (3), wild (8)
1987 disease (10)
1988 far-fetched (2)
1990 fringe (3)
1991 despicable (2), insane (3)
1992 crazy (4)
1994 bigot (2)
1995 extreme (4), right-wing (8)
2004 unhinged (4)
2009 birther (4), truther (1)

Generally speaking, given that the total number of articles approaches two thousand, this is a relatively small amount of ridicule and labeling. However, the attack on conspiracy beliefs, as limited as it is, has been quite harsh. Conspiracy beliefs are associated with mental illness, including paranoia, obsession, psychosis, insanity, craziness, and being unhinged; with being outside the mainstream, including radical, left-wing, right-wing, fringe, and extreme; with being implausible as in far-fetched; with being antisocial, including crackpots and despicable and bigoted people; and with being fanatical, as in cults, birthers, and truthers.

As the term's use has expanded, its application has become arbitrary and defensive. The subjective nature of the conspiracy-theory label's pejorative associations is evident in the changes that occur in associations as the partisan political context shifts from a Republican to a Democratic White House. As shown in the above list of pejoratives, in 1975, not long after President Nixon had resigned and President Ford was being criticized for pardoning him, conspiracy theories were said to be left-wing. In other words, the people who

GRANTING PARDON TO RICHARD NIXON

BY THE PRESIDENT OF THE UNITED STATES OF AMERICA

A PROCLAMATION

Richard Nixon became the thirty-seventh President of
the United States on January 20, 1969 and was reelected in
1972 for a second term by the electors of forty-nine of the
fifty states. His term in office continued until his resignation on August 9, 1974.

Pursuant to resolutions of the House of Representatives,
its Committee on the Judiciary conducted an inquiry and
investigation on the impeachment of the President extending
over more than eight months. The hearings of the Committee
and its deliberations, which received wide national publicity
over television, radio, and in printed media, resulted in
votes adverse to Richard Nixon on recommended Articles of
Impeachment.

As a result of certain acts or omissions occurring before
his resignation from the Office of President, Richard Nixon
has become liable to possible indictment and trial for
offenses against the United States. Whether or not he shall
be so prosecuted depends on findings of the appropriate grand
jury and on the discretion of the authorized prosecutor.
Should an indictment ensue, the accused shall then be entitled
to a fair trial by an impartial jury, as guaranteed to every
individual by the Constitution.

It is believed that a trial of Richard Nixon, if it became
necessary, could not fairly begin until a year or more has
elapsed. In the meantime, the tranquility to which this
nation has been restored by the events of recent weeks could
be irreparably lost by the prospects of bringing to trial
a former President of the United States. The prospects of such

2

trial will cause prolonged and divisive debate over the
propriety of exposing to further punishment and degradation
a man who has already paid the unprecedented penalty of
relinquishing the highest elective office of the United States.

NOW, THEREFORE, I, Gerald R. Ford, President of the
United States, pursuant to the pardon power conferred upon
me by Article II, Section 2, of the Constitution, have granted
and by these presents do grant a full, free, and absolute
pardon unto Richard Nixon for all offenses against the
United States which he, Richard Nixon, has committed or may
have committed or taken part in during the period from
January 20, 1969 through August 9, 1974.

IN WITNESS WHEREOF, I have hereunto set my hand this
eighth day of September, in the year of our Lord nineteen
hundred and seventy-four, and of the Independence of the
United States of America the one hundred and ninety-ninth.

Gerald R. Ford

Richard Nixon's pardon. (Source: National Archives)

believed in conspiracy theories were alleged to be liberals. Twenty years later, when President Bill Clinton was being targeted by conspiracy theories about Whitewater, Vince Foster, and Monica Lewinski, conspiracy theories were considered a right-wing phenomenon, since Clinton was being criticized by conservatives. Thus the conspiracy-theory label has become a powerful smear that, in the name of reason, civility, and democracy, preempts public discourse, reinforces rather than resolves disagreements, and undermines popular vigilance against abuses of power. Put in place in 1967 by the CIA, the term continues to be a destructive force in American politics.

5

STATE CRIMES
AGAINST DEMOCRACY

The civilization from which America derives many of its values and institutions places confidence in science and philosophy over tradition and sentiment. With science, we have successfully corrected our worldview many times despite the sometimes difficult implications for our established beliefs. This chapter considers the possibility that the reactions many people experience today toward SCAD theory are similar to people's reactions when told by Galileo and Darwin that the earth is spinning and human beings are descended from apes.

This not to say the SCAD construct is comparable to some of the great ideas in the history of science. The point is, rather, to try to learn from these earlier, revolutionary advances in knowledge, how they overcame people's very plausible objections to claims by the scientists that on their face seemed ludicrous. It is understandable people would have some doubts about the idea that all animals evolved from primitive organisms. Common sense also said the earth could not be spinning and flying through space, just as common sense today says 9/11 could not have been an inside job.

How did Galileo and Darwin convince us of the truth when it was so counterintuitive?

Science, which can be understood as a way of seeing, [1, 2] has historically helped us overcome our misconceptions and prejudices by reconceptualizing everyday experience and pointing out unnoticed facts that have been more or less in plain sight all along. Galileo opened people's eyes with the concept of gravity along with some surprising but irrefutable observations. This chapter is intended to do this, in a small way, with the SCAD concept and some novel observations about patterns in political crimes.

At the end of the chapter, the focus turns to the implications of these crime patterns for investigating the most important unsolved crime since the assassination of President Kennedy: the cluster of attacks on America that have come to be referred to collectively as "9/11."

Scientific Conceptualization

Although science is based on observation, scientific observation is more than merely looking and seeing. Modern science says the earth is spinning on its axis and revolving around the sun, and yet, clearly, the earth does not feel to us as if it were moving.

If the earth is spinning, why do we not fly off? What holds us to the ground?

"Gravity," you say.

But can you show me this gravity? What does it look like? Where can I find it?

"It is invisible," you reply.

But surely you jest. You ask me to believe in a mysterious force that I cannot see, that operates at a distance like a spirit, and the only reason you have for claiming the force exists is that (you say) the earth is spinning, when it obviously is not.

The concept of gravity is essential to the sun-centered

model of the planetary system. It explains what holds people to the spinning earth as well as what holds the planets in their orbits around the sun. However, gravity is not something we can observe directly; it is a postulated force.

Galileo convinced people that gravity exists by showing them something remarkable that they could see with their own eyes but had never noticed. The concept of gravity implied that, when dropped, physical objects would fall at the same rate of acceleration regardless of their size or weight because they are all pulled down by the same uniform force—the uniform force of the earth's "gravity," not the varying force of the objects' "weight." Galileo is said to have proved this by dropping objects from the Leaning Tower of Pisa. The fact that objects of different weights fell at the same speed was an astounding discovery; people had seen objects fall countless times, but they had always assumed heavier objects fell faster than lighter objects. Thus, the concept of gravity pointed to an observable phenomenon that people's conventional beliefs had prevented them from seeing. The SCAD construct functions similarly in positing invisible elite schemes, which then lead to discoveries of patterns in political crimes in which state offices may play a role.

This is also how the theory of evolution overturned the accepted idea that all the plants and animals on earth had been created in the form and diversity they display today. Contradicting the biblical account of creation, Darwin said plants and animals evolved from simple life forms to more complex, differentiated forms (or "species") through the process of natural selection. However, most people initially considered it ludicrous, not to say insulting, to suggest that humankind came from apes. Some people are still offended by the idea. Moreover, speciation itself cannot be observed; it is something that has already happened.

We came to accept evolutionary theory not because we actually saw evolution, but because the theory led to a number of novel discoveries that had been more or less in plain sight all along. One was the fact that the characteristics of animals vary with their environments. Rabbits in snowy regions are white while in sandy regions they are tan. Another discovery was the fossil record of dinosaurs and of intermediary species between apes and human beings.

The theory of evolution also allowed us to see things about ourselves that we had never considered. Darwin himself would point out to audiences that the origin of human beings from animals is evident in our bodies. Apes and dogs have a crease in their ears where their ears bend and they can raise and lower the tips. If you feel the back of your own ear, you will probably find an atavistic remnant of this same crease. It is a small indentation along the back of your ear about a third of the way down.

These examples show that it is often the surprising discovery or novel observation that persuades people to accept scientific theories and abandon their taken-for-granted, commonsense beliefs about how the world works. Uncovered by concept-driven and theory-driven observation, these discoveries take two forms. Some are macro-discoveries in the sense that they zoom *out* and point to missing pieces that fill in a larger theoretical picture. For example, in biology, the intermediary species between apes and human beings, or in astronomy, Kepler's discovery that the planets move in elliptical orbits. Based on the SCAD construct and its premises about elite political criminality, our discovery that the assassination of President Kennedy was followed quietly by adoption of the Twenty-Fifth Amendment was a macro-discovery of an outlying connection hitherto unnoticed.

Other discoveries are micro-discoveries in the sense that they zoom *in*, bringing obscure phenomena into focus. For example, the crease in the human ear and the uniform acceleration of falling objects. Similarly, the SCAD construct—the theory that sometimes public officials in democracies will lie, cheat, and kill to get their way—directed our observation to the behavior of Lyndon Johnson at the crime scene, and we saw Johnson take charge of Kennedy's body, something most people have overlooked because of their preoccupation with questions about the number of bullets and shooters. In both cases, macro- and micro-, the world is seen in a new way because new concepts highlight overlooked facts and cause old perceptions to be reinterpreted. Where previously we saw the earth as stationary and the sun as rising and setting, we now realize the sun is stationary and the earth is spinning. Where previously we saw political crimes and tragedies individually and in isolation, we now see, or shall soon see, a series of comparable events.

The Victim's Perspective

The SCAD concept is intended to function like a corrective lens to shift the standpoint and widen the angle of political crime observation. In effect, everyday (case-by-case) perceptions of assassinations, defense failures, election fiascos, and similar events view these events from the perspective of a victim, a perspective that magnifies the threat and/or the vulnerability of the target.

The victim's perspective is frequently evident in the photographic images of SCADs that become iconographic: President and Mrs. Kennedy in their limo with the Texas School Book Depository rising above them in the background; a close-up, full-body picture taken from below eye level of Lee Harvey Oswald holding a rifle; Robert Kennedy prostrate on the floor, dying, surrounded by horrified onlookers.

To this day, when we are reminded of 9/11, the images that come to mind "see" the destruction "from below." If they are images of the Twin Towers, their perspective is from street level looking up. Of course, in the case of 9/11, the natural tendency to magnify the threat and see it "from below" was enhanced by the fact that the threat came from the sky, but it was also abetted by a decision of the U.S. government to sequester photos that looked down on the carnage. Before, during, and after the Twin Towers imploded, thousands of photos were taken of the World Trade Center from a police helicopter flying overhead. These are the only images in existence that show the destruction from above, and yet the photos were withheld from the public for over eight years. They came out only because *ABC News* filed a request under the Freedom of Information Act with the National Institute of Standards and Technology (NIST), the agency responsible for investigating the World Trade Center destruction.

Significantly, no official explanation for sequestering these photos has been offered despite a *New York Times* editorial criticizing the action after the photographs were released in February 2010. The editorial focused on how these photos would have changed popular perceptions of 9/11 had they been released sooner. The editorial was titled "9/11 from Above" (February 14, 2010). It is a troubled and troubling missive that flirts with dark suspicions but ultimately leaves them unspoken. The editorial says it is "surprising to see these photographs now in part because we should have seen them sooner." Pointing out that "9/11 has resolved itself into a collection of core images," the authors imply that these images have left Americans with a picture of events that is blurry and too close up. Implicitly contrasting this "collection of core images" with the new photos, the editorial says, because the photos from the helicopter were "shot from on high, they capture with startling clarity both the voluminousness of the pale cloud that swallowed Lower Manhattan and the sharpness of its edges." The authors do not explain what this reveals about 9/11, but they clearly believe it is significant, for they conclude by saying the photos "remind us of how important it is to keep enlarging our sense of what happened on 9/11, to keep opening it to history."

SCAD Conceptualization

The SCAD concept and SCAD research operate similarly in reconceptualizing accepted perceptions of American politics and government. Americans are largely unaware of it, but they have been trained by the nation's increasingly defensive political elites, with the help of a complicit media, to avoid seeing or looking for connections between political crimes. In contrast, SCAD research begins by looking at SCADs and suspected SCADs collectively and comparatively.

SCAD-TAINTED ELECTIONS

A variety of SCADs and suspected SCADs have occurred in the United States since the nation's founding. Table 5.1 (page 210) lists twenty-seven known SCADs and other counter-democratic crimes, tragedies, and suspicious incidents for which evidence of U.S. government involvement has been uncovered. The table identifies tactics, suspects, policy consequences or aims, and includes a summary assessment of the degree to which official complicity has been confirmed. The criteria used to select these cases are discussed at length in the academic papers written on this topic. [3, 4] Suffice it to say here that the focus is on more or less notorious cases in U.S. domestic politics where democratic accountability was misdirected, subverted, preempted, or evaded by public officials, political candidates, or other political insiders. Over half (56 percent) of the SCADs are highly confirmed, typically by court rulings, official documents, recordings, or memoirs. Only three of the events have limited confirmation for state involvement: the assassinations of Senators Paul Wellstone and Robert Kennedy; and the attempted assassination of Ronald Reagan. Nevertheless, even in these cases, there is circumstantial evidence suggestive of state capabilities or connections.

Before we examine some telling patterns in Table 5.1, note

that it is obvious that American democracy in the post-WWII era has been riddled with elite political crimes. (References are cited in table.) *SCADs have greatly increased in frequency since 1945 and especially since 1960.* Seventy percent of all SCADs in the table occurred in the post–World War II era. Clearly, American politics in the post-WWII era cannot be understood without recognizing the role of high crimes.

Most Americans, if they thought about it, might suspect that elite political crime has gone up, for they would recall the assassinations and assassination attempts in the 1960s and 1970s. But they would undoubtedly be surprised by the frequency and clustering of crimes around certain events, such as elections. A simple review of elections makes it clear that American democracy has been repeatedly undermined by violence and insider manipulations. Presidential elections were impacted by assassinations, election tampering, and/or intrigues with foreign powers in 1964, 1968, 1972, 1980, 2000, and 2004. This amounts to over a third of all presidential elections since 1948 and fully half of all elections since 1964. Moreover, two-thirds of these tainted elections were marred by *multiple* events:

- 1964 included the assassinations of President John F. Kennedy and Lee Harvey Oswald, plus the Gulf of Tonkin incident, which had a rally-'round-the-president effect shortly before the election;
- 1968 included the assassination of Robert Kennedy plus the 1968 October Surprise;
- 1972 included the stalking of Ellsberg, the crimes of Watergate, and the attempted assassination of Wallace; and
- 2004 included false terror alerts plus election tampering.

When we stop looking at SCADs one by one; when we telescope out and look at them collectively or, so to speak, "from above," we see a nation repeatedly abused. This abuse is another reason for the citizenry's failure to recognize obvious connections; trauma fragments memory because traumatic events loom too large to be kept in perspective. Just as victims of child abuse and spousal abuse tend to have fragmented recollections of the abuse, so America's collective memory of assassinations, defense failures, and other shocking events—the people's shared narrative and sense of history—is shattered into emotionally charged but disconnected bits and pieces.

Comparative analysis of the SCADs and suspected SCADs in Table 5.1 reveals the patterns discussed below. Since World War II, the main effect of most SCADs and suspected SCADs has been to foster social panic and militarism in the American mass public and belligerency in U.S. foreign policy. [3]

POLICY CONSEQUENCES

Many SCADs and suspected SCADs are associated with foreign policy and international conflict. They include the following events or alleged events: passing the 1798 Sedition Act in the context of growing tension with Great Britain; contriving a pretext for the Mexican-American War; allowing the sinking of the *Maine* to provide a pretext for the Spanish-American War; failing to warn commanders in the Pacific about the impending Japanese attack on Pearl Harbor; the assassinations of John Kennedy and Robert Kennedy; the Gulf of Tonkin incident; the burglary of Daniel Ellsberg's psychiatrist's office; the 1968 October Surprise; Iran-Contra; 9/11; the anthrax letter attacks; Iraq-gate; and the bogus terror alerts in 2004. All of these SCADs and suspected SCADs contributed to the initiation or continuation of military conflicts. (The assassination of President Lincoln almost falls into this category, but the killers, although suspected of receiving support from the president's bodyguards, were from states in rebellion and insurrection.)

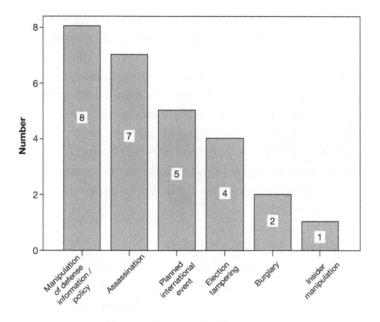

Figure 5.1. Modus operandi of U.S. SCADs and suspected SCADs.

MODUS OPERANDI

SCADs are fairly limited in their modus operandi (MOs). Figure 5.1 is a bar chart showing the breakdown of MOs for the events listed in Table 5.1. SCAD MOs listed by order of frequency are mass deceptions by manipulating defense information or policy (8), assassinations (7), planned international-conflict events (5), election tampering (4), burglaries (2), and insider manipulation (to influence the wording of the Fourteenth Amendment) (1). SCAD MOs have shifted noticeably in the post-WWII era. Prior to the end of World War II, there were only two mass deceptions regarding defense information, but in the post-WWII era, there have been six, which constitute about a third of all post-WWII SCADs. In addition, assassinations have been a more common MO in recent decades than earlier. Both of these MOs

are indicative of groups with expertise in the skills of espionage and covert, paramilitary operations. Consistent with
the analysis in Chapter 2, the post-WWII proliferation of
SCADs employing deception may be attributable in part to
the growing scale and centralization of government and business in political-economic complexes, and the holographic
character of discourse in a public sphere that is increasingly "virtual," that is, packaged in carefully crafted catchphrases (sound bites) as opposed to spontaneous, unpolished
sense-making, and disseminated in electronic as opposed to
printed form. [5]

PRESIDENTS NIXON AND BUSH

Many SCADs in the post-WWII era indicate both direct
and nested connections to two presidents: Richard Nixon
and George W. Bush. Not only was Nixon responsible for
Watergate and the illegal surveillance of Daniel Ellsberg,
he benefited directly from the assassination of Robert Kennedy in 1968 and the attempted assassination of George
Wallace in 1972. RFK was assassinated on the night he won
the California Democratic primary. He was favored to win
the national Democratic Party nomination and would have
been a formidable candidate in the general election against
Nixon. In 1972, running as a third-party candidate, Wallace
posed a threat to Nixon because he appeared likely to win a
number of states in the South, potentially preventing Nixon
from gaining a majority of votes in the Electoral College. The
SCADs and suspected SCADs that benefited Bush include the
election administration problems in Florida in 2000 and in
Ohio in 2004; the events of 9/11; the anthrax letter attacks
on top Senate Democrats in October 2001; Iraq-gate; and the
series of specious terror alerts that rallied support for Bush
before the 2004 presidential election. Were it not for election
administration problems in urban centers where Democrats
are concentrated (as well as glitches in computer-based vote-

tabulation equipment that tended to favor Bush), Bush might not have been declared winner of Florida in 2000 or Ohio in 2004. [6] All of the other SCADs benefiting Bush fomented fear and anger toward terrorism, produced a "rally-'round-the-president" effect, buoyed Bush's popularity, and played into his agenda for waging war in the Middle East.

There is also reason for thinking the behavior of the Nixon and Bush-Cheney administrations was connected by enduring networks of political insiders in the upper echelons of the bureaucracy who were inclined to push the limits of the law. George H. W. Bush was chairman of the Republican National Committee during the Nixon Administration. Bush was appointed director of the CIA by President Ford, who of course had pardoned Nixon in a deal apparently brokered by Alexander Haig. The latter served as Reagan's secretary of state. Bush Senior was suspected of having helped arrange the 1980 October Surprise. [8] Also rumored to have been involved was Robert Gates, who became assistant director of the CIA for Reagan and later secretary of defense for Bush-Cheney. He was kept on in that capacity by President Obama. As vice president, Bush appears to have been the person in charge of the Iran-Contra program, information he withheld from investigators. [9] Some of the people he pardoned for participating in Iran-Contra ended up serving in the Bush-Cheney administration. The extent to which this multigenerational network was united by the teachings of Leo Strauss is unclear, but Strauss' students from the 1950s and 1960s, students such as Paul Wolfowitz, did end up in influential positions as this network took root. Russ Baker covers much of this ground in his book *Family of Secrets*. [10]

The Democrats also have political criminality—Lyndon Johnson was possibly a principal in the assassination of President Kennedy, and he misled Congress and the American people about the Gulf of Tonkin incident. But the Democrats do not appear to have developed, at least not yet, a political philosophy that condones high crimes in the name of policy objectives.

ASSASSINATION TARGETS

The range of officials targeted for assassination in the post-WWII era is limited to those most directly associated with foreign policy: presidents (and presidential candidates) and senators. High-ranking officials in the federal government have seldom been murdered even though many have attracted widespread hostility and opposition. No vice presidents have been assassinated, nor have any U.S. Supreme Court justices. The only member of the U.S. House of Representatives who has been targeted is Gabrielle Giffords in January 2011.

The science for estimating the likelihood of events occurring by chance is called "statistics." In probability theory, events are assumed to have a finite range of variation. A flipped coin can land on only heads or tails. The probability of any given variant occurring by chance is the proportion that variant comprises of the total number of variants in the range of variation. The flipped coin landing on heads is one variant out of two; the other variant is tails. So the probability of a flipped coin landing on heads is one out of two, or .5. Common sense tells us that the odds of similar multiple events occurring together by chance are low, but the science of statistics can help us estimate how low. As the number of coincidences increases, the odds of them occurring by chance rapidly becomes infinitesimal, which is to say, almost impossible. The odds of one variant occurring twice are equal to the odds of it occurring once *squared*. The odds of getting two heads in two flips are one in four (.5 × .5 = .25). The odds of something occurring three times are the odds of it occurring once *cubed*. The odds of getting three heads in three flips are one in eight (.5 × .5 × .5 = .125). Ten heads out of ten flips would be expected to occur one time in 1,024 tries.

Let us calculate some rough estimates of assassination probabilities. If one assassination of a top public official were committed each year, and if targets were randomly selected, the odds of a president being killed in any given year would be 1 in 546. (There are 100 senators, 435 representatives, 9 Supreme Court justices, 1 vice president, and 1 president.) The odds of two presidents (Kennedy and Reagan) being shot by chance since 1948 are roughly 1 in 274,000. If Robert Kennedy is included (as a president-to-be), the odds of three presidents being targeted by chance since 1948 are approximately 1 in 149 million. The upshot is that targets are not being selected randomly. [11]

A related pattern has to do with the particular presidents who have been targeted for elimination, as opposed to the many who have not. Since the end of WWII, presidents have been targeted only when their elimination would benefit military and pro-war interests. Because a president who is killed or dies in office is automatically succeeded by the vice president, a presidential assassination would benefit military interests only if the vice president's background or policy positions were dramatically better for the military than the president's. This situation has existed only twice in the post-WWII era—during the presidencies of John F. Kennedy and Ronald Reagan. Unlike Kennedy, who was trying to end the Cold War, Lyndon Johnson was a well-known hawk and Pentagon supporter. Similarly, although Reagan and George H. W. Bush had similar positions on the Cold War, Bush's background as director of the CIA gave him much closer ties than Reagan to the military establishment.

Embodied in the pejorative conspiracy-theory label, powerful norms discourage just about everyone from voicing serious suspicions that any of the nation's leaders have been involved in political conspiracies to assassinate their colleagues or to use other criminal means to achieve political objectives they could not achieve democratically. The assumptions tend to be that there is no evidence of guilt and that in the Anglo-American legal tradition, people who have not been proven guilty are supposed to be presumed innocent. This widely shared attitude is mistaken in at least two respects.

One is its view that there is no evidence of elite involvement in America's post-WWII political assassinations. The evidence is difficult to see in individual assassinations when they are examined one at a time, but evidence of elite involvement is quite clear when assassinations are examined together and comparatively. The targets of assassinations are officials who control foreign policy. Dovish presidents with hawkish vice presidents are assassinations waiting to happen. Since the shooting of Ronald Reagan, presidential candidates have been rather careful to avoid tempting fate. They pick running mates who are clones of themselves, have a history of heart attacks, or who, like Dan Quayle and Sarah Palin, have questionable competency.

The other problem with the premises underlying the taboo against conspiracy theories is that the presumption of innocence was never intended to outlaw suspicions. Rather, it calls for suspicions to be tested with thorough and fair investigations grounded by procedural rules for procuring and presenting evidence more substantial than hearsay. In contrast, the conspiracy-theory label is applied not to categorize a position that will actually be considered, but to head off argumentation before it begins.

SENATORIAL ASSASSINATIONS

A similar pattern is observed in assassinations and attempted assassinations of senators. Three senators have been confirmed to have been targeted for assassination since 1948: Robert Kennedy, Patrick Leahy, and Tom Daschle. Senators have been assassinated only when running for president (Robert Kennedy) or when the Senate was closely divided and the death of a single senator from the majority party could significantly impact policy. Aside from RFK, the only well-confirmed senatorial assassinations or attempted assassinations in the post-WWII era occurred in 2001, when Democrats controlled the Senate by virtue of a one-vote advantage over Republicans. In May of 2001, just four months after George W. Bush gained the presidency in a SCAD-ridden disputed election, Republican Jim Jeffords left the party to become an independent, and the Senate shifted to Democratic control for the first time since 1994. Five months later, on October 9, 2001, letters laced with anthrax were used in an unsuccessful attempt to assassinate two leading Senate Democrats, Majority Leader Tom Daschle and Judiciary Committee Chairman Patrick Leahy. And in 2002, the Democratic senator Paul Wellstone died in a suspicious plane crash. Assassination scholar and philosophy professor Jim Fetzer argues in a coauthored book, *American Assassination*, that Wellstone may have been the victim of foul play.

TRENDS IN FREQUENCY AND SCOPE

Ominously, the frequency of SCADs has recently increased sharply, and the number of SCADs with wide government complicity has been growing. Figure 5.2 graphs the frequency of SCADs by decade, with wide versus narrow government complicity. SCAD frequency surged in the 1960s, declined in the 1970s and 1980s, dropped to zero when the Cold War ended in the 1990s, and then jumped dramatically in the 2000s. To some extent, the SCAD sprees of the 1960s and the 2000s reflect the behavior associated with Presidents Richard Nixon and George W. Bush. However, the widening scope of government complicity across the decades suggests that creeping corruption may be amplifying the untoward implications of morally unrestrained presidential administrations.

The expanding scope of government complicity in elite political intrigues can be observed in the trajectory from

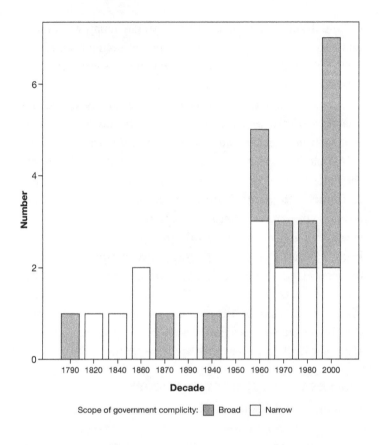

Figure 5.2. Number of SCADs with narrow versus wide government complicity, by decade (excluding decades with no known SCADs or suspected SCADs), 1790–2000.

Watergate through Iran-Contra to Iraq-gate. [12, 13] The crimes of the Nixon administration were driven by the president's personal fears and animosities, and involved only a handful of top officials, most of whom participated only in cover-ups and, even then, reluctantly. Furthermore, Republican and Democratic members of Congress joined together to investigate and condemn the president's actions. In contrast, the Iran-Contra episode was systemic, organized, and carefully planned, and its investigation was impeded by partisan opposition even though (or perhaps because) it was very likely connected both to the alleged 1980 October Surprise [8, 9] and to the importation of cocaine into America's inner cities. [14, 15] Motivated by ideology, Iran-Contra emanated from the White House and garnered enthusiastic participation by high-ranking officials and career professionals within the State Department, the CIA, and the military. Even wider in scope and more deeply woven into governing institutions were the crimes apparently committed by the Bush-Cheney administration. [16–18] Attacking the organs of deliberation, policymaking, oversight, and legal review, they appear to have involved officials throughout the executive branch and perhaps leaders in Congress as well.

Searching for Novel Facts in 9/11

The observations drawn above about SCAD patterns are macro-discoveries showing that what at first look like random events, when examined collectively and comparatively, are not random at all. Many political crimes and suspicious events affecting or involving elites in America share various characteristics. They often employ military skills and tactics, cause social panic and militarism in the American mass public, and encourage belligerency in U.S. foreign policy. [3] SCAD patterns that have been consistent for decades point to the military-industrial complex.

A controversial possible SCAD today is 9/11. It is viewed officially as an attack in the war against al-Qaeda. In this theoretical context, the search has been on for masterminds in the caves of Afghanistan and also sympathizers in the United States, its allies, and other developed nations.

If 9/11 is viewed as a SCAD, however, the focus shifts to the United States, and specifically to the CIA and other intelligence agencies, the military (and especially to those services

*The Twin Towers from above. (Source: National
Institute of Standards and Technology)*

with aviation skills and resources), possibly to the White
House, and to any political-economic complexes that stood
to benefit from or would be favorably impacted by a U.S. invasion of the Middle East. Two complexes are obvious: oil and
armaments. Pharmaceuticals became suspect because of
the anthrax letter attacks that began about a week after 9/11.

In the absence of the SCAD construct, the range of possible domestic connections to 9/11 is very large. The SCAD construct offers some simplifying assumptions.

Three lines of inquiry are suggested: (1) follow the U.S. investigators and other officials, and look for guilty knowledge, hidden agendas, and the like; (2) search for parallels in related SCADs; and (3) check for unique CIA capabilities, such as the meme planting observed in the CIA propaganda program that stigmatized the idea of conspiracy theories.

IMMEDIATE ACTIONS OF INVESTIGATORS AND TOP OFFICIALS

With the SCAD construct, we make the cynical assumptions that (1) officials in investigative positions will actively avoid evidence of government involvement and will, instead, gather supporting evidence for theories that exonerate officials who may be suspect; and (2) officials in operational positions will exploit the crimes to serve their agendas, hidden and otherwise.

Focusing on the NIST investigators, we learn that, despite signs of controlled demolition (or because of them), the government failed to investigate the debris at the World Trade Center for signs of explosives and incendiaries. This failure has been decried by many scientists, engineers, architects, and other experts. A leading voice in this regard is physicist Steven E. Jones, who critiqued the NIST investigation in a chapter in the 2007 book, *9/11 and American Empire*. Arguably, the decision by federal investigators not to check for chemical indications of controlled demolition amounts to nonfeasance indicative of guilty knowledge. In other words, investigators may have avoided examining the debris because they knew that such an inquiry would reveal trace elements of explosives and incendiaries and did not want the evidence to be discovered.

The observed actions of other officials in the aftermath of

9/11 include immediately invading Afghanistan, adopting an official policy of preemptive war (in the 2002 National Security Strategy Report), and manipulating intelligence to justify the invasion and occupation of Iraq. [19, 20] With these actions, operational officials may have simply been exploiting the 9/11 attacks while having played no role in facilitating the attacks. Of course the evidence is also consistent with a preexisting agenda to contrive a pretext for waging wars of aggression in the Middle East to gain control of diminishing energy supplies. As troubling as it may be to consider, the possibility cannot be ruled out that 9/11 could have been an inside job driven by imperial ambitions. For researchers, the question to be asking next is, if 9/11 was a SCAD, who, specifically, are the main suspects and what were they doing at the time?

THE ANTHRAX LETTER ATTACKS

SCAD research suggests that SCADs are committed in pairs or clusters. Examples include the assassination of John Kennedy, which was followed two days later by the assassination of Lee Harvey Oswald and a year after that by the Gulf of Tonkin incident; the stalking of Daniel Ellsberg, which was followed by the crimes of Watergate and the attempted assassination of George Wallace; and the 1980 October Surprise, which was followed by Iran-Contra. In the case of Watergate and Ellsberg, we know that the crimes in question were committed by the exact same group of people, and that this group committed other crimes as well.

If this pattern were to hold for 9/11, then other crimes closely related in time or employing similar tactics were probably planned and organized by the same people. An obvious place to start looking for connections to 9/11 is with the anthrax letter attacks, but consideration should also be given to investigating other events and venues, such as who approved the flights for bin Laden's family to leave the

United States. The bin Laden family members should have been thoroughly interrogated. Also, why not hold them for an extended period while their finances were being investigated? At the very least, exposing the family to inconvenience would have embarrassed bin Laden and probably would have made his family reluctant to associate with him. For that matter, in war the U.S typically takes advantage of opportunities to harm or inconvenience its enemies. Arlington Cemetery, for example, was established during the Civil War by expropriating the plantation of Robert E. Lee, the top general of the Confederacy. The plantation came into the Union's hands, and in a single stroke the Union leadership made Lee's family homeless and created a lasting symbol that laid hundreds of thousands of deaths at Lee's feet. It is therefore quite shocking that bin Laden's family was given special treatment so they could leave the country quickly and quietly.

Officially, the anthrax letter attacks have been attributed to Bruce Ivins, a bio-weapons expert who allegedly had psychological problems. However, the case against Ivins contains several gaps. [21] The anthrax in the letters has not been conclusively connected to the anthrax in Ivins' control; the high amount of silicon in the mailed anthrax, which enhanced its lethality, may have required equipment and skills Ivins lacked; and Ivins did not have direct control of the equipment allegedly used to dry the anthrax.

Like 9/11, the anthrax letter attacks played into the Bush-Cheney agenda for invading Iraq. In fact, the administration immediately suggested that the anthrax had come from Iraq. This effort to implicate the regime of Saddam Hussein was thwarted only because the FBI investigation concluded that the anthrax had come from a strain developed by the U.S. military at the Army Medical Research Institute of Infectious Diseases at Fort Detrick, Maryland. [7]

There is already circumstantial evidence in the public domain suggesting federal officials had foreknowledge of the anthrax letter attacks. In the evening on 9/11, weeks before the anthrax mailings were discovered, medical officers at the White House distributed a powerful antibiotic (Cipro) to the president and other officials. [22] Officials might claim that Cipro was administered simply as a precaution, but this innocent explanation is belied by the failure of anyone in the White House to tell Congress and the public that an anthrax attack was feared. Investigators should determine what kind of anthrax attack was of concern; who issued the warning; who suggested that Cipro should be administered; to whom Cipro was given and for how long; and why other officials and the public were not warned. For investigators, those officials who were responsible for these decisions, especially those earliest in the decision chain, would be considered persons of interest in both 9/11 and the anthrax letter attacks, and their whereabouts and contacts on and immediately before and after 9/11 should be carefully tracked.

LINGUISTIC THOUGHT CONTROL

The 1967 CIA propaganda program shows that the United States government has been actively engaged in engineering America's civic culture and has been alarmingly effective at doing so. It appears that one of its methods is to insert memes into the culture through a global network of media contacts and assets. The scholar most directly familiar with this propaganda machine has compared it to a giant pipe organ, or "Wurlitzer." [23]

The possibility of cultural engineering in relation to 9/11, the anthrax letter attacks, and other associated crimes should be investigated. It should be assumed that covert cultural operations involve inserting debilitating memes and perhaps other forms of weaponized language into the discursive arena to skew the search for meaning, agreement, and collective action in the public sphere. These destructive memes may have characteristics similar to those of the conspiracy-theory label, which is normatively powerful but conceptually flawed and alien to America's civic culture.

A number of memes have been introduced by the military as part of the war on terror (including the phrase "war on terror" and "global war on terror"), but, at least when considered in isolation, they do not appear to qualify as linguistic thought control because they were not released into the public sphere surreptitiously. These memes skew and hamper communication, but they are recognized as artificial constructs, and hence their ability to distort public discourse is mitigated. In contrast, memes warranting inspection as possible linguistic containers for surreptitious cognitive structuring are those that are taken for granted as natural products of sense-making in civil society.

Of immediate concern should be the term "9/11." If it was inserted into the organs of opinion formation during or immediately after the day of the hijackings, prior planning would probably have been necessary, which could be construed as evidence of official complicity in the events of 9/11 themselves.

Today, the term "9/11" is accepted as simply a straightforward name for the events on September 11, 2001. However, as a label for "terrorist attacks upon the United States" (the phrase used in the official title of the 9/11 Commission), "9/11" has characteristics of a conceptual Trojan horse similar to those of the conspiracy-theory meme. On the surface, the term "9/11" says almost nothing; it is not even a complete date. And yet it carries hidden associations and implications that reverberate in the national psyche.

First, the term "9/11" contains emotionally charged symbolism. The numbers 9-1-1 correspond to the phone number for emergencies in the United States. This means references to 9/11 subliminally provoke thoughts among Americans about picking up the phone and calling for an ambulance or for help from police or firefighters. The 9/11 label would not have been possible if the events had not occurred on September 11; this itself suggests prior planning for a date with emotional connections. Nevertheless, state intervention into the discursive processes of civil society would have been necessary both to suggest the date as the label for the events and to drop the year from "9-11-01."

As a matter of fact, the connection between the abbreviated date (9/11) and the emergency phone number (9-1-1) was highlighted in what had to be one of the very first times the term "9/11" was used in the media. The 9/11 label was included in the headline of a story in the *New York Times* on September 12, 2001. The headline was "America's Emergency Line: 9/11." The first sentence of the article referred to "America's aptly dated wake-up call." Since then, the connection between the date and the emergency number has been mentioned in the *New York Times* only one other time—in an article published in February 2002.

A second characteristic of the 9/11 label indicative of cognitive infiltration is that it deviates from America's naming conventions for the type of event it designates. With the possible exception of Independence Day, which is often referred to as "July Fourth," the 9/11 label marks the first time Americans have called a historic event by an abbreviated form of the date on which the event occurred. 9/11 is a first-of-its-kind "numeric acronym." Americans do not call Pearl Harbor "12/7," even though President Roosevelt declared December 7, 1941, to be "a date that will live in infamy." Americans do not refer to the (John) Kennedy assassination as "11/22." Historically, as these examples suggest, Americans have referred to crimes, tragedies, and disasters by their targets, locations, methods, or effects—not their dates. Americans remember the Alamo and the sinking of the *Maine*. They speak of Three Mile Island, Hurricane Katrina, the Oklahoma City bombing, and Watergate.

If Americans had followed this pattern for 9/11, the events

would probably have been called "the hijacked airplane attacks." Americans would tell themselves to remember the World Trade Center and the Pentagon.

Even when Americans want to refer to a specific day because of its historical significance, they seldom use the date. They speak of Independence Day, D-Day, VE Day, Election Day, and so on. If they had done this for September 11, it would have been called the Day of the Hijackings or something like that.

Third, the term "9/11" should be suspect and should therefore be subjected to scientific and forensic investigation because the term is so powerful while at the same time so simple and compact. It is like a verbal bullet, loaded with explosive implications and shaped for penetration. It is a very short phrase; three numbers and a slash. And yet, in evoking thoughts of the emergency telephone number, it conveys a comprehensive conception of the relationship between citizen and government. The government's actions are dictated by the emergency and not statutory and constitutional requirements. The government is defined as a rescuer, a protector. The citizen's role is to call for help and to wait for it to come.

In modern political philosophy, the emergency situation was analyzed by Carl Schmitt, a leading Nazi legal scholar and political theorist with whom Leo Strauss corresponded and whose writings influenced Strauss or at least attracted his attention. Schmitt defined an emergency as an existential threat to the nation conceived as a political and biological community. He argued that emergencies brought into sharp relief what politics is really about, which is survival of the community against enemies seeking to annihilate it. [24] Schmitt assumed that government has an absolute right to survival, which means that when survival is at stake there are no limits to political authority.

Thus, in effect, the 9/11 meme with its connection to 9-1-1

contains within it an entire political philosophy. This philosophy says there is a national emergency and it requires
a national emergency response; the government alone is
responsible for choosing a course of action, defining who
is an enemy, and deciding what actions are necessary from
moment to moment to preserve the political entity in its
struggle to overcome the emergency. The judge of the emergency and of the state's response to it is the state itself. It
alone will judge the legitimacy of its actions.

This political philosophy is based on ideas about the
nature of politics, but it makes empirical claims about how
people and governments actually behave in emergencies.
They take extreme actions, they designate friends and enemies, they disregard legal restrictions.

This may indeed be so; Schmitt may be correct that this
is exactly how political entities respond in emergencies. But
what is left out by Schmitt is a discussion of when events are
seen as emergencies and when they are seen as simply challenges to be processed by the established political institutions. America changed after 9/11 because it internalized the
belief that came with the 9/11 meme, namely, that we are in
a state of emergency with no end in sight. We are not at war
in the conventional sense of the term, because the oppo-
nent is not another nation. We are not in a state of war; we
are in a state of emergency, which poses a far greater threat
to our democracy than an ordinary conflict. The connection
between 9/11 the date, and 9-1-1 the emergency telephone
number, by planting the idea that 9/11 created an emergency,
turned September 11 into an event of world-historic propor-
tions: the beginning of an endless emergency.

Fourth, the term "9/11" should be suspected of being an
artifact of linguistic thought control because the term shapes
perceptions in ways that play into elite agendas for global
military aggression. Just as SCAD research asks who benefits from an assassination, an election breakdown, and so on,

so it asks who benefits from an event being framed in a certain way. The 9/11 meme played into elite agendas for military action in the Middle East. In drawing attention to a date as opposed to the method or location of the destruction, the term "9/11" suggests there has been a shift in the flow of history. 9/11 is a historical marker. There is the world before 9/11, and the world after 9/11. As Vice President Cheney and other officials said, "9/11 changed everything." Clearly, this framing suggests the need for a dramatic U.S. response and a determined, hardened attitude. Think how less convincing and urgent it would be to say the *hijackings* changed everything, or the *collapse of the Twin Towers and Building 7* changed everything. When you refer to hijackings and buildings, you cannot avoid the realization that the threat of terrorism is in no way comparable to the threat the Allies faced in World War II or to the dangers in the standoff between the United States and the Soviet Union in the Cold War. Using the term "9/11" to refer to the destruction at the World Trade Center and the Pentagon has the effect of exaggerating the threat posed by people who hijack airplanes and use them as weapons.

Fifth, by stressing the date, the term "9/11" draws our attention away from the victims, the destruction, and the military response. Imagine if we referred to the events in question as the "Airplane Mass Murders," or the "Multiple Skyscraper Collapse," or the "National Air-Defense Failure." Each of these names points to a different investigative focus. "9/11," as a name, causes us to think in terms of chronology and historic change instead of failures and culpability. The armed services of the United States, especially the Air Force, which is the branch of the military most responsible for the nation's air defenses, benefited greatly from the focus on the date, because the focus ignored the failure of the Air Force that day.

As with SCADs generally, memes should be analyzed collectively and comparatively on the assumption that they may be the products of the same group or of cooperating groups. The United States has had an extensive program of cultural manipulation and influence overseas since the end of World War II, and the CIA routinely uses this overseas megaphone to influence U.S. domestic opinion indirectly. Howard Hunt claimed to have been a high-ranking executive in the operation near the end of his career with the CIA. [25] The U.S. also manipulates opinion at home and abroad by fabricating or exaggerating attacks on U.S. military forces.

If national security elites are manipulating public discourse and public perceptions of military actions like these to generate popular support for global military aggression, they are almost certainly developing and planting concepts in public discourse. It is very unlikely that the conspiracy-theory label was a unique instance of CIA concept creation and deployment. Recall the language used to sell the Iraq War. Could President Bush and Condoleezza Rice come up with the line, "We don't want the smoking gun to be a mushroom cloud"? We know that some orchestration of messaging was carried out by the White House Iraq Group. But it is unlikely that even this specially tasked working committee, whose job was to make the case for invading Iraq, could have come up with the full package of concepts and themes that quickly emerged around the war on terror in the aftermath of 9/11 and the anthrax letter attacks.

Considered together, the nomenclature for the aggressive wars in the Middle East was thematic, integrated, and invested with emotion still attached to World War II. Many of the terms used during the early years of the war on terror had direct connections to this war, which is remembered as a good war, a necessary war, and a war that was won decisively and in only four years. Examples of World War II linguistic connections include such terms as "homeland," "axis of evil" (as in the Axis powers), and "ground zero." Moreover, it was not just that the language was nostalgic for a particular era; the language was also woven together in ways that created depth and emotional complexity. For example, the term "homeland security" evokes an identification with home that divides America from the rest of the world, and when this identification is connected in speech with the war on terror, the image conjured tends to be of the United States isolated and besieged. Similarly, the president's and Condoleezza Rice's warnings about the mushroom cloud conjured images of the atomic bombs exploding in Hiroshima and Nagasaki, while the reference to the site of the Twin Towers and Building 7 as "ground zero" drew a line from the destruction in Japan to the destruction in New York. These connections are laden with deeply complicated and ambivalent feelings. Yes, we won WWII, but we dropped enormously powerful radioactive bombs on a defeated people. Ground zero? Was this our punishment? Or is Ground Zero the new Pearl Harbor, and if so, is this not a conflicted emblem for a national calling?

Thus the 9/11 meme was the nucleus and seed for a web of terms that conceptualized the hijacked airplane attacks as a world-historic event initiating a "global war on terror" in which America's role would be comparable in significance and righteousness to the nation's role in World War II. The language of this new world contest was rolled out over the course of about two years. The language included entire new lexicons for preemptive war, torture ("enhanced interrogations") of prisoners ("detainees," "enemy combatants"), the enemy ("Islamofascism," "Jihadists," "al Qaeda"), national defense ("Homeland Security"), and more. It took the masterminds of the Cold War several years longer to develop their policies and terminology. NSC 68, which was adopted in 1950, introduced the policy of containment to deal with "communist expansionism." Churchill had already introduced, in 1946, the imaginative term "the iron curtain." The "domino theory" had yet to be fully articulated until the Korean War or later.

A SCAD approach to memes assumes further that the CIA and other possibly participating agencies are formulating memes well in advance of operations, and therefore SCAD memes appear and are popularized very quickly before any competing concepts are on the scene. The tendency in meme analysis for marketing research is to track the life cycle of memes from obscurity to popularity and then fadeout. SCAD memes would be expected to become widely used very quickly, block new memes from entry, and consequently have a much longer longer shelf life than standard memes.

The rapidity with which the new language of the war on terror appeared and took hold; the synergy between terms and their mutual connections to WWII nomenclatures; and above all the connections between many terms and the emergency motif of "9/11" and "9-1-1"—any one of these factors alone, but certainly all of them together—raise the possibility that work on this linguistic construct began long before 9/11. The decision had to be made that the core concept would be the world-historic emergency before planning could be set in motion around the September 11 date and downstream terminology could be framed accordingly. In short, once we recognize the centrality of 9/11 as a symbol and linguistic core for what has materialized as a new paradigm of American government (an endless emergency) and an American-dominated world order backed by military forces deployed around the globe; once we recognize that NSC 68 put America on the path of constructing U.S. civic culture to stand firm against the threat of global thermonuclear warfare; once we see that U.S. policy both domestically and internationally has become subordinate to military plans and calculations that envision the future, decades in advance, 9/11 itself is put in a larger perspective, as is the hope and fate of American democracy. It turns out that elite political crime, even treason, may actually be official policy.

6

RESTORING
AMERICAN DEMOCRACY

N ow that troubling symbolism in the timing and naming of the hijacked airplane attacks has been spoken of openly, and evidence has been introduced indicating possible official foreknowledge of the anthrax letter attacks, we should be able, in this concluding chapter, to examine two explosive but open secrets about antidemocratic elite conspiracies in modern American politics. These are like family secrets that are not discussed and resolved because they have the potential to tear the family apart. And yet this lack of resolution prevents the family from getting along well and being happy.

America's Family Secrets

One of America's secrets about SCADs has to do with the real reasons why conspiracy theories have become so popular and why public officials are considering police actions to infiltrate and disrupt conspiracy-theory groups and networks—and this despite the horrendous experience in the 1960s with police infiltration of the civil rights and antiwar movements. At the risk of oversimplifying the situation, the unvarnished truth is that conspiracy theories are and have long been a matter of intense official concern, not necessarily because they are false but dangerously appealing to mass paranoia, but because they are often true, or come close to the truth, and are therefore difficult to disprove.

As an epithet or insult, the conspiracy-theory label is not really intended to influence those who would speak of conspiracies. For one thing, there are too many conspiracy believers to silence. The conspiracy-theory label does something else; it targets the audience, not the speaker. It inculcates in people who are undecided about conspiracies—or who have never considered such matters—a propensity to dismiss conspiracy claims out of hand. In this way, conspiracy statements that are actually quite compelling go unheard.

America's second open secret about SCADs is that the demos is ambivalent about elite conspiracies and cover-ups. If the U.S. electorate were united in opposing conspiracies by the political class, most of the elite intrigues and duplicity in domestic politics would have ended long ago, but the truth is that many Americans support U.S. officials and institutions even when they are implicated in antidemocratic conspiracies targeting U.S. policymaking. Simply put, there is an element in American society, perhaps a large element, that trusts the government to do what is best for the nation, and that believes state manipulation of domestic politics, at least in relation to foreign affairs, is necessary even though it is usually illegal.

This group can be called "conspiracy realists," not because they are more realistic than conspiracy believers or deniers, but because they base their political actions and attitudes on what they consider to be the existing realities of power. They speak as if they support the aspirations of the Founders for liberty and popular control of government, but they are quite happy if the government secretly snoops on their neighbors to enhance their own security. Although few conspiracy realists would be familiar with the ideas of Leo Strauss, their philosophy is Straussian in important respects. Conspiracy realists might reject some of the conclusions drawn in the previous chapter's analysis of SCAD patterns, 9/11, and the anthrax letter attacks, but this is not the key reason for their continued support of America's amoral national security elites. Their main considerations are that the government has information we lack; the agencies being accused of complicity in murder, treason, and other high crimes are essentially the same organizations that led America to victory in both World War II and the Cold War using those very tactics; and the growing availability of thermonuclear, biological, and chemical weapons of mass destruction exposes the U.S. to extreme and perhaps existential threats from any number of enemies. Conspiracy realists would want to protect what they see as the gains of the past decade, principal among them that America's national security elites and top elected officials have successfully shaped a new world order around the idea of a "war on terror" that allows the United States to attack its enemies preemptively despite UN Charter provisions to the contrary.

Reform Where Law and Politics Meet

To be clear going in, the position taken in this final chapter is that political reform should aim at aiding the democratic elements of the demos against the conspiracy realists and national security elites, who are, however well intentioned, betraying the nation's Founders and founding principles. The United States of America was established as a nation of laws, and the rule of law means that the law applies, not merely to the people, but to government as well.

The notion of State Crimes against Democracy is intended to capture this simple idea, with the added requirement that the laws be formulated and enacted with meaningful input by the people in the true spirit of popular government. This requires that the president and others with privileged access to information level with the American people about the actual state of affairs surrounding the questions at issue. When President Bush and his subordinates told the nation that Iraq possessed weapons of mass destruction, he committed a SCAD or, if you prefer, a high crime, for he deprived Congress and the people of the information necessary to make an informed decision about whether to support or oppose military action. At the very least, the people should have been told that the intelligence about Iraqi weapons of mass destruction was ambiguous, that some of it had been extracted from prisoners under harsh methods of interrogation, and that United Nations inspectors believed they could make an accurate determination if given more time. As Abraham Lincoln said of President Polk's statement to Congress about the need for the Mexican-American War, if President Bush told the truth, he did not tell the whole truth, and what he left out was essential to judging the merits of the point he was making. According to former federal prosecutor Elizabeth de la Vega in her 2006 book, *United States v. George W. Bush et al.*, this is fraud, pure and simple. In presenting a fraudulent case for war, federal officials subverted American democracy to gain support for a war of aggression, the type of crime for which, as we have seen, the United States and its allies tried, convicted, and executed Nazi leaders after World War II. [1] As a result of the U.S. invasion of Iraq, thousands if not hundreds of thousands of people died, among them American soldiers, sailors, airmen, and Marines. Experienced prosecutors have argued that officials responsible for the invasion of Iraq, including the president, should be tried for murder. [2]

The people cannot have meaningful input into national decision making if decisions, mandated by the Constitution to be debated and made in public, are deals made in secret.

The treaties into which the United States enters with other nations must be brought before the Senate for ratification and, once ratified, become the highest laws of the land. There is no room in the Constitution for a secret deal between U.S. president George W. Bush and British prime minister Tony Blair to invade Iraq in the spring of 2003, as reported in the Downing Street Memos. [3 pp. 6–12, 211–220] Charles Beard [4 p. 582] pointed out in his book on decisions preceding America's entry into World War II that President Roosevelt had made secret deals with the British to enter the war in the Pacific under certain conditions, and had failed to submit the plans for Senate approval. Beard warned that, if ignored, this usurpation of authority would set a precedent, and it clearly did, for despite the outcry about the Bush administration misleading the country into war in Iraq, no comparable complaints were heard about bringing the United States into a secret alliance with the United Kingdom.

Nor can the people control the government if presidents ignore the crimes of their predecessors or use their pardon powers to protect themselves or their agents from accountability. With the possible exception of Thomas Jefferson, who encouraged federal prosecution of Aaron Burr (Jefferson's vice president during his first term), no U.S. president has chosen to investigate or prosecute possible high crimes or war crimes of top officials from previous administrations. When faced with this issue as he took office in 2009, President Barack Obama explained that he was going to look "forward rather than backward."[5] He did not say that no high crimes or war crimes had been committed. President Ford avoided further investigation and prosecution of Richard Nixon by granting him a pardon that included "all offenses against the United States" that Nixon "committed or may have committed or taken part in" while he was president. The presidential proclamation announcing this blanket pardon said that it was necessary to avoid "a prolonged and divisive debate over the propriety" of subjecting a former president to a trial. As independent counsel Lawrence Walsh recounted in his 1997 book *Firewall*, when the senior President Bush pardoned the defendants who had been or were being prosecuted in connection with Iran-Contra, Bush claimed that prosecution in these cases amounted to turning policy differences into crimes. In Walsh's view, however, the pardons prevented equal application of the law to political appointees in high office who had lied to help a president evade congressional restrictions on executive action.

The Constitution places special responsibility on the president to maintain the rule of law. In America, all public officials except the president swear an oath to "support" the Constitution (Article VI). The president swears to "preserve, protect, and defend" the Constitution (Article II, Section 1). The Constitution further instructs the president to "take care that the laws be faithfully executed" (Article II, Section 3). Presidents are not supposed to be above the law; they are supposed to be the guardians of the law and the defenders of the constitutional order.

The family fight America has been trying to avoid at least since the end of World War II is about presidents and other political elites obeying the law. The Constitution contains a few provisions for emergencies. Habeas corpus can be suspended, and Congress can meet in secret. But the budget must be published in full, and military action requires in most cases a congressional declaration of war, something Congress has not done since World War II, notwithstanding the wars in Korea, Vietnam, Laos, Cambodia, and Afghanistan, and the two wars in Iraq. America does not have a separate constitution for emergencies. In fact, the point of being a government of laws is that the laws are enforced most carefully *during emergencies.*

America's political class has been operating with disregard for the constitutional framework for almost sixty years, if not longer. This is why the assassination of President Kennedy may have happened as speculated earlier, that is, because impeachment was considered impractical and the Constitution was considered expendable. This is probably why Nixon had to be pardoned: he knew too much; he was too guilty to jail. This may also be the reason so many questions remain unanswered about 9/11 and the anthrax letter attacks. No one—not Congress, not the people, not even presidents elected specifically to bring about change—seems capable or willing to hold this government accountable.

There are two main arguments against this criticism. One is that investigation and prosecution of political crimes tends to be partisan. This is the idea that if one party investigates the leaders of the other party, they are criminalizing policy differences. The reality, however, is that the law actually tends to be interpreted very cautiously, and public officials are reluctant to police their own. Moreover, the people have a proven ability to discern when prosecution is malicious. The people had no difficulty telling the difference between the Watergate hearings and the impeachment of President Clinton. Moreover, investigative hearings provide an opportunity for public officials and the people alike to differentiate legal and political issues and to weigh their relative importance.

The second criticism of this call for accountability in high office is that if an incoming president were to investigate his or her predecessor, all incoming presidents would investigate their predecessors if they were from different political parties, and America would become a banana republic. There may be some truth to the idea that investigations would spawn subsequent investigations, but this would be problematic today only because presidents routinely commit crimes and therefore are vulnerable to investigation and prosecution when they leave office. If presidents knew they would be investigated at the end of their terms, then presumably they would take the simple precaution of obeying the law.

Presidents have set themselves above the law when in practice the law should apply to them more forcefully than to people in ordinary positions in the government. The Constitution includes a reference to high crimes, which are much more loosely defined than felonies and misdemeanors. The latter must be specifically spelled out in statute, whereas high crimes have to do with betrayal of the public trust, abuse of power, and other failures related to general expectations of rectitude given the public trust vested in top leaders. The reason for being so open-ended about potential criminality in high office is because those who hold high office have command of the prosecutorial machinery and other administrative organs that can be used to destroy or hide evidence and silence witnesses. Over the years since World War II, if not earlier, the political class somehow slipped free of the public's rightful expectations for honorable behavior in office, and officials created the impression that for top leaders to be impeached, they must violate a specific statute and the evidence must be beyond a reasonable doubt. In the hearings surrounding President Nixon's high crimes, members of Congress asked, what did he know and when did he know it? The implication was that to be guilty he had to have authorized the crimes of the Watergate burglars, but from a legal perspective that is a ridiculous standard. After all, he approved hiring Hunt and Liddy, he knew they were working for the committee to reelect the president, and he knew the character of the former attorney general, John Mitchell. Evidencing his familiarity with Howard Hunt, he complained that Hunt knew too much about the Kennedy years. Nixon was ultimately responsible for what his henchmen did. To define the situation otherwise leads to these absurd, hairsplitting questions about culpability when the office itself should be held responsible for the actions of its appointees. The questions should have been turned around to ask, if the president was unaware of the criminal activities his people were engaging in, why did he not suspect something, why was he out of the loop, why was he so incurious about what former FBI and CIA agents were doing working in the White House for his political advisor, Charles Colson?

The notion of "plausible deniability" shows where this ludicrous line of thinking leads. In the early cloak-and-dagger years of the Cold War, this concept referred to the ability of the U.S. government to convincingly deny responsibility for assassinations, terrorist attacks, and other covert actions it had sponsored or carried out. The Bay of Pigs invasion was an example. However, the idea gradually evolved into the practice of shielding U.S. presidents from knowledge of the details of illegal actions on the self-serving assumption that this would relieve them of responsibility for actions they have only approved in general or set in motion organizationally. Some variant of this strategy was used to protect not only Nixon in Watergate, but also President Reagan in Iran-Contra and the second President Bush in the outing of Valerie Plame as a CIA agent. Of course, since the first President Bush pardoned the Iran-Contra defendants, there has been a very strong incentive for underlings to protect the president from impeachment so that pardons will be available if necessary. But saying the president is not responsible for crimes he did not approve in detail is like a Mafia boss saying he is innocent because he did not know his people were going to hijack a specific truck on such and such a date. No prosecutor or jury would give credence to a defense like this. They would say, well, you may not have known about this particular crime, but you are the head of the organization that assembled the team that committed this whole string of crimes. This is what it has come to in the modern White House. Once again, the central cause of this breakdown in the rule of law is a failure to adhere to the Constitution, but this breakdown is not limited to the White House; it is pervasive, for in general the legal requirements on the president are interpreted very narrowly, which is contrary to the Constitution's intent.

But there may be a way to restore the rule of law that takes advantage of this commitment to legal technicalities.

The solution suggested here is that, when confronted by a suspected SCAD (a political crime in which the government appears to be implicated), we begin by enforcing the laws that govern criminal investigations. For example, we take the procedures we use in ordinary murders, and apply them to assassinations. This includes crime-scene control, interrogation of suspects, cutting deals with one suspect to catch another, and so on. There is more to the proposal than this, for we must deal with a national security apparatus that has learned how to influence us behind our backs. But this is the basic idea: start at the point of contact between public officials and the law; start with the police, the medical examiners, and the prosecutors. When the Secret Service came to take President Kennedy's body, the person who tried to uphold the law was the medical examiner. The Watergate burglars were discovered breaking into the National Democratic Party headquarters because a security guard at the Watergate office building discovered tape on an unlocked door and called the police (see guard log book page 127). In reality, when it comes to crimes in high office, street-level officers and investigators are our first line of defense against tyranny.

Selective Totalitarianism

Families that avoid openly acknowledging intractable issues from the past are often said to have "an elephant in the living room," an elephant that no one mentions and in a sense no one sees, but that everyone steps around, which means they do see it even if they do not say so. Thus the metaphor implies that everyone somehow sees without noticing.

The elephant in America's living room is the well-known but seldom acknowledged fact that the nation's citizens do not believe much of what their government says, especially about events with which the government itself is in some way connected. In the post–World War II era, Americans have learned that the government has misled them about provoking wars, assassinating foreign leaders, wiretapping American citizens, stealing elections, collaborating with organized crime, and much more. The people recognize that, as shocking as these disclosures were at the time, they may be only the tip of the iceberg. Certainly there is no reason to assume that all of the government's significant deceptions, domestic intrigue, international crimes, and other wrongdoings have been exposed. The one thing of which we can be certain is that the government treats the American people to some degree as the conspiracy realists argue, that is, it manipulates information and events to generate support for U.S. government policies and priorities. The actual nature and extent of this manipulation are unclear, but we know it occurs and that it can have very serious consequences, including leading the nation into unjustified wars.

Nevertheless, most Americans take some solace in their belief that U.S. government manipulation of events and information is relatively rare. The idea is that this is still a free country because for the most part we are left alone to interpret events as they come. On, say, 99 percent of the issues, the U.S. government lets history unfold naturally and provides the most complete and accurate information it possesses. In other words, the USA is not like the USSR because the government of the former Soviet Union controlled everything, whereas the government of the USA controls just a little.

This assumes, however, that all events and information that might be subject to government control are equally important, and therefore that what matters is *how much* is controlled and not *what*. But the truth is that events and information vary greatly in their importance, and hence a more or less totalitarian system can be achieved with a bare minimum of government intrigue and propaganda if the political apparatus and specifically the organs of manipulation are focused on society's key levers and choke points. This might be called "smart" or "selective" totalitarianism. In such a system, the government rarely intervenes into domestic or international affairs for domestic effect, but when it does, it orchestrates hugely important events that set the frame for policy and politics for years or even decades to come.

Is this not perhaps the system of government that America has today? For the U.S. government to control the flow of history, the nation's political priorities, and the character of the civic culture, its leaders need not have a grip on every individual or organization; quite the opposite, SCAD networks need only stage, facilitate, or execute events that discipline politics and policy at key moments and at crucial points by changing either the lineup of top policymakers or the perceived constellation of major problems and threats facing the social order. The Vietnam War was started with a false report that American ships had been attacked by North Vietnamese gunboats in the Gulf of Tonkin; over fifty thousand American soldiers lost their lives. Half or more died after 1968, when, in the first October Surprise, Nixon sabotaged peace talks that were on the verge of ending the war. As reported by Anthony Summers in *The Arrogance of Power,* his definitive study of Nixon's life and career, Nixon feared peace in Vietnam would give the edge to Vice President Hubert Humphrey in the 1968 presidential election, so Nixon sent word to South Vietnam's president that if the latter withdrew from the peace talks, Nixon would negotiate a better deal for South Vietnam after he was elected. The main effect of most SCADs and suspected SCADs has been to foster social panic and militarism in the American mass public and belligerency in U.S. foreign policy. Presumably, this is why, as Bacevich observes, U.S. policies toward international relations and America's global military presence have not changed despite many shifts in partisan control of the White House since the end of World War II. [6]

When Jack Ruby was interviewed by the Warren Commission in Dallas, he was allowed to speak to the press, and he said that Americans did not realize it, but an entirely new form of government had been installed. Of course most people dismissed this comment as the ravings of a sick mind, but it may be that Ruby knew of what he spoke. For America's distrust of its own government appears to have begun with the Kennedy assassination. As with other family secrets, the people seem to know this instinctively; they know something changed fundamentally when President Kennedy was assassinated and when his alleged assassin was killed two days later while in police custody. They know they were never given a believable account of the basic facts.

SEEING THE KENNEDY ASSASSINATION FROM ABOVE

The Kennedy assassination still haunts Americans because they do not understand it. They generally believe government elements were involved, but they do not see a clear motive. They remain confused because they have yet to look at it from the viewpoint of elites, and especially the military elites, and to consider what these men had been saying all along before young Mr. Kennedy took the helm.

We have seen how the norms condemning conspiracy theorizing distort perceptions of elite political crimes by causing observers to focus on one event at a time. The norms do this because they discourage suspicion of elites, and suspicion is a prerequisite to looking for repeat offenders and crime sprees. In a similar way, the conspiracy-theory label also skews perceptions of the political class; it directs attention away from the elite strata. Although the victim is often one of the political elites, as Kennedy was, the focus is always on the crimes and not on the political class and its motives. We ask, who killed Kennedy, but not whom did Kennedy provoke. And even if we ask whom Kennedy provoked, we do not ask what actions could drive men in high office, men who were patriots and war heroes, to commit murder and treason.

The SCAD construct is useful in pulling back the curtain so that antidemocratic elite conspiracies can be seen in their larger contexts and studied comparatively. By delineating a general crime category, the construct automatically directs attention to multiple examples that qualify, and of course this helps observers rise above a case-by-case orientation. It also directs our attention to elite motives and behavior and inter-elite rivalries relative to political crimes. It assumes that political elites are capable of committing SCADs but that they usually do so only when in their view circumstances call for it and there is little likelihood of detection. Presumably, political elites are capable of "reading" their own circumstances and the circumstances of others through the others' eyes, so they are able to recognize how incentives and disincentives are lined up for the relevant players. Consequently, they are likely to check and balance one another by anticipating moves and blocking them or minimizing their effects. This means that in all likelihood, President Kennedy saw his murder coming but was powerless to prevent it.

No one could say this publicly in the immediate aftermath of the assassination, but there were obvious indications JFK was dangerously out of synch with the government's military and intelligence leadership. The Bay of Pigs invasion in 1961 was followed a little over a year later by the Cuban missile crisis in 1962 and one more year later, in 1963, by the president's assassination. Not long before the assassination, the Kennedy administration signed a treaty with the Soviet Union, strongly opposed by the nation's military leaders because they said the Soviets would cheat, [7] banning nuclear tests in the atmosphere. The sequence is striking if not telling. Kennedy had refused to authorize additional airstrikes during the Bay of Pigs invasion for fear of starting a nuclear war, but this had left all of the expatriate Cubans on the beaches to be killed or captured by Castro's forces. He had forbidden his military commanders from invading Cuba to take control of nuclear weapons placed there by the Soviets, weapons that put millions of American lives at risk. During the Cuban missile crisis, President Kennedy placed civilian officials on the U.S. ships to stand alongside Navy commanders because he feared the commanders might intentionally provoke a battle so that America would be pushed by circumstances into launching a nuclear first strike against the Soviet homeland. To end the crisis, Kennedy agreed to withdraw nuclear missiles from Turkey in return for a promise by the Soviets to take their missiles out of Cuba, a promise the fulfillment of which could not be confirmed because inspections were not included in the deal, much to the consternation of military commanders. General Curtis LeMay, a man of few words, went out of his way to criticize the president to his face in an official meeting. [7]

All indications are that Kennedy was trying to end the Cold War. This might seem like a laudable aspiration, but *ending the Cold War was not the policy of the United States government*. The policy was *containment*. The policy was to stand up to the Soviets at every turn, to engage them in regional wars and if necessary to launch a first-strike nuclear attack. [8] The U.S. had a capacity at least through 1963 to take out, in a surprise attack, almost all of the nuclear weapons of the Soviet Union and leave the Soviets without the ability to effectively respond. The generals and admirals believed Kennedy was negotiating away this advantage. He was sending personal envoys to Khrushchev, bypassing the State Department, our own diplomats, and our military commanders. Who knows what kind of deals he was cutting?

U.S. game theorists and the nation's best minds may have

Thirteen months after the assassination of President Kennedy and four months after the Tonkin Gulf incident, military leaders meet with President Johnson at his ranch. The president is leaning over the table on his elbows. Secretary of Defense Robert McNamara is in white short-sleeved shirt. General Curtis LeMay is at far end of table smoking a cigar. (Source: Lyndon B. Johnson Library)

concluded that Kennedy's propensity to equivocate, his reluctance to initiate a first strike while the United States retained its advantage in nuclear weapons, and his willingness to sign a peace treaty with the Soviets to end the testing of nuclear weapons in the atmosphere—all of these and similar considerations may have been inviting a Soviet nuclear buildup so the Soviets could hit the United States while it was still headed by this easily manipulated president. Howard Hunt later claimed [9 p. 132] that Kennedy's decisions in the Bay of Pigs operation had encouraged Moscow to erect the Berlin Wall and place nuclear missiles in Cuba. General LeMay said Kennedy's actions in the Cuban missile crisis and his agreement to remove U.S. missiles from Turkey amounted to "appeasement." This was no minor observation. It could have been a warning. Also, LeMay was politically ambitious. He was the running mate of George Wallace in 1968.

In short, other top leaders in the government may have concluded that President Kennedy himself posed an existential threat to the United States. Game theorists at RAND were advising military commanders that the slightest opportunity to destroy the enemy would be very tempting to either side. The policy developed to prevent nuclear war was called "mutually assured destruction." [10 pp. 281–282] The upshot was that as long as both sides knew they would be annihilated in a nuclear war no matter which side initiated the conflagration, neither would act. LeMay had been responsible for organizing the Strategic Air Command, which had nuclear armed bombers headed toward the USSR with strict orders to continue on to their targets and drop their bombs unless specifically called back by their commanders. [10 p. 46] This was to ensure that, even if the Soviets attacked and everyone in the U.S. was killed, retaliation would proceed and the Soviet people would be completely obliterated. In theory, if the Soviets thought we lacked the courage to act—to kill hundreds of millions of people—they would, according to our own experts, be foolish not to strike and end the existential threat we posed *to them.*

At the time, the Constitution provided no quick means to remove President Kennedy from office. Any effort to do so would have led to a protracted political dispute and would have required disclosure of military judgments about the president that simply could not bear airing. Kennedy's drug abuse and womanizing were relevant because they testified to his recklessness. Probably more important were his blatant efforts to position his brother to follow in his presidential footsteps by appointing him attorney general. This was not only inappropriate, but also raised the possibility of another twelve years of Kennedy rule (four more for John and eight for Robert) and perhaps eight more after that if Teddy proved competent. If John Kennedy was the victim of a state crime, he was almost certainly killed because of his behavior at the height of the Cold War when the United States and the Soviet Union were in a thermonuclear stand-off. Incidentally, after Robert Kennedy vacated the position of attorney general, Congress passed a law prohibiting presidents from appointing members of their immediate families to high-level positions within their administrations.

CONTRIBUTING FACTORS TO KENNEDY'S MURDER

There were also a number of circumstantial factors at work in Kennedy's murder. One was the tension between Kennedy and Johnson. Howard Hunt said American politics is a struggle between East Coast finance and western oil. The Kennedy administration was a witch's brew of both. Kennedy was East Coast finance, very wealthy, and born to privilege. Lyndon Johnson was Western oil, an unpolished outsider who had long coveted the presidency and who, according to extensive research by Phillip Nelson, was considered by those who knew him well to be dishonest and perhaps murderous. [11 pp. 227–299] The Kennedy-Johnson ticket put the main competitors of American politics together, but Kennedy marginalized Johnson once they took office. Rumors that Johnson might be dropped from the ticket in 1964 were an insult to the western wing of the East-West coalition. Thus it may be no coincidence that JFK was assassinated in a western city.

The SCAD construct points to yet another consideration. As Kennedy learned about the losses that would result from nuclear war, he turned into a dove, while Johnson remained a hard-line hawk. A reluctant warrior with a militaristic VP is an invitation for assassination, independent of other factors.

One last criminogenic contributing factor was an embittered CIA. The agency had had strong ties and access to President Eisenhower. This all changed with Kennedy and the many Eastern intellectuals he brought in with the New Frontier (the name of the 1960 Democratic Party platform). Hunt said his colleagues in the CIA were dismayed by the young president's decision to withdraw air support from the Bay of Pigs, and doubly incensed at being blamed for the invasion's failure. [9] John and Robert Kennedy were noted for leaving no sleeping dogs un-kicked. Perhaps they should have passed over agencies with lethal skills.

LIFE IMITATING ART

A final influence in President Kennedy's assassination is art, especially cinema and television. This is not a cause or a contributing factor in the traditional sense of the term as a motive rooted in self-interest, but to overlook it is to miss an important dimension of experience and history. Art is a Cassandra to politics. It foretells the future and to some extent causes the future by articulating narratives that vividly interpret our circumstances and help us understand the meaning of our subjective experiences. The characters depicted in art both reflect and become social roles we play in real life.

John Kennedy fulfilled an iconic role of his era and perhaps of all eras: the young man butting heads with his father or his father's generation. Kennedy's struggle, if not his death, was foretold many times over before he was even elected. This may be why, although he had many personal weaknesses, he is remembered to this day as a sort of innocent, struck down by dark forces, as if he were a sacrificial lamb who shed his blood to evoke the guilt and conjure the remorse of his father's generation, a generation that had been too hardened to recognize that a new era was dawning, an age of peace and prosperity founded on love rather than power.

In cinema, the men of the father's generation were cynical and distant. They made their fortunes in hardscrabble times and shielded their sons from such struggles and from the knowledge that the world is brutal and unforgiving. Although John Kennedy was a war hero, he was not responsible for making decisions that resulted in literally millions of deaths. During the U.S. firebombing of Japan, one hundred thousand Japanese were killed every night—one hundred thousand men, women, and children burned alive, night after night. Curtis LeMay was responsible for this. [7] He made the decision for Americans to fly in low and drop incendiary bombs on the Japanese civilian population centers and their wooden houses. Flying in low meant more of his men would be killed. Bombing population centers was a war crime. LeMay was willing to make the hardest of choices to win the war. He was also deeply involved in selecting the type of plane to use and the cities to target when the atomic bombs were dropped on Japan. [7] LeMay was an extreme case, but many military commanders sent their forces into battle knowing that the precious lives of American boys would be lost by the tens of thousands. These were definitely hard men, and now they were confronting the Soviets, an enemy as ruthless as and even more powerful than the Nazis, and nuclear weapons had made the stakes all or nothing.

Kennedy talking restraint to such men was beyond naïve, but Kennedy did it anyway. He was the president, the voice of a new generation. That is what he said in his inaugural address; the torch had been passed to a new generation.

Apparently, others in addition to officials in the White House can "read" the circumstances and anticipate the actions of different players. For in 1962 a bestselling book was published that was about a military takeover of the United States government. Titled *Seven Days in May*, the book was made into a movie in 1964. [12] The plot and characters resembled the situation in the Kennedy White House very much. The military was concerned that the president was moving too quickly on peace, placing too much trust in the enemy, and putting the security of the country in jeopardy. A small but strategically located network of officers decided they had to take charge. It was only because their plans were discovered that their coup was foiled. The only parallel to the Kennedy administration that was not in the movie or the book was the equivalent of Vice President Johnson, a super ambitious, morally ambiguous hawk. That role was played by the general who organized the coup.

President Kennedy knew he was in danger. He encouraged the director to make the bestselling book into a movie, and when the movie was being filmed, he and his family went to Camp David to allow the cast and director to have easy access to the White House for filming.

Another parallel is to the television show *Gunsmoke*. According to Stanley Rosen, one of Leo Strauss' students, Strauss would leave class early to get home in time to watch the most popular weekly television show in America at the time of JFK's assassination. [13] Strauss said the show taught important moral lessons similar to noble lies. *Gunsmoke* was a Western about a marshal who routinely broke the law to enforce the law and keep the peace in Dodge City during the cowboy days. Dodge had a base population of farmers, merchants, artisans, and others who possessed the values and embraced the societal roles of Western civilization. However, coming into the city occasionally to conduct business, meet a stagecoach, pick up supplies, and sometimes just to get drunk were ranch hands, gunslingers, wooly old trappers, and other less civilized elements. Generally, the good town folk came into contact with these dangerous men from the hinterlands at various bars and dancehalls, which gave the ruffians a certain degree of superficial respect, offered them tables and cards for gambling, aroused their desire for women, and sold them liquor straight from the bottle. Much of the marshal's time was spent in the bars settling conflicts and arresting patrons who became too disorderly. The marshal did not try to prevent fights, but did try to make sure they were fair and that both sides were willing participants, and to keep them from getting out of hand and ending in someone's death. His favorite bar was run and owned by his girlfriend and was where his friend, the town doctor, could often be found drinking. The marshal drank socially but never so much as to affect his sensibilities.

The partially civilized bar where the city people mingled with the ruffians for purposes of gambling, prostitution, and other forms of moneymaking and where the marshal was often needed was similar to the semi-lawless frontier of international relations; conflict was governed by a natural law that allowed a fair fight. To maintain his status as hegemonic peacekeeper, the marshal had to be prepared to meet paid killers for a shootout in the street. He also had to watch out for back shooters.

This cultural backdrop seems eerily present in JFK's murder. President Kennedy was shot at high noon in the middle of a downtown street in a western city by a back-shooting communist sympathizer. It was as if the moral lesson being taught to the people was that Kennedy's efforts to make peace with a ruthless enemy resulted, not in peace, but in dirty fighting and death.

The morning of the visit to Dallas, President Kennedy delivered a speech at a breakfast meeting in nearby Fort Worth. At its conclusion he was given a Stetson cowboy hat as a memento, and the crowd urged him to put it on, but he tactfully refused, saying he would try it on when he was back in Washington. Why say Washington? Why not just say he would try it on later? The implication was that he did not want to wear a cowboy hat in Texas. Did he sense that he was being ushered into a deadly role?

THE DIALECTIC OF SUSPICION

Lyndon Johnson and the Warren Commission would have been poorly received from the start if the civic culture's wariness toward political elites had not been weakened by the influence of Karl Popper and the behavioral movement in the social sciences. The citizenry's skittish attitude toward leaders in high office was inherited from the Founders, expressed in the Declaration of Independence, and written into the U.S. Constitution in the system of checks and balances. It was also embodied in the pragmatic political science employed by subsequent generations to deal with the challenges to democratic governance brought by political parties, the spoils system, industrialization, and monopolies.

However, by the time of President Kennedy's assassination, America's leaders had largely abandoned this ethos. The Founders were honorable men who took oaths seriously. They had worried about isolated tyrants and oppressive factions, even oppressive majorities. But they had not envisioned a time when the nation's leaders, as a class, would come to see the people not as sovereign, but as an external threat to the political order.

In the early decades of the Cold War, perhaps influenced by the teachings of Leo Strauss, the country's leaders decided they knew what was best for America, and that the people were actually a potential obstacle to the nation's survival. These antidemocratic sentiments were reinforced by Karl Popper and the "behavioral movement" in the social sciences, a movement that abandoned the research program of Charles Beard, who had taught a generation of Americans to be on the alert for self-serving elites and to root out upper-class advantages in laws and political institutions. The men who had led the United States through World War II saw John Kennedy as a threat to the nation's military victory in the Cold War, which they had come to believe would probably require a surprise nuclear attack on the Soviet Union. [8] For them, Kennedy was indeed the voice of a new generation, but it was a sheltered generation that lacked experience with ruthless totalitarian regimes.

After JFK's murder, other elite political crimes were committed, and they reflect the creeping criminalization of America's political class that was unleashed by the JFK assassination. Lying to justify war in Vietnam. The many crimes of Watergate. The cases of election tampering by manipulating foreign affairs during presidential election campaigns. The stalking of Daniel Ellsberg. The plans, although called off, to murder investigative reporter Jack Anderson and Senator Ted Kennedy. [14 pp. 207–211, 15 p. 406] Another victim may have been George Wallace, who believed strongly that Nixon was behind the attempted assassination that left him crippled. [16 pp. 106–107]

Naturally, popular suspicions mounted, but they all went back to Kennedy. The questions about his death needed to be dealt with before it would be possible to silence the others. Hence America's national security elites deployed the conspiracy-theory label and used propaganda to develop associated norms against doubts about the lone-gunman and magic-bullet theories underpinning the official account of JFK's murder.

Then came the investigations of Watergate and Iran-Contra, the reinvestigation of the assassination of President Kennedy, and the Church Committee hearings on CIA assassinations of foreign leaders and domestic operations against the civil rights and antiwar movements. These exposures gave credibility to the idea that conspiracy theories might be closer to the truth than the conclusions of official commissions. In response to the findings of these and other inquiries, the mass public became increasingly skeptical and cynical about top leaders, and public officials became increasingly defensive and alarmed about mass suspicions.

Nevertheless, the CIA's campaign against conspiracy theory, launched in 1967, was a riveting success. The conspiracy-theory label eventually became normative in polite society, and comments about signs of elite crimes of almost any kind were driven from the media. But people are funny in both senses of the term: humorous and odd. They can be intimidated and silenced, but then, somehow, their suppressed thoughts manage to escape, just a little bit, in slips of the tongue, jokes, talking in their sleep. So as conspiracy theories themselves became prohibited in the public sphere, concepts from those theories entered the lexicon of political speech: "lone gunman," "grassy knoll," "magic bullet," "Manchurian candidate," "false-flag terrorism," "limited hang out," "wag-the-dog," "let-it-happen," "Iraq-gate" and "Plame-gate," "October Surprise," and so on. Furthermore, although it is considered bad form to speak of the assassination of President Kennedy as an inside job, no one objects to use of the term "magic bullet" or "magic-bullet theory." By the 1990s if not earlier, Americans had become accustomed to using all of these terms even though the narratives they come from are considered off limits in public discourse. It is as if a nation of preachers went around cursing.

This peculiar behavior did not arise from ignorance about the terms' origins in conspiracy theories. The movies *JFK* and *Conspiracy Theory* came out in the 1990s. This language pattern reflected the conflicted views Americans had come to hold about their government. They needed to trust their leaders, but they also needed to be wary of deception and betrayal. And America's leaders, too, acknowledged this elephant in the living room even as they tried to walk around it. President Clinton certainly knew that dark rumors circulated about the death of Vince Foster, the airplane crash that killed his commerce secretary, and of course the Whitewater investment as well as his actions with Monica Lewinsky. The First Lady went so far as to complain about a "vast rightwing conspiracy." [17]

This was the context, this mutual distrust between the people and the political class, when, beginning in 2000, a cascading series of troubling events further intensified popular suspicions to the point that Sunstein, Vermeule, and others started calling for government actions to suppress conspiracy theorizing. [18] The events included the disputed 2000 and 2004 presidential elections; the seemingly inexplicable defense failures on 9/11; revelations about warnings preceding 9/11; evidence that anthrax mailed in October 2001 had come from a strain developed by the U.S. military; the failure to locate Osama bin Laden for almost a decade; pictures of tortured prisoners at Abu Ghraib despite official denials of torture; the absence of weapons of mass destruction in Iraq; the exposure in 2005 of warrantless wiretapping that had been active since 9/11; sole-source contracts for Halliburton and other politically connected military contractors; publication of the Downing Street Memos documenting a conspiracy to justify the invasion of Iraq [8]; and publication of the "torture memos" written by lawyers in the Bush-Cheney administration. Questions also arose about the bungled response to Hurricane Katrina, the 2008 financial crisis and bailouts, and the BP oil disaster in the Gulf of Mexico.

The Struggle Ahead

So this is where things stand. On the one hand, there is growing pressure for an American *glasnost*. It is no coincidence that the idea for SCAD research—the idea of looking at political crimes collectively and comparatively—emerged in the past decade. The nation is regaining its vision. It is becoming difficult not to notice the spiraling corruption that somehow came with the war on terror. Each additional unconnected dot placed on the page makes pattern perception more likely. The Internet is also a factor. It not only brings suspicious minds together, but also offers to the average person rapid-search access to vast archives of newspapers and magazines, a resource never before available to anyone except military and intelligence analysts. The U.S. citizenry is increasingly like the people in the story of the emperor's new clothes. It would seem to be only a matter of time before the electorate sees what it is looking at.

On the other hand, the assertion that the pressure for reform is building assumes that shocking events have been accumulating, that is, that assassinations, election breakdowns, October surprises, and so on, have been perceived, at least faintly or occasionally, as repeat instances of the same basic type of improbable event, thus making it increasingly difficult to convincingly attribute additional occurrences to chance.

The CIA, though, may well have developed techniques that prevent serial SCADs, SCAD sprees, and SCAD connections in general from being noticed. This could have devastating consequences, because it could bring an end to the citizenry's ability to learn from experience; but just because it is undesirable does not make it impossible. [19 pp. 131–133] The enormous success of the conspiracy-theory label in suppressing public perception of elite political crime has been noted previously. What should also be recognized is that the propaganda program outlined in CIA Dispatch 1035-960 was devised almost fifty years ago. If the CIA has been weaponizing and experimenting with concepts, catchphrases, memes, and so on; if it has been learning to swarm Internet sites, infiltrate online groups, automate monitoring and disruption of virtual communities; if it has been experimenting and learning, its capabilities are undoubtedly much further along.

Hence journalists, scholars, SCAD researchers, and others interested in this field should remain alert to the possibility that the U.S. government is deeply and widely involved in linguistic and computer-based manipulation of the civic culture. In some respects this capacity and interest in using it are evident, for example, in the attention the military pays to naming military operations. But these types of manufactured phrases are recognized at the doorstep. The danger is when they enter the lexicon surreptitiously and are mistaken for authentic products of sense-making. Similarly, programs where the government sends out speakers to community forums and maintains propagandistic websites are not problematic for the civic culture in the same way surreptitious programs are.

The advances of the CIA in cognitive manipulation cannot be determined, but advancement would probably take only one form: the basic approach would be to disrupt logical systems of thought and self-regulating systems of discourse and argumentation. The conspiracy-theory label preempts the normal reasoning of people when they witness a longer-than-usual series of chance events, whether good or bad. If we see a husband lose a series of wives to various accidents, we naturally wonder about foul play.

The conspiracy-theory label does not try to form a new pattern of thought. It simply tries to and does interfere with a logic that would unfold naturally were it not for the presence of an unnatural impediment. In this respect, the choice of words used by Sunstein and Vermeule about "cognitive infiltration" and "disrupting conspiracy theory groups and networks" is worrisome. [18] The thinking that has come out of the RAND Corporation has focused on how collective action does or does not take place when self-interested individuals are located in a contained social setting with an array of possible actions open to them. [10] This rational choice framework has proven to be a powerful method for understanding and therefore being able to manipulate conditions that can make collective action more or less likely. Collective action is democracy in action. Democracy is people forming into groups to protect their collective interests and to accomplish large-scale objectives beyond their capacities as individuals. To be able to disrupt collective action is to be able to dismantle democracy or play it like a pipe organ.

Also important to keep in mind is the possibility that

the government's capacity to track public opinion may be far greater than anything we have seen in public opinion research. Public opinion research uses sampling methods to be able to accurately generalize about a large population from a small number of interviews. However, to follow subsets of opinion, to see how opinion changes, to see how it moves from a small group to a large population, to identify tipping points and the effects of polarization and groupthink—to study such processes would take the kinds of industrial-scale efforts that the military and intelligence organs are noted for undertaking.

In this respect it may be significant that CIA Dispatch 1035-960 refers vaguely to observations of opinions that appear to be drawn from a very sophisticated method of opinion tracking. In discussing the idea that President Johnson is being blamed for the Kennedy assassination, the dispatch says, "There seems to be an increasing tendency to hint that President Johnson himself, as the one person who might be said to have benefited, was in some way responsible for the assassination."

The kind of opinion tracking this suggests is one where people are in conversations that they do not know are being monitored. This has always been a problem with survey research; respondents are alerted upfront that they are being interviewed for a study. This raises the possibility of their opinions being self-censored. In cases where respondents are asked to express racial and ethnic prejudices, such self-censoring tends to occur. It sounds as if the CIA may have been conducting interviews without notifying the respondents. The results would be candid and subtle. Rather than getting simple responses of "yes," "no," or other standard survey options, responses could be judged in terms of how open they were, how emphatic they were, whether they were withdrawn when challenged, and so on.

German social scientists did something like this as they

developed a theory called the "spiral of silence." [20] They rode on trains during election season with buttons visibly displayed in support of one or another candidate. They observed whether people commented either for or against the candidate. They found that people quit standing up for the losing candidate about twelve hours in advance of when public opinion was explicitly expressed indicating that support for the candidate had deteriorated. The spiral of silence strikes quickly and apparently unconsciously in the sense that it is not verbalized when people are asked about it.

Survey research capabilities of this kind, which would allow for very large samples to get at some groups, which would not notify respondents that they were being interviewed, and which would delve deeply into the nuances of opinion in both substance and strength, could provide a "public-opinion-scope" that could foresee opinion changes further in advance than standard methodologies allow, and that could identify opinion nodes or switches that could be manipulated to prevent these changes or to channel them in different directions. The possibilities are truly frightening. There are rumors in academia that this kind of research is being conducted on Internet searches and the like.

This is not to say that such methods definitely exist and are being engaged. But it is to suggest that they are possible, and that scholars, journalists, and others in the civil society who want to protect the integrity of the formation of opinion and mobilization of collective action should be on the lookout for these kinds of possibilities. Forensic sciences that track memes may offer the best hope for detecting and eventually investigating and prosecuting antidemocratic government invasions of civil society. Of course, criminalizing subversion of civil society would require an expansive understanding of democracy and of the obligations of oaths of office. In my view, this is the current horizon of SCAD theory and research.

A Simple Proposal for Reform

Having acknowledged all this about the government's possible abilities to undermine pressures for reform by disrupting pattern recognition, Internet communication, and collective action, we should remind ourselves that the truth does not disappear beneath its misinterpretation. Smart or selective totalitarianism depends on SCADs not being objectively and thoroughly investigated. A simple reform that would go far toward ending the history of SCADs in America, allowing civil society to reason freely, and restoring vigor to the nation's democratic governing institutions, would be to allow political crimes and suspicious events to be investigated objectively and thoroughly by law enforcement professionals who are free to do their jobs without interference or influence from above. In the long run it would be helpful if State Crimes against Democracy were singled out for special investigations by a law enforcement agency established for that purpose that would be both constrained and protected by a rigorous system of checks and balances. SCADs should also be targeted for special punishment, like hate crimes and racketeering.

In the short run, however, it would be enough to produce dramatic change to simply apply the same forensic protocols to elite crimes and tragedies that are now routinely applied in investigations of ordinary cases of murder, fraud, arson, and the like. For this is essentially what has been missing from our system for holding elites accountable. Evidence has not been gathered, inventoried, and protected in a careful, responsible manner. It should go without saying that in these incredibly important cases, rigorous forensic protocols should be followed. In actual practice today, however, this happens sporadically at best. In the case of President Kennedy, the body itself was not protected, and the limousine in which he was riding was washed. Similarly, a major question in the assassination of Robert Kennedy was how many shots were fired, for there appeared to be more bullets altogether in Kennedy, in wounded bystanders, and in doors and walls than the alleged assassin's pistol could hold. In an egregious slipup, the police failed to check the weapons of security guards to make sure none had been fired. Then, in yet another failure of protocol, a bullet-ridden doorframe from the room where the shooting occurred was lost after having been taken into police custody. [21]

In addition to these examples, public officials or their agents misplaced, discarded, or destroyed critical evidence in World Trade Center debris from 9/11, [22] the anthrax samples used to trace the anthrax in the anthrax letter attacks to domestic laboratories, [23] and computer records from the office of the Florida secretary of state from the disputed 2000 presidential election. [24, 25]

There are a number of other ways in which investigations of political crimes, tragedies, and suspicious events fall short of even minimal investigative standards. Suspects are not interrogated, witnesses are not interviewed, assertions and alibis are not checked. Sometimes inquiries are delayed by the very people who are to be evaluated. For over a year after 9/11, the Bush-Cheney administration resisted demands for a 9/11 commission before finally acceding to pressures from the victims' families, at which point the administration gave the commission a very small budget and placed it under unrealistic deadlines. [26 pp. 25, 29–31, 36–38] Later, eyebrows were raised when President Bush and Vice President Cheney insisted on testifying together, in private with the 9/11 Commission, and not under oath.

The important point is that Americans need to start demanding proper investigations. If political elites are truly concerned about growing distrust of government; if they have nothing to hide, then surely they will not object to thorough and impartial inquiries. And if we, as citizens, can begin to enforce the laws at the point of contact between our investigators and the nation's top officials; if we can become accustomed to treating our presidents like public servants rather than royalty, the return to representative democracy and the rule of law should neither require nor lead to social convulsions; it should occur incrementally and be less a deferred day of judgment than steps on a path we have already chosen.

It should be noted, though, that the crimes of the past, not just those in the future, must be dealt with. Otherwise, America will be moving forward with a false impression of its past. There is no statute of limitations for murder. If the nation does not have the stomach to see present or former leaders punished, they could be pardoned, but prosecution is necessary to correct the historical record. An American *glasnost* should include revisiting all major investigations in which public officials were dubiously exonerated. A glaring example is the failure of officials to investigate for signs of explosives and incendiaries in the debris at the World Trade Center. Another is the investigation of the anthrax letter attacks, an investigation that has avoided focusing on the one or two labs in the U.S. that actually have the capability to produce anthrax that is as airborne as the mailed anthrax was initially said to be.

The American "family" can handle the truth. Enforcing the law will not turn us into a banana republic. To be a great democracy, we must become a good democracy, and that means a democracy that is truly open: open to knowledge of its errors as well as its achievements.

≡ APPENDIX ≡
CIA Dispatch #1035-960

This retyped copy of CIA Dispatch #1035-960 was checked against http://www.jfklancer.com/CIA.html (accessed May 2012).

Marked "PSYCH" and "Destroy when no longer needed"
RE: Concerning Criticism of the Warren Report

1. Our Concern. From the day of President Kennedy's assassination on, there has been speculation about the responsibility for his murder. Although this was stemmed for a time by the Warren Commission report (which appeared at the end of September 1964), various writers have now had time to scan the Commission's published report and documents for new pretexts for questioning, and there has been a new wave of books and articles criticizing the Commission's findings. In most cases the critics have speculated as to the existence of some kind of conspiracy, and often they have implied that the Commission itself was involved. Presumably as a result of the increasing challenge to the Warren Commission's report, a public opinion poll recently indicated that 46% of the American public did not think that Oswald acted alone,

while more than half of those polled thought that the Commission had left some questions unresolved. Doubtless polls abroad would show similar, or possibly more adverse results.

2. This trend of opinion is a matter of concern to the U.S. government, including our organization. The members of the Warren Commission were naturally chosen for their integrity, experience and prominence. They represented both major parties, and they and their staff were deliberately drawn from all sections of the country. Just because of the standing of the Commissioners, efforts to impugn their rectitude and wisdom tend to cast doubt on the whole leadership of American society. Moreover, there seems to be an increasing tendency to hint that President Johnson himself, as the one person who might be said to have benefited, was in some way responsible for the assassination.

Innuendo of such seriousness affects not only the individual concerned, but also the whole reputation of the American government. Our organization itself is directly involved: among other facts, we contributed information to the investigation. Conspiracy theories have frequently thrown suspicion on our organization, for example by falsely alleging that Lee Harvey Oswald worked for us. The aim of this dispatch is to provide material countering and discrediting the claims of the conspiracy theorists, so as to inhibit the circulation of such claims in other countries. Background information is supplied in a classified section and in a number of unclassified attachments.

3. Action. We do not recommend that discussion of the assassination question be initiated where it is not already taking place. Where discussion is active [business] addresses are requested:

a. To discuss the publicity problem with [?] and friendly

elite contacts (especially politicians and editors), point-ing out that the Warren Commission made as thorough an investigation as humanly possible, that the charges of the critics are without serious foundation, and that further speculative discussion only plays into the hands of the opposition. Point out also that parts of the conspiracy talk appear to be deliberately generated by Communist propa-gandists. Urge them to use their influence to discourage unfounded and irresponsible speculation.

b. To employ propaganda assets to [negate] and refute the attacks of the critics. Book reviews and feature articles are particularly appropriate for this purpose. The unclas-sified attachments to this guidance should provide use-ful background material for passing to assets. Our ploy should point out, as applicable, that the critics are (I) wedded to theories adopted before the evidence was in, (II) politically interested, (III) financially interested, (IV) hasty and inaccurate in their research, or (V) infatuated with their own theories. In the course of discussions of the whole phenomenon of criticism, a useful strategy may be to single out Epstein's theory for attack, using the attached Fletcher [?] article and Spectator piece for back-ground. (Although Mark Lane's book is much less convinc-ing than Epstein's and comes off badly where confronted by knowledgeable critics, it is also much more difficult to answer as a whole, as one becomes lost in a morass of unrelated details.)

4. In private to media discussions not directed at any par-ticular writer, or in attacking publications which may be yet forthcoming, the following arguments should be useful:

a. No significant new evidence has emerged which the Commission did not consider. The assassination is some-times compared (e.g., by Joachim Joesten and Bertrand

Russell) with the Dreyfus case; however, unlike that case, the attacks on the Warren Commission have produced no new evidence, no new culprits have been convincingly identified, and there is no agreement among the critics. (A better parallel, though an imperfect one, might be with the Reichstag fire of 1933, which some competent historians (Fritz Tobias, A. J. P. Taylor, D. C. Watt) now believe was set by Vander Lubbe on his own initiative, without acting for either Nazis or Communists; the Nazis tried to pin the blame on the Communists, but the latter have been more successful in convincing the world that the Nazis were to blame.)

b. Critics usually overvalue particular items and ignore others. They tend to place more emphasis on the recollections of individual witnesses (which are less reliable and more divergent—and hence offer more hand-holds for criticism) and less on ballistics, autopsy, and photographic evidence. A close examination of the Commission's records will usually show that the conflicting eyewitness accounts are quoted out of context, or were discarded by the Commission for good and sufficient reason.

c. Conspiracy on the large scale often suggested would be impossible to conceal in the United States, esp. since informants could expect to receive large royalties, etc. Note that Robert Kennedy, Attorney General at the time and John F. Kennedy's brother, would be the last man to overlook or conceal any conspiracy. And as one reviewer pointed out, Congressman Gerald R. Ford would hardly have held his tongue for the sake of the Democratic administration, and Senator Russell would have had every political interest in exposing any misdeeds on the part of Chief Justice Warren. A conspirator moreover would hardly choose a location for a shooting where so much depended on conditions beyond his control: the route, the speed of the cars, the moving target, the risk that the assassin would be discovered. A group of wealthy conspirators could have arranged much more secure conditions.

d. Critics have often been enticed by a form of intellectual pride: they light on some theory and fall in love with it; they also scoff at the Commission because it did not always answer every question with a flat decision one way or the other. Actually, the make-up of the Commission and its staff was an excellent safeguard against over-commitment to any one theory, or against the illicit transformation of probabilities into certainties.

e. Oswald would not have been any sensible person's choice for a co-conspirator. He was a "loner," mixed up, of questionable reliability and an unknown quantity to any professional intelligence service.

f. As to charges that the Commission's report was a rush job, it emerged three months after the deadline originally set. But to the degree that the Commission tried to speed up its reporting, this was largely due to the pressure of irresponsible speculation already appearing, in some cases coming from the same critics who, refusing to admit their errors, are now putting out new criticisms.

g. Such vague accusations as that "more than ten people have died mysteriously" can always be explained in some natural way e.g.: the individuals concerned have for the most part died of natural causes; the Commission staff questioned 418 witnesses (the FBI interviewed far more people, conduction 25,000 interviews and re interviews), and in such a large group, a certain number of deaths are to be expected. (When Penn Jones, one of the originators of the "ten mysterious deaths" line, appeared on television, it emerged that two of the deaths on his list were from heart attacks, one from cancer, one was from a head-on collision on a bridge, and one occurred when a driver drifted into a bridge abutment.)

5. Where possible, counter speculation by encouraging reference to the Commission's Report itself. Open-minded foreign readers should still be impressed by the care, thoroughness, objectivity and speed with which the Commission worked. Reviewers of other books might be encouraged to add to their account the idea that, checking back with the report itself, they found it far superior to the work of its critics.

Table 2.1. Eras of corruption and reform in American history

TIME PERIOD	VEHICLE OF CORRUPTION	FORM OF CORRUPTION
1796–1830	Political parties	Primarily antidemocratic
1830–1890	Political "machines"	Primarily pecuniary
1890–1946	Iron triangles (political-economic conglomerates, usually specific to particular industries being regulated or to particular sectors or groups receiving benefits)	Primarily pecuniary
1946–	Political-economic complexes	Both antidemocratic and pecuniary

SPECIFIC TYPE OF CORRUPTION	EXAMPLE	REFORMS
Oppressive faction: Antidemocratic legislation to suppress dissent, opposition, or unwanted advocacy or inquiry	The Alien and Sedition Acts	Procedures for partisan competition that protect minority rights
Perfidious and mercenary officials: Misuse of administrative resources for electoral advantage	The spoils system	Professionalizing public administration
Special-interest manipulation: Insider manipulation of legislative and administrative technicalities, usually for economic gain	The conspiracy theory of the Fourteenth Amendment; Teapot Dome	Regulation of stakeholder-government relations, i.e., restrictions on campaign finance, lobbying, government rulemaking, etc.
SCADs in high office to subvert whole governments, branches: Conspiracies by high officials to commit fraud, treason, murder, etc., usually for a combination of ideological, economic, and bureaucratic reasons	Watergate; Iran-Contra; possibly assassinations of President John Kennedy and Senator Robert Kennedy	Restricting presidential powers, e.g., the War Powers Act and the Foreign Intelligence Surveillance Act

Table 3.1. Conspiracy-theory perspectives of Beard, Popper, and Strauss

ASPECTS/IMPLICATIONS OF THEORIES	BEARD
Political ideal	Upper-class manipulations exposed, and all economic bias stripped from political institutions. Shown in Fig. 3.1 as "Popular Govt. in Public Interest."
Conceptualization of conspiracies	Plots by political insiders to protect privileges of propertied classes, often by rigging political processes.
Conceptualization of conspiracy theories	Hypotheses about the economic basis of political decisions.
Results of conspiracy theories	Increased democracy and equality.
Explanation of WWII	President Roosevelt conspired to bring U.S. into war by provoking Pearl Harbor attack and not warning Pacific commanders.

POPPER	STRAUSS
All social and political myths critiqued. Conspiracy theories excluded as unscientific because cannot be true in all circumstances. Shown in Fig. 3.1 as "Open."	Mythos protected from scientific critique. Science limited normatively by respect for religion and tradition. Shown in Fig. 3.1 as modern representative democracies with "Balance of Inquiry."
Plots by powerful people that almost always fail because individual action is embedded in "brittle" institutions such as markets and political systems, which tend to counteract efforts of individual actors, e.g., buyers seek low prices but prices rise because demand increases.	Elite conspiracies reconceptualized as actions taken to protect society, sometimes by allowing harm so as to avoid greater harm by awakening the society to a gathering danger.
Secularized religious superstitions. A version of the historicist theory that mobilizes totalitarian political movements.	Misguided attempts on the part of non-elites/citizens to discredit legitimate political authority by exposing noble lies.
Fanatical social movements and totalitarianism.	Noble lies and salutary myths threatened.
Inevitable conflict between open and closed societies. The simple existence of open societies threatens closed societies.	Modern philosophers failed to conceal their dangerous truths from ordinary men, which led to the emergence of tyrants as elites cast aside moral restraints on competing for, and exercise of, authority.

Table 3.1. Conspiracy-theory perspectives of Beard, Popper, and Strauss (continued)

ASPECTS/IMPLICATIONS OF THEORIES	BEARD
Historical parallels of WWII	Wilson maneuvered U.S. into World War I.
Basic view of conspiracy theories	Conspiracy believer (thinks conspiracies exist and should be exposed and their consequences corrected).

POPPER	STRAUSS
War between open Athens and closed Sparta.	Tension between Athens and Jerusalem in Roman Empire and Western civilization generally. (Athenian democracy founded on philosophy/science; Jerusalem founded on religious faith.)
Conspiracy denier or "dismisser" (does not believe that conspiracies, if they do occur, succeed in achieving their goals).	Conspiracy realist (thinks elite conspiracies occur but are a necessary part of leadership in modern representative democracies).

Table 5.1. Crimes against American democracy committed or allegedly committed by elements of the U.S. government

CRIME OR SUSPICIOUS EVENT, TIME FRAME, AND MODUS OPERANDI	PERPETRATOR MOTIVE OR POLICY IMPLICATION
Sedition Act passed. 1798. Outlaws antigovernment speech unless proven true. *Manipulation of defense information/policy*	Federalist Party seeks to entrench itself by suppressing antigovernment speech. *Political opportunism*
"Corrupt Bargain." 1824. No presidential candidate wins majority in the Electoral College (EC), so decision goes to House, where Speaker Henry Clay gives presidency to number-two EC vote getter J. Q. Adams in return for appointment as secretary of state. *Election tampering*	Federalist Party fends off for four more years a wave of popularity for Democratic Party based on enfranchisement of citizens with little property. *Political opportunism*
Mexican-American War. 1846. President Polk works with military commanders to manufacture pretext for war against Mexico. *Manipulation of defense information/policy*	War extends U.S. territory to Pacific Ocean, thereby extending slavery, since much of the annexed territory (e.g., Texas) is slaveholding. *Control war policy*
Assassination of Abraham Lincoln. 1865. *Assassination*	Andrew Johnson, a southerner, becomes president. Unsuccessful aim was to throw the Union into confusion and renew the South's willingness to fight. [2] *Control war policy*
Fourteenth Amendment passed. 1868. Amendment crafted to favor corporate interests. *Insider manipulation*	Amendment gives corporations the same constitutional protections as persons. [4] *Political opportunism*

SUSPECTED OR CONFIRMED PERPETRATOR	DEGREE OF CONFIRMATION OF GOVERNMENT ROLE
President John Adams and the emergent Federalist Party, led principally by the framers of the U.S. Constitution.	High [1 p. 5]
John Quincy Adams and House Speaker Henry Clay.	Medium, in that the allegation of the bargain was never documented but was seemingly acknowledged by the silence of those accused.
President Polk, working with military commanders.	Medium. Evidence is extensive but entirely circumstantial. Congressman Abraham Lincoln makes case for conspiracy on floor of House, but allegations never substantiated.
John Wilkes Booth and others, with help from the Secret Service and other insiders, possibly including the vice president.	High for the Secret Service; low for the vice president. [3]
Members of Congress and railroad owners and their representatives are alleged to have drafted the Fourteenth Amendment so that it might apply to corporations.	Medium [4–6]

Table 5.1. Crimes against American democracy committed or allegedly committed by elements of the U.S. government (continued)

CRIME OR SUSPICIOUS EVENT, TIME FRAME, AND MODUS OPERANDI	PERPETRATOR MOTIVE OR POLICY IMPLICATION
Disputed presidential election of 1876. Suppression of black vote in Florida and submission of fraudulent returns in white counties give Florida electoral college vote to Democratic candidate. *Election tampering*	Florida votes in Electoral College rejected by federal commission and presidency is awarded to the Republican. In response to threats by South to start another civil war, Reconstruction ends. Federal soldiers are withdrawn from South, which is then free to disenfranchise blacks and expropriate their property. *Control war policy*
Sinking of the *Maine*. 1898. U.S. battleship sunk to precipitate war. *Planned international event*	Spanish-American War is initiated. McKinley is reelected. *Control war policy*
Pearl Harbor. 1941. Roosevelt forewarned of attack but fails to alert Pacific commanders. *Planned international event*	Congress declares war on Japan. Germany declares war on U.S., which reciprocates. *Control war policy*
McCarthyism. 1950–1955. Senator Joseph McCarthy leads anticommunist crusade. *Manipulation of defense information/policy*	Large-scale purge of leftists from government and business boosts careers of McCarthy and Senator Richard Nixon. Power of FBI director Hoover increases. Fuels social panic/fear of communist infiltration. *Political opportunism*

SUSPECTED OR CONFIRMED PERPETRATOR	DEGREE OF CONFIRMATION OF GOVERNMENT ROLE
Florida county election officials in conjunction with new Democratic governor.	High [7]
Official account is that the ship was sunk by a Spanish mine. Other theories blame spontaneous combustion of coal dust, U.S. agents, and groups seeking Cuban independence.	Low [8]
President Franklin D. Roosevelt, Secretary of State Hull, Secretary of War Stimson, and top military leaders.	Medium [9]
Joseph McCarthy, with others. Nixon hinted in tapes that FBI's Hoover framed Hiss and fed Nixon incriminating evidence. [10]	High [11, 12]

Table 5.1. Crimes against American democracy committed or allegedly committed by elements of the U.S. government (continued)

CRIME OR SUSPICIOUS EVENT, TIME FRAME, AND MODUS OPERANDI	PERPETRATOR MOTIVE OR POLICY IMPLICATION
Assassination of President Kennedy. 1963. *Assassination*	Lyndon Johnson becomes president. Vietnam War escalates. *Control war policy*
Assassination of Lee Harvey Oswald. 1963. *Assassination*	Oswald's ties to the CIA remain hidden. Trial of Oswald is avoided. *Conceal crime*
Gulf of Tonkin incident. 1964. President Johnson and Defense Secretary McNamara falsely claim that North Vietnam attacked a U.S. military ship in neutral waters. *Planned international event*	Vietnam conflict escalates. *Control war policy*
Assassination of Senator Robert Kennedy. 1968. *Assassination*	With RFK out of the way, weak Democratic nominee (Humphrey) is ensured. Nixon is reelected. Further investigation of JFK assassination is halted. Vietnam conflict escalates. *Control war policy*
October Surprise of 1968. South Vietnam withdraws from Johnson's peace negotiations to end Vietnam War. *Manipulation of defense information/policy*	Secure election of Richard Nixon as president. *Political opportunism*

SUSPECTED OR CONFIRMED PERPETRATOR	DEGREE OF CONFIRMATION OF GOVERNMENT ROLE
Right-wing elements in CIA, FBI, military, and Secret Service, and possibly higher officials.	Medium [13–18]
Jack Ruby, who had ties to the CIA and organized crime.	Medium [17]
President Johnson and Defense Secretary McNamara, with tacit support of upper levels of intelligence agencies and armed services.	High [19]
Right-wing elements in the CIA and FBI, and possibly higher officials.	Low [20, 21]
Nixon and intermediaries with South Vietnam leadership.	High [22]

Table 5.1. Crimes against American democracy committed or allegedly committed by elements of the U.S. government (continued)

CRIME OR SUSPICIOUS EVENT, TIME FRAME, AND MODUS OPERANDI	PERPETRATOR MOTIVE OR POLICY IMPLICATION
U.S. government burglary of Daniel Ellsberg's psychiatrist's office. 1971. *Burglary*	Goal was to discredit former military analyst Daniel Ellsberg, who had leaked the Pentagon Papers to the *New York Times*. *Control war policy*
Attempted assassination of presidential candidate George Wallace. 1972. *Assassination*	With Wallace out of the way, Nixon is reelected. Wallace was likely to win seven southern states, forcing the election to be decided by a Democratically controlled Congress. *Political opportunism*
Watergate. 1972. Burglary and wiretapping of Democratic National Headquarters, and subsequent cover-up. *Burglary/wiretapping*	Sought to maneuver weakest Democratic nominee (McGovern) into the nomination to aid Nixon reelection. *Political opportunism*
October Surprise of 1980. Iran is offered an arms deal if they agree to postpone release of hostages until after presidential election. *Manipulation of defense information/policy*	Goal was to secure election of Ronald Reagan as president. *Political opportunism*
Attempted assassination of Ronald Reagan. 1981. *Assassination*	Goal was to strengthen Vice President Bush's role in administration, especially in relation to covert operations in Middle East and Latin America. *Control war policy*

SUSPECTED OR CONFIRMED PERPETRATOR	DEGREE OF CONFIRMATION OF GOVERNMENT ROLE
President Nixon, White House staff, and CIA operatives or former operatives.	High [19]
Arthur Bremer. Some circumstantial evidence points to involvement of Nixon via the "plumbers." Evidence includes comments of Nixon on his audiotapes.	Medium [23, 24]
President Nixon, White House staff, and CIA operatives or former operatives.	High [23]
Reportedly arranged in a meeting in Paris attended by high-ranking officials.	High [25, 26]
John Hinkley. Involvement of ambiguous elements in the intelligence community is suspected on the basis of a variety of circumstantial evidence.	Low [27, 28]

Table 5.1. Crimes against American democracy committed or allegedly committed by elements of the U.S. government (continued)

CRIME OR SUSPICIOUS EVENT, TIME FRAME, AND MODUS OPERANDI	PERPETRATOR MOTIVE OR POLICY IMPLICATION
Iran-Contra. 1984–1986. Senior Reagan administration officials secretly facilitate sale of arms to Iran, the subject of an arms embargo, using proceeds to fund Nicaraguan Contras, which had been prohibited by Congress. *Manipulation of defense information/policy*	Goal was to circumvent arms embargo against Iran (in order to obtain release of Iranian hostages) and congressional prohibition against funding Nicaraguan Contras. *Control war policy*
Disputed 2000 presidential election. 2000. Florida officials suppress vote and falsify election results. *Election tampering*	Goal was to block legally mandated recount. G. W. Bush becomes president through U.S. Supreme Court decision. *Political opportunism*
Events of 9/11. 2001. High-ranking U.S. government officials possibly involved in attacks on U.S. *Planned international event*	Bush popularity rises. Defense spending increases. Republicans gain in off-year elections. U.S. invades Afghanistan. U.S. invades Iraq. *Control war policy*

SUSPECTED OR CONFIRMED PERPETRATOR	DEGREE OF CONFIRMATION OF GOVERNMENT ROLE
Senior officials, CIA, military.	High [29–31]
Florida officials developed flawed felon disenfranchisement program and colluded to block recount. They also facilitated counting of fraudulent overseas military ballots.	High [32, 33]
High-ranking government officials.	Medium [34, 35] Eyewitness, chemical, and visual evidence possibly indicates the Twin Towers and Building 7 at the World Trade Center were brought down by controlled demolition. Visual evidence: videos publicly available show (1) the Twin Towers explode into dust from the top down, and (2) Building 7 collapses symmetrically and initially at free-fall acceleration into its own footprint. Chemical evidence of incendiary and explosives in the debris. [36] Eyewitnesses reported explosions inside the buildings prior to their collapse. [37 pp. 32–37] Government failure to look for chemical evidence of controlled demolition is possible indication of "guilty knowledge."

Table 5.1. Crimes against American democracy committed or allegedly committed by elements of the U.S. government (continued)

CRIME OR SUSPICIOUS EVENT, TIME FRAME, AND MODUS OPERANDI	PERPETRATOR MOTIVE OR POLICY IMPLICATION
Anthrax letter attacks. 2001. Letters containing anthrax sent to high-ranking Democratic senators. *Planned international event*	Failed assassination of Senate Majority Leader Tom Daschle and Judiciary Committee Chairman Patrick Leahy. Attack was first blamed on Iraq and fed social panic related to recent 9/11 attacks. Bush popularity rises. Defense spending increases. Republicans gain in off-year elections. U.S. invades Afghanistan. U.S. invades Iraq. *Control war policy*
Assassination of Senator Paul Wellstone. 2002. *Assassination*	Republicans regain control of Senate after Wellstone is replaced. *Control war policy*
Iraq-gate. 2003. Bush administration fixes intelligence to justify war against Iraq, claiming Iraq sought to purchase uranium in Niger and possesses weapons of mass destruction. *Manipulation of defense information/policy*	U.S. gains control of Iraq oil production. Iran surrounded by U.S. forces. Other Middle East nations are intimidated. *Control war policy*
False terror alerts. 2004. Government issues false terror alerts in advance of presidential election. *Manipulation of defense information/policy*	Bush wins reelection. Support is maintained for war on terror. *Political opportunism*

SUSPECTED OR CONFIRMED PERPETRATOR	DEGREE OF CONFIRMATION OF GOVERNMENT ROLE
Bush-Cheney first blamed Iraq. When FBI discovered that anthrax had been developed by the U.S. Army, blame shifted to bio-weapons expert Bruce Ivins, who allegedly had psychological problems. Possibly, anthrax letter attacks were part of overall 9/11 operation, involving high-ranking government officials.	High for involvement of U.S. bio-weapons expert(s) [38] Medium for officials, who were administered antibiotics on the night of 9/11.
Intelligence operatives.	Low [39]
President George W. Bush, Vice President Dick Cheney, CIA director.	High [40–42]
Bush administration officials.	High [43]

Table 5.1. Crimes against American democracy committed or allegedly committed by elements of the U.S. government (continued)

CRIME OR SUSPICIOUS EVENT, TIME FRAME, AND MODUS OPERANDI	PERPETRATOR MOTIVE OR POLICY IMPLICATION
Disputed 2004 presidential election. Election officials impede voting in Democratic precincts in Ohio. *Election tampering*	Bush wins EC vote with a 118,000-vote margin in Ohio. *Political opportunism*

1. Levy, L. W., *Freedom of Speech and Press in Early American History: Legacy of Suppression.* 1963, New York: Harper and Row.

2. Bingham, J. A., *Trial of the Conspirators for the Assassination of President Lincoln: Argument of John A. Bingham, Special Judge Advocate.* 1865, Washington, DC: Government Printing Office.

3. Winkler, H. D., *Lincoln and Booth: More Light on the Conspiracy.* 2003, Nashville, TN: Cumberland House.

4. Beard, C., and M. Beard, *The Rise of American Civilization: Volume 2: The Industrial Era.* 1927, New York: Macmillan.

5. Graham, H. J., The "Conspiracy Theory" of the Fourteenth Amendment. *Yale Law Journal* 1938 47(3): 371–403.

6. Russell, J. F. S., The Railroads in the "Conspiracy Theory" of the Fourteenth Amendment. *Mississippi Valley Historical Review* 1955 41(4): 601–622.

7. Shofner, J. H., *Nor Is It Over Yet: Florida in the Era of Reconstruction, 1863–1877.* 1974, Gainesville: University Press of Florida.

8. Eggert, G. G., Our Man in Havana: Fitzhugh Lee. *Hispanic American Historical Review* 1967 47(4): 463–485.

9. Borch, F., and D. Martinez, *Kimmel, Short, and Pearl Harbor: The Final Report Revealed.* 2005, Annapolis, MD: Naval Institute Press.

10. Kutler, S. I., *The Wars of Watergate: The Last Crisis of Richard Nixon.* 1990, New York: W. W. Norton.

11. Fried, R. M., *Nightmare in Red: The McCarthy Era in Perspective.* 1990, New York: Oxford University Press.

12. Johnson, H., *The Age of Anxiety: McCarthyism to Terrorism.* 2005, New York: Harcourt.

13. Fetzer, J. H., Smoking Guns and the Death of JFK, in *Murder in Dealey Plaza: What We Know Now That We Didn't Know Then about the Death of JFK*, J. H. Fetzer, Editor. 2000, Chicago: Catfeet Press. 1–16.

14. Groden, R. J., *The Killing of a President: The Complete Photographic Record of the JFK Assassination, the Conspiracy, and the Cover-up.* 1993, New York: Penguin.

15. Garrison, J., *On the Trail of the Assassins: My Investigation and Prosecution of the Murder of President Kennedy.* 1988, New York: Sheridan Square Press.

16. Lane, M., *Rush to Judgment: A Critique of the Warren Commission's Inquiry into the Murders of President John F. Kennedy, Officer J. D. Tippit, and Lee Harvey Oswald.* 1966, New York: Holt, Rinehart, and Winston.

17. Scott, P. D., *Deep Politics and the Death of JFK.* 1993, Berkeley: University of California Press.

18. White, R. F., Apologists and Critics of the Lone Gunman Theory: Assassination Science and Experts in Post-Modern America, in *Assassination Science: Experts Speak out on the Death of JFK*, J. H. Fetzer, Editor. 1998, Chicago: Catfeet Press. 377–413.

19. Ellsberg, D., *Secrets: A Memoir of Vietnam and the Pentagon Papers.* 2002, London: Penguin.

20. Pease, L., The RFK Plot Part I: The Grand Illusion, in *The Assassinations: Probe Magazine on JFK, MLK, RFK, and Malcolm X*, J. P. DiEugenio and L. Pease, Editors. 2003, Los Angeles: Feral House. 536–570.

SUSPECTED OR CONFIRMED PERPETRATOR	DEGREE OF CONFIRMATION OF GOVERNMENT ROLE
Election officials in Ohio possibly in collusion with federal-level elites.	High [44]

21. Pease, L., The RFK Plot Part II: The Rubik's Cube, in *The Assassinations: Probe Magazine on JFK, MLK, RFK, and Malcolm X*, J. P. DiEugeio and L. Pease, Editors. 2003, Los Angeles: Feral House. 571–610.

22. Summers, A., *The Arrogance of Power: The Secret World of Richard Nixon*. 2000, New York: Viking.

23. Bernstein, C., and B. Woodward, *All the President's Men*. 1974, New York: Simon and Schuster.

24. Carter, D., *The Politics of Rage: George Wallace, the Origins of the New Conservatism, and the Transformation of American Politics*. 2000, Baton Rouge: Louisiana State University Press.

25. Parry, R., *Trick or Treason: The October Surprise Mystery*. 1993, New York: Sheridan Square Press.

26. Sick, G., *October Surprise: America's Hostages in Iran and the Election of Ronald Reagan*. 1991, New York: Random House.

27. Bowen, R. S., *The Immaculate Deception: The Bush Crime Family Exposed*. 1991, Chicago: Global Insights.

28. Wiese, A., and M. Downing, Bush's Son Was to Dine with Suspect's Brother. *Houston Post*, 1981.

29. Kornbluh, P., and M. Byrne, eds., *The Iran-Contra Scandal: The Classified History*. 1993, New York: New Press.

30. Martin, A., *The Conspirators: Secrets of an Iran-Contra Insider*. 2001, Pray, MT: National Liberty Press.

31. Parry, R., *Lost History: Contras, Cocaine, the Press and Project Truth*. 1999, Arlington, VA: The Media Consortium.

32. Barstow, D., and D. J. Van Natta, *How Bush Took Florida: Mining the Overseas Absentee Vote*. New York Times, 2001.

33. deHaven-Smith, L., *The Battle for Florida*. 2005, Gainesville: University Press of Florida.

34. Griffin, D. R., *The New Pearl Harbor: Disturbing Questions about the Bush Administration and 9/11*. 2004, Northampton, MA: Olive Branch Press.

35. Tarpley, W. G., *9/11 Synthetic Terror*. 2005, Joshua Tree, CA: Progressive Press.

36. Jones, S. E., Why Indeed Did the Buildings at the World Trade Center Collapse, in *9/11 and American Empire: Intellectuals Speak Out*, D. R. Griffin and P. D. Scott, Editors. 2007, Northampton, MA: Olive Branch Press. 33–62.

37. Marrs, J., *Inside Job: Unmasking the 9/11 Conspiracies*. 2004, San Rafael, CA: Origin Press.

38. Spertzel, R., *Bruce Ivins Wasn't the Anthrax Culprit*. Wall Street Journal, 2008.

39. Arrows, F., and J. H. Fetzer, *American Assassination: The Strange Death of Senator Paul Wellstone*. 2004, Brooklyn: Vox Pop.

40. Clarke, R. A., *Against All Enemies: Inside America's War on Terror*. 2004, New York: Free Press.

41. Dean, J. W., *Worse than Watergate: The Secret Presidency of George W. Bush*. 2004, New York: Little, Brown.

42. Wilson, J., *The Politics of Truth: Inside the Lies That Led to War and Betrayed My Wife's CIA Identity*. 2004, New York: Carroll and Graf.

43. Hall, M., *Ridge Reveals Clashes on Alerts*. USA Today, 2005.

44. Miller, A., *What Went Wrong in Ohio: The Conyers Report on the 2004 Presidential Election*. 2005, Chicago: Academy Publishers.

≡ NOTES ≡

INTRODUCTION

1. Hofstadter, R., The Paranoid Style in American Politics, *Harper's Magazine*, 1964.

2. The Warren Commission was a blue ribbon panel appointed by President Johnson to investigate the assassination of President Kennedy. It is generally referred to by the name of its chair, Earl Warren, chief justice of the U.S. Supreme Court. Its findings were issued in a report titled *Report of the President's Commission on the Assassination of President John. F. Kennedy*. The report is commonly known as the Warren Commission report or the Warren report.

3. Waldron, M., *FBI Chiefs Linked to Oswald File Loss, New York Times*, 1975.

4. Douglass, J. W., *JFK and the Unspeakable: Why He Died and Why It Matters*. 2008, Maryknoll, NY: Orbis Books.

5. Bugliosi, V., *Reclaiming History: The Assassination of President John F. Kennedy*. 2007, New York: Norton.

6. Kay, J., *Among the Truthers: A Journey through America's Growing Conspiracist Underground*. 2011, New York: Harper's.

7. Avlon, J., *Wingnuts: How the Lunatic Fringe Is Hijacking America*. 2010, Philadelphia: Beast Books.

8. Sunstein, C. R., and A. Vermeule, Conspiracy Theories: Causes and Cures, *Journal of Political Philosophy* 2009 17(2): 202–227.

9. Sunstein, C. R., *Going to Extremes: How Like Minds Unite and Divide*. 2009, New York: Oxford.

10. Bernstein, C., and B. Woodward, *All the President's Men*. 1974, New York: Simon and Schuster.

11. Kornbluh, P., and M. Byrne, eds. *The Iran-Contra Scandal: The Classified History*. 1993, New York: New Press.

12. Rich, F., *The Greatest Story Ever Sold*. 2006, New York: Penguin.

13. deHaven-Smith, L., When Political Crimes Are Inside Jobs: Detecting State Crimes against Democracy, *Administrative Theory and Praxis* 2006 28(3): 330–355.

14. Husting, G., and M. Orr, Dangerous Machinery: "Conspiracy Theorist" as a Transpersonal Strategy of Exclusion, *Symbolic Interaction* 2007 30(2): 127–150.

15. Gray, L. P., *In Nixon's Web: A Year in the Crosshairs of Watergate*. 2008, New York: Henry Holt.

16. Kutler, S. I., *The Wars of Watergate: The Last Crisis of Richard Nixon*. 1990, New York: W. W. Norton.

17. Summers, A., *The Arrogance of Power: The Secret World of Richard Nixon*. 2000, New York: Viking.

18. Parry, R., *Trick or Treason: The October Surprise Mystery*. 1993, New York: Sheridan Square Press.

19. Isikoff, M., and D. Corn, *Hubris: The Inside Story of Spin, Scandal, and the Selling of the Iraq War*. 2006, New York: Crown.

20. Wilson, J., *The Politics of Truth: Inside the Lies That Led to War and Betrayed My Wife's CIA Identity*. 2004, New York: Carroll and Graf.

21. Heyman, J. M. E., ed., *States and Illegal Practices*. 1999, Oxford: Berg.

22. Johnson, L. K., Covert Action and Accountability: Decision-Making for America's Secret Foreign Policy, *International Studies Quarterly* 1989 33(1): 81–109.

23. Ginsberg, B., and M. Shefter, *Politics by Other Means: Politics, Prosecutors, and the Press from Watergate to Whitewater*. 2002, New York: W. W. Norton.

24. The term "false flag" originally referred to pirate ships that flew flags of the home countries (or allied countries) of the ships they were approaching to attack and board. The pirates used the false flag as a disguise to prevent their victims from fleeing or preparing for battle. The term today extends beyond naval encounters to include

countries that organize attacks on themselves and make the attacks appear to be by enemy nations or terrorists, thus giving the nation that was supposedly attacked a pretext for domestic repression and foreign military aggression. In the wake of the hijacked airplane attacks on September 11, 2001, the term was stretched further by some commentators to include terrorist attacks that a government knew were coming and could have stopped but allowed to succeed so that the nation would be primed for war. In general, the term "false-flag terrorism" today can even refer to quasi-military violence carried out against civilians by groups that, whether they know it or not, are being influenced, supported, controlled, or tricked by the victim nation. The language has become looser because, in the context of contemporary terrorism and international intrigue, the duplicity of nations has become increasingly complex and disjointed.

25. Gould, J., TV: Truman Capote Defines His Concept of Justice: He Offers Theories on the Assassinations, *New York Times*, 1968. Note how Capote is ridiculed for connecting the dots.

26. Freeman, S. F., and J. Bleifus, *Was the 2004 Presidential Election Stolen? Exit Polls, Election Fraud, and the Official Count.* 2006, New York: Seven Stories.

27. Broad, W. J., et al., Anthrax Probe Hampered by FBI Blunders, *New York Times*, 2001.

28. Cable Sought to Discredit Critics of Warren Report, *New York Times*, 1977.

CHAPTER ONE

1. Appleton, S., Trends: Assassinations, *Public Opinion Quarterly* 2000 64(4): 495–522.

2. Lane, M., *Rush to Judgment: A Critique of the Warren Commission's Inquiry into the Murders of President John F. Kennedy, Officer J. D. Tippit, and Lee Harvey Oswald.* 1966, New York: Holt, Rinehart and Winston.

3. Langguth, J., Twelve Perplexing Questions about Kennedy Assassination Examined, *New York Times*, 1964.

4. Lawyer Disputes Warren Findings: Article Says at Least Two Persons Fired at Kennedy, *New York Times*, 1965.

5. Copeland, M., *The Game of Nations: The Amorality of Power Politics.* 1969, New York: Simon and Schuster.

6. The awesome capability of the CIA is not due to the exceptional

abilities of individuals but to their ability to apply very large numbers of people to research and operations. The agency approaches issues with industrial-scale efforts.

7. Nelson, P. F., *LBJ: Mastermind of JFK's Assassination*. 2010, Bloomington, IN: Xlibris.

8. Phillips, C., Major Political Scandal Looming in the Bobby Baker Case, *New York Times*, 1964.

9. Baker, R., Kennedy Backs Johnson for '64: Says Texan Can Have Spot on Ticket if He Wishes, *New York Times*, 1962.

10. Loftus, J. A., Johnson Promised Place on a '64 Kennedy Ticket, *New York Times*, 1963.

11. Nixon, R. M., *Six Crises*. 1962, New York: Doubleday. See chapter on 1960 election.

12. See Chapter 1 of the Warren Commission report for a narrative timeline.

13. Warren Commission, *Report of the President's Commission on the Assassination of President Kennedy*. 1964, New York: St. Martin's Press.

14. Sunstein, C. R., and A. Vermeule, Conspiracy Theories: Causes and Cures, *Journal of Political Philosophy* 2009 17(2): 202–227.

15. McCullough, D., *Truman*. 1992, New York: Simon and Schuster.

16. Hunt, E. H., *Undercover: Memoirs of an American Secret Agent*. 1974, New York: G. P. Putnam's Sons.

17. Liddy, G. G., *Will: The Autobiography of G. Gordon Liddy*. 1980, New York: St. Martin's Press.

18. Kay, J., *Among the Truthers: A Journey through America's Growing Conspiracist Underground*. 2011, New York: HarperCollins.

19. Pipes, D., *Conspiracy: How the Paranoid Style Flourishes and Where It Comes From*. 1997, New York: Simon and Schuster.

20. Arnold, G. B., *Conspiracy Theory in Film, Television, and Politics*. 2008, Westport, CT: Praeger.

21. Fenster, M., *Conspiracy Theories: Secrecy and Power in American Culture*. 1999/2008, Minneapolis: University of Minnesota Press.

22. Barkun, M., *A Culture of Conspiracy: Apocalyptic Visions in Contemporary America*. 2003, Berkeley: University of California Press.

23. Ellsberg, D., *Secrets: A Memoir of Vietnam and the Pentagon Papers*. 2002, London: Penguin.

24. Rich, F., *The Greatest Story Ever Sold*. 2006, New York: Penguin.

25. Aaronovitch, D., *Voodoo Histories: The Role of Conspiracy Theory in Shaping Modern History*. 2010, New York: Riverhead Books.

26. Olmsted, K. S., *Real Enemies: Conspiracy Theories and American Democracy*. 2009, Oxford: Oxford University Press.

27. Marrs, J., *The Terror Conspiracy: Deception, 9/11 and the Loss of Liberty*. 2006, New York: Disinformation.

28. Summers, A., *The Arrogance of Power: The Secret World of Richard Nixon*. 2000, New York: Viking.

29. Weldon, D., The Kennedy Limousine: Dallas 1963, in *Murder in Dealey Plaza: What We Know Now That We Didn't Know Then about the Death of JFK*, J. H. Fetzer, Editor. 2000, Chicago: Catfeet Press. 129–158.

30. Groden, R. J., *The Killing of a President: The Complete Photographic Record of the JFK Assassination, the Conspiracy, and the Cover-up*. 1993, New York: Penguin.

31. Talbot, D., *Brothers: The Hidden History of the Kennedy Years*. 2007, New York: Free Press.

32. Burleigh, N., *A Very Private Woman: The Life and Unsolved Murder of Presidential Mistress Mary Meyer*. 1998, New York: Bantam Books.

33. Coffey, T. M., *Iron Eagle: The Turbulent Life of General Curtis LeMay*. 1986, New York: Avon Books.

34. Tanner, H., Nixon, Back in Moscow, Debates Again, *New York Times*, 1965.

35. Upton, L., Nixon's Reply to Russian Criticized, *New York Times*, 1965.

CHAPTER TWO

1. deHaven-Smith, L., State Crimes against Democracy in the War on Terror: Applying the Nuremberg Principles to the Bush-Cheney Administration, *Contemporary Politics* 2010 16(4): 403–420.

2. Bailyn, B., *The Ideological Origins of the American Revolution*. 1967/1997, Cambridge: Harvard University Press.

3. Tackett, T., Conspiracy Obsession in a Time of Revolution: French Elites and the Origins of the Terror, 1789–1792, *American Historical Review* 2000 105(3): 691–713.

4. Quoted in Bailyn, 145.

5. The sermon or poem is "First They Came," by Martin Niemoller.

It is on display at the U.S. Holocaust Museum in Washington, DC, and its history is discussed on the museum's website.

6. Polk, W. R., *The Birth of America: From before Columbus to the Revolution*. 2006, New York: HarperCollins.

7. Polk, W. R., *Violent Politics: A History of Insurgency, Terrorism and Guerrilla War, from the American Revolution to Iraq*. 2007, New York: Harper Perennial.

8. Quotes and references are from the Classic Original Edition of *The Federalist Papers*, by James Madison, Alexander Hamilton, and John Jay, 2012, Lindenhurst, NY: Tribeca Books.

9. Fisher, L., *The Constitution and 9/11: Recurring Threats to America's Freedoms*. 2008, Lawrence: University Press of Kansas.

10. Bingham, J. A., *Trial of the Conspirators for the Assassination of President Lincoln: Argument of John A. Bingham, Special Judge Advocate*. 1865, Washington, DC: Government Printing Office.

11. Beard, C., and M. Beard, *The Rise of American Civilization, Volume 2: The Industrial Era*. 1927, New York: Macmillan.

12. Crosby, E. H., Destruction of the Maine: Mr. Crosby Thinks Spain's Guilt as Yet Unproven, *New York Times*, 1904.

13. Rohter, L., Havana Journal: Remember the *Maine*? Cubans See an American Plot to This Day, *New York Times*, 1998.

14. deHaven-Smith, L., Beyond Conspiracy Theory: Patterns of High Crime in American Government, *American Behavioral Scientist* 2010 53(6): 795–825.

15. Rogow, A. A., and H. D. Lasswell, *Power, Corruption, and Lies*. 1963, Englewood Cliffs, NJ: Prentice Hall.

16. Lowi, T., *The End of Liberalism*. 1969, New York: Norton.

17. deHaven-Smith, L., and C. E. Van Horn, Subgovernment Conflict in Public Policy, *Policy Studies Journal* 1984 12(4): 627–642.

18. McCool, D., The Subsystem Family of Concepts: A Critique and a Proposal, *Political Research Quarterly* 1998 51(2): 551–570.

19. Dahl, R., and C. E. Lindblom, *Politics, Economics, and Welfare*. 1976/1946, New Haven: Yale University Press.

20. Eisenhower, D., *Farewell Address*. 1961. Available on the Eisenhower Library website (eisenhower.library@nara.gov).

21. Black, W. K., *The Best Way to Rob a Bank Is to Own One*. 2005, Austin: University of Texas Press.

22. Calavita, K., H. N. Pontell, and R. H. Tillman, *Big Money Crime: Fraud and Politics in the Savings and Loan Crisis*. 1997, Berkeley: University of California Press.

23. Munson, R., *From Edison to Enron: The Business of Power and What It Means for the Future of Electricity*. 2005, Westport, CT: Praeger.

24. Harris, W. R., *Tyranny on Trial: The Evidence at Nuremberg*. 1954, Dallas: Southern Methodist University Press.

25. Marrus, M. R., *The Nuremberg War Crimes Trial, 1945–46: A Documentary History*. 1997, Boston: Bedford/St. Martin's.

26. Persico, J. E., *Nuremberg: Infamy on Trial*. 1994, New York: Penguin.

27. Conot, R. E., *Justice at Nuremberg*. 1983, New York: Basic Books.

28. Tusa, A., and J. Tusa, *The Nuremberg Trial*. 1983, New York: McGraw-Hill.

29. Shirer, W. L., *The Rise and Fall of the Third Reich: A History of Nazi Germany*. 1959, New York: Simon and Schuster.

CHAPTER THREE

1. Popper, K. R., *The Open Society and Its Enemies, Volume II: The High Tide of Prophecy*. 1962, Princeton, NJ: Princeton University Press.

2. Strauss, L., *Studies in Platonic Political Philosophy*. 1983, Chicago: University of Chicago Press.

3. Strauss, L., *On Tyranny*. 1963, Ithaca, NY: Cornell University Press.

4. Strauss, L., *Liberalism Ancient and Modern*. 1989/1968, Chicago: University of Chicago Press.

5. Beard, C., *President Roosevelt and the Coming of the War, 1941: Appearances and Realities*. 1948/2003, New Brunswick: Transaction.

6. Mann, J., *The Rise of the Vulcans: The History of Bush's War Cabinet*. 2004, New York: Viking.

7. Norton, A., *Leo Strauss and the Politics of American Empire*. 2004, New Haven: Yale University Press.

8. Drury, S. B., *The Political Ideas of Leo Strauss*. 1988, New York: St. Martin's Press.

9. Strauss, L., *Natural Right and History*. 1950, Chicago: University of Chicago Press.

10. Strauss, L., *Persecution and the Art of Writing*. 1952, Chicago: University of Chicago Press.

11. Mills, C. W., *The Power Elite*. 1959, New York: Oxford University Press.

12. Popper, K. R., *The Open Society and Its Enemies, Volume I: The Spell of Plato*. 1962, Princeton, NJ: Princeton University Press.

13. Beard, C., *An Economic Interpretation of the Constitution of the United States*. 1913, New York: Free Press.

14. Beard, C., and M. Beard, *The Rise of American Civilization, Volume II: The Industrial Era*. 1927, New York: Macmillan.

15. Campbell, C., Introduction, in *President Roosevelt and the Coming of War*. 2003, New Brunswick, NJ: Transaction. pp. vii–xvii.

16. Pigden, C., Popper Revisited, or What Is Wrong with Conspiracy Theories? *Philosophy of the Social Sciences* 1995 25(1): 3–34.

17. Strauss, L., *An Introduction to Politial Philosophy*. 1989, Detroit: Wayne State University Press.

18. Habermas, J., *Legitimation Crisis*. 1973, Boston: Beacon Press.

19. Catlaw, T. J., *Fabricating the People: Politics and Administration in the Biopolitical State*. 2007, Tuscaloosa: University of Alabama Press.

20. Foucault, M., Governmentality, in *Power: Essential Works of Foucault, 1954–1984*, J. D. Faubio, Editor. 2000, New York: New Press. 201–222.

21. deHaven-Smith, L., When Political Crimes Are Inside Jobs: Detecting State Crimes against Democracy, *Administrative Theory and Praxis* 2006 28(3): 330–355.

22. deHaven-Smith, L., and M. T. Witt, Preventing State Crimes against Democracy, *Administration and Society* 2009 41(5): 527–550.

23. Wolin, S., *Democracy Incorporated: Managed Democracy and the Specter of Inverted Totalitarianism*. 2008, Princeton, NJ: Princeton University Press.

CHAPTER FOUR

1. Garrison, J., *On the Trail of the Assassins: My Investigation and Prosecution of the Murder of President Kennedy*. 1988, New York: Sheridan Square Press.

2. Lawyer Disputes Warren findings: Article Says at Least Two Persons Fired at Kennedy, *New York Times*, 1965.

3. Lane, M., *Rush to Judgment: A Critique of the Warren Commission's Inquiry into the Murders of President John F. Kennedy, Officer*

J. D. Tippit, and Lee Harvey Oswald. 1966, New York: Holt, Rinehart, and Winston.

4. Janson, D., The Dallas Mystery: The Events in Dallas: Large Questions Remain Unanswered about Oswald and Ruby, *New York Times*, 1963, p. 247.

5. Appleton, S., Trends: Assassinations, *Public Opinion Quarterly* 2000 64(4): 495–522.

6. Cable Sought to Discredit Critics of Warren Report, *New York Times*, 1977.

7. Strauss, L., *The Rebirth of Classical Political Rationalism: An Introduction to the Thought of Leo Strauss*. 1989, Chicago: University of Chicago Press.

8. Strauss, L., *Persecution and the Art of Writing*. 1952, Chicago: University of Chicago Press.

9. The role of philosophers in society in Strauss' account, it might be argued, is essentially the same as the role of national security elites acting as the "guardian class." See L. deHaven-Smith, *The Guardian Elite*, presentation at the Public Administration Theory Network 23rd annual conference, Omaha, NB, 2010.

10. Miller, M. C., *The Bush Dyslexicon: Observations on a National Disorder*. 2001, New York: W. W. Norton.

11. Ellsberg, D., *Secrets: A Memoir of Vietnam and the Pentagon Papers*. 2002, London: Penguin.

12. Hunt, E. H., *Undercover: Memoirs of an American Secret Agent*. 1974, New York: G. P. Putnam's Sons.

13. Liddy, G. G., *Will: The Autobiography of G. Gordon Liddy*. 1980, New York: St. Martin's Press.

14. Converse, P. E., The Nature of Belief Systems in Mass Publics, in *Ideology and Discontent*, D. E. Apter, Editor. 1964, New York: Free Press.

15. Talbot, D., *Brothers: The Hidden History of the Kennedy Years*. 2007, New York: Free Press.

16. The *Time* magazine article is posted at http://www.time.com /time/magazine/article/0,9171,837645,00.html.

17. From 1875 through 2011, the *New York Times* published 1,943 stories that mention conspiracy theory; *Time* magazine published 193 such stories from 1913 through 2011.

18. The *New York Times* and *Time* magazine archives were queried for articles with "conspiracy theory" (or "conspiracy theories," "conspiracy theorist," or "conspiracy theorists") anywhere in the headline,

the abstract, or the full text. The query results were converted to a dataset with a "case" or "record" for each article containing any variant of the phrase.

19. *Pentagon Papers: The Defense Department History of United States Decisionmaking on Vietnam.* 4 vols. Senator Gravel edition. 1971, Boston: Beacon Press.

20. Adams, S., *War of Numbers: An Intelligence Memoir.* 1994, South Royalton, VT: Steerforth Press. This is a rare, insider's account of how the CIA's information about battlefield statistics and prognosis for victory was withheld.

21. Husting, G., and M. Orr, Dangerous Machinery: "Conspiracy Theorist" as a Transpersonal Strategy of Exclusion, *Symbolic Interaction* 2007 30(2): 127–150.

CHAPTER FIVE

1. Toulmin, S., *Foresight and Understanding: An Enquiry into the Aims of Science.* 1961, New York: Harper and Row.

2. Kuhn, T. S., *The Structure of Scientific Revolutions.* 1962, Chicago: University of Chicago Press.

3. deHaven-Smith, L., When Political Crimes Are Inside Jobs: Detecting State Crimes against Democracy, *Administrative Theory and Praxis* 2006 28(3): 330–355.

4. deHaven-Smith, L., Beyond Conspiracy Theory: Patterns of High Crime in American Government, *American Behavioral Scientist* 2010 53(6): 795–825.

5. Witt, M. T., and L. deHaven-Smith, Conjuring the Holographic State: Scripting Security Doctrine for a (New) World of Disorder, *Administration and Society,* 2008 40(6): 547–585.

6. deHaven-Smith, L. *The Battle for Florida.* 2005, Gainesville: University Press of Florida.

7. Broad, W. J., et al., Anthrax Probe Hampered by FBI Blunders, *New York Times,* 2001.

8. Parry, R., *Trick or Treason: The October Surprise Mystery.* 1993, New York: Sheridan Square Press.

9. Walsh, L. E., *Firewall: The Iran-Contra Conspiracy and Cover-up.* 1997, New York: W. W. Norton.

10. Baker, R., *Family of Secrets: The Bush Dynasty, the Powerful Forces That Put Them in the White House, and What Their Influence Means for America.* 2009, New York: Bloomsbury Press.

11. Of course, lone gunmen might be drawn to presidents because of their visibility and power, but this does not explain the pattern of presidents with hawkish vice presidents being targeted, or senators being killed when the Senate is evenly divided. These patterns are indicative of the interests of political insiders who have a stake in the direction of foreign policy.

12. Wise, D., *The American Police State: The Government against the People*. 1976, New York: Vintage Books.

13. Raskin, M. G., Democracy versus the National Security State, *Law and Contemporary Problems* 1976 40(3): 189–220.

14. Parry, R., *Lost History: Contras, Cocaine, the Press and Project Truth*. 1999, Arlington, VA: Media Consortium.

15. Webb, G., *Dark Alliance: The CIA, the Contras, and the Crack Cocaine Explosion*. 1998, New York: Seven Stories Press.

16. Fisher, L., The Way We Go to War: The Iraq Resolution, in *Considering the Bush Presidency*, G. L. Gregg and M. J. Rozell, Editors. 2004, New York: Oxford University Press. 107–124.

17. Goldsmith, J., *The Terror Presidency: Law and Judgment inside the Bush Administration*. 2007, New York: W. W. Norton.

18. Greenwald, G., *A Tragic Legacy: How a Good vs. Evil Mentality Destroyed the Bush Presidency*. 2007, New York: Crown.

19. Isikoff, M., and D. Corn, *Hubris: The Inside Story of Spin, Scandal, and the Selling of the Iraq War*. 2006, New York: Crown.

20. Rich, F., *The Greatest Story Ever Sold*. 2006, New York: Penguin.

21. Spertzel, R., Bruce Ivins Wasn't the Anthrax Culprit, *Wall Street Journal*, 2008.

22. Sobieraj, S., White House Mail Machine Has Anthrax, *Washington Post*, 2001.

23. Wilford, H., *The Mighty Wurlitzer: How the CIA Played America*. 2008, Cambridge: Harvard University Press.

24. Schmitt, C., *The Concept of the Political*. 1996, Chicago: University of Chicago Press.

25. Hunt, E. H., *Undercover: Memoirs of an American Secret Agent*. 1974, New York: G. P. Putnam's Sons.

CHAPTER SIX

1. deHaven-Smith, L., State Crimes against Democracy in the War

on Terror: Applying the Nuremberg Principles to the Bush-Cheney Administration. *Contemporary Politics* 2010 16(4): 403–420.

2. Bugliosi, V., *The Prosecution of George W. Bush for Murder*. 2008, Cambridge, MA: Vanguard Press.

3. Wright, A., and S. Dixon, *Dissent: Voices of Conscience*. 2008, Kihei, HI: Koa Books.

4. Beard, C., *President Roosevelt and the Coming of the War, 1941: Appearances and Realities*. 1948/2003, New Brunswick: Transaction.

5. Savage, C., Obama Reluctant to Look into Bush Programs, *New York Times*, 2009.

6. Bacevich, A. J., *Washington Rules: America's Path to Permanent War*. 2010, New York: Metropolitan Books.

7. Morris, E., *The Fog of War*. 2004, Sony Pictures Home Entertainment.

8. Galbraith, J. K., Did the U.S. Military Plan a Nuclear First Strike for 1963? *The American Prospect* 1994 5(19).

9. Hunt, E. H., *Undercover: Memoirs of an American Secret Agent*. 1974, New York: G. P. Putnam's Sons.

10. Abella, A., *Soldiers of Reason: The Rand Corporation and the Rise of the American Empire*. 2008, Boston: Mariner Books.

11. Nelson, P. F., *LBJ: Mastermind of JFK's Assassination*. 2010, Bloomington, IN: Xlibris.

12. Knebel, F., and C. I. Bailey, *Seven Days in May*. 1962, New York: Harper and Row.

13. Curtis, A., *The Power of Nightmares*, 2004, British Broadcasting System.

14. Liddy, G. G., *Will: The Autobiography of G. Gordon Liddy*. 1980, New York: St. Martin's Press.

15. Summers, A., *The Arrogance of Power: The Secret World of Richard Nixon*. 2000, New York: Viking.

16. Fulsom, D., *Nixon's Darkest Secrets: The Inside Story of America's Most Troubled President*. 2012, New York: St. Martin's Press.

17. Maraniss, D., First Lady Launches Counterattack, *Washington Post*, 1998.

18. Sunstein, C. R., and A. Vermeule, Conspiracy Theories: Causes and Cures. *Journal of Political Philosophy* 2009 17(2): 202–227.

19. Habermas, J., *Legitimation Crisis*. 1973, Boston: Beacon Press. Habermas raises this issue in more general terms as a change in the form and purpose of verbal communication, but his observations are relevant.

20. Noelle-Neumann, E., *The Spiral of Silence*. 1993, Chicago: University of Chicago Press.

21. Pease, L., The RFK Plot Part I: The Grand Illusion. In *The Assassinations: Probe Magazine on JFK, MLK, RFK, and Malcolm X*, J. P. DiEugenio and L. Pease, Editors. 2003, Los Angeles: Feral House. 536–570.

22. Griffin, D. R., *The New Pearl Harbor: Disturbing Questions about the Bush Administration and 9/11*. 2004, Northampton, MA: Olive Branch Press.

23. Broad, W. J., et al., Anthrax Probe Hampered by FBI Blunders, *New York Times*, 2001.

24. Barstow, D., and D. J. Van Natta, How Bush Took Florida: Mining the Overseas Absentee Vote, *New York Times*, 2001.

25. deHaven-Smith, L., *The Battle for Florida*. 2005, Gainesville: University Press of Florida.

26. Shenon, P., *The Commission: The Uncensored History of the 9/11 Investigation*. 2008, New York: Twelve.

≡ BIBLIOGRAPHY ≡

Aaronovitch, D. *Voodoo Histories: The Role of Conspiracy Theory in Shaping Modern History*. 2010, New York: Riverhead Books.

Abella, A. *Soldiers of Reason: The Rand Corporation and the Rise of the American Empire*. 2008, Boston: Mariner Books.

Ackerman, B., and D. Fontana. Thomas Jefferson Counts Himself into the Presidency. *Virginia Law Review* 2004 90(2): 551–643.

Adams, S. *War of Numbers: An Intelligence Memoir*. 1994, South Royalton, VT: Steerforth Press.

Appleton, S. Trends: Assassinations. *Public Opinion Quarterly* 2000 64(4): 495–522.

Arnold, G. B. *Conspiracy Theory in Film, Television, and Politics*. 2008, Westport, CT: Praeger.

Arrows, F., and J. H. Fetzer. *American Assassination: The Strange Death of Senator Paul Wellstone*. 2004, Brooklyn: Vox Pop.

Avlon, J. *Wingnuts: How the Lunatic Fringe Is Hijacking America*. 2010, Philadelphia: Beast Books.

Bacevich, A. J. *Washington Rules: America's Path to Permanent War*. 2010, New York: Metropolitan Books.

Bailyn, B. *The Ideological Origins of the American Revolution*. 1967/1997, Cambridge: Harvard University Press.

Baker, R. *Family of Secrets: The Bush Dynasty, the Powerful Forces That Put Them in the White House, and What Their Influence Means for America*. 2009, New York: Bloomsbury Press.

Baker, R. Kennedy Backs Johnson for '64: Says Texan Can Have Spot on Ticket if He Wishes. *New York Times*, 1962.

Barkun, M. *A Culture of Conspiracy: Apocalyptic Visions in Contemporary America*. 2003, Berkeley: University of California Press.

Barstow, D., and D. J. Van Natta. How Bush Took Florida: Mining the Overseas Absentee Vote. *New York Times*, 2001.

Beard, C. *An Economic Interpretation of the Constitution of the United States*. 1913, New York: Free Press.

Beard, C. *President Roosevelt and the Coming of the War, 1941: Appearances and Realities*. 1948/2003, New Brunswick: Transaction.

Beard, C., and M. Beard. *The Rise of American Civilization: Volume 2: The Industrial Era*. 1927, New York: Macmillan.

Bernstein, C., and B. Woodward. *All the President's Men*. 1974, New York: Simon and Schuster.

Bingham, J. A. *Trial of the Conspirators for the Assassination of President Lincoln: Argument of John A. Bingham, Special Judge Advocate*. 1865, Washington, DC: Government Printing Office.

Black, W. K. *The Best Way to Rob a Bank Is to Own One*. 2005, Austin: University of Texas Press.

Borch, F., and D. Martinez. *Kimmel, Short, and Pearl Harbor: The Final Report Revealed*. 2005, Annapolis, MD: Naval Institute Press.

Bowen, R. S. *The Immaculate Deception: The Bush Crime Family Exposed*. 1991, Chicago: Global Insights.

Broad, W. J., et al. Anthrax Probe Hampered by FBI Blunders. *New York Times*, 2001.

Bugliosi, V. *The Prosecution of George W. Bush for Murder*. 2008, Cambridge, MA: Vanguard Press.

Bugliosi, V. *Reclaiming History: The Assassination of President John F. Kennedy*. 2007, New York: Norton.

Burleigh, N. *A Very Private Woman: The Life and Unsolved Murder of Presidential Mistress Mary Meyer*. 1998, New York: Bantam Books.

Cable Sought to Discredit Critics of Warren Report. *New York Times*, 1977.

Calavita, K., H. N. Pontell, and R. H. Tillman. *Big Money Crime: Fraud and Politics in the Savings and Loan Crisis*. 1997, Berkeley: University of California Press.

Campbell, C. Introduction. In *President Roosevelt and the Coming of the War*. 2003, New Brunswick, NJ: Transaction. pp. vii–xvii.

Carter, D. *The Politics of Rage: George Wallace, the Origins of the New*

Conservatism, and the Transformation of American Politics. 2000, Baton Rouge: Louisiana State University Press.

Catlaw, T. J. *Fabricating the People: Politics and Administration in the Biopolitical State.* 2007, Tuscaloosa: University of Alabama Press.

Clarke, R. A. *Against All Enemies: Inside America's War on Terror.* 2004, New York: Free Press.

Coffey, T. M. *Iron Eagle: The Turbulent Life of General Curtis LeMay.* 1986, New York: Avon Books.

Conot, R. E. *Justice at Nuremberg.* 1983, New York: Basic Books.

Converse, P. E. The Nature of Belief Systems in Mass Publics. In *Ideology and Discontent,* D. E. Apter, Editor. 1964, New York: Free Press.

Copeland, M. *The Game of Nations: The Amorality of Power Politics.* 1969, New York: Simon and Schuster.

Crosby, E. H. Destruction of the Maine: Mr. Crosby Thinks Spain's Guilt as Yet Unproven. *New York Times,* 1904.

Curtis, A. *The Power of Nightmares.* 2004, British Broadcasting Corporation.

Dahl, R., and C. E. Lindblom. *Politics, Economics, and Welfare.* 1976/1946, New Haven: Yale University Press.

Dean, J. W. *Worse than Watergate: The Secret Presidency of George W. Bush.* 2004, New York: Little, Brown.

deHaven-Smith, L. *The Battle for Florida.* 2005, Gainesville: University Press of Florida.

deHaven-Smith, L. Beyond Conspiracy Theory: Patterns of High Crime in American Government. *American Behavioral Scientist* 2010 53(6): 795–825.

deHaven-Smith, L. *The Guardian Elite.* Presentation at the Public Administration Theory Network 23rd annual conference, Omaha, NB, 2010.

deHaven-Smith, L. *Philosophical Critiques of Policy Analysis: Lindblom, Habermas, and the Great Society.* 1988, Gainesville: University of Florida Press.

deHaven-Smith, L. Show Us the Votes: Election Results Don't Add Up. *Miami Herald,* 2004.

deHaven-Smith, L. State Crimes against Democracy in the War on Terror: Applying the Nuremberg Principles to the Bush-Cheney Administration. *Contemporary Politics* 2010 16(4): 403–420.

deHaven-Smith, L. When Political Crimes Are Inside Jobs: Detecting State Crimes against Democracy. *Administrative Theory and Praxis* 2006 28(3): 330–355.

deHaven-Smith, L., and C. E. Van Horn. Subgovernment Conflict in Public Policy. *Policy Studies Journal* 1984 12(4): 627–642.

deHaven-Smith, L., and M. T. Witt. Preventing State Crimes against Democracy. *Administration and Society* 2009 41(5): 527–550.

Douglass, J. W. *JFK and the Unspeakable: Why He Died and Why It Matters.* 2008, Maryknoll, NY: Orbis Books.

Drury, S. B. *The Political Ideas of Leo Strauss.* 1988, New York: St. Martin's Press.

Eggert, G. G. Our Man in Havana: Fitzhugh Lee. *Hispanic American Historical Review* 1967 47(4): 463–485.

Eisenhower, D. *Farewell Address.* 1961.

Ellsberg, D. *Secrets: A Memoir of Vietnam and the Pentagon Papers.* 2002, London: Penguin.

Fenster, M. *Conspiracy Theories: Secrecy and Power in American Culture.* 1999/2008, Minneapolis: University of Minnesota Press.

Fetzer, J. H. Smoking Guns and the Death of JFK. In *Murder in Dealey Plaza: What We Know Now That We Didn't Know Then about the Death of JFK*, J. H. Fetzer, Editor. 2000, Chicago: Catfeet Press. 1–16.

Fisher, L. *The Constitution and 9/11: Recurring Threats to America's Freedoms.* 2008, Lawrence: University Press of Kansas.

Fisher, L. The Way We Go to War: The Iraq Resolution. In *Considering the Bush Presidency*, G. L. Gregg and M. J. Rozell, Editors. 2004, New York: Oxford University Press. 107–124.

Foucault, M. Governmentality. In *Power: Essential Works of Foucault, 1954–1984*, J. D. Faubio, Editor. 2000, New York: New Press. 201–222.

Freeman, S. F., and J. Bleifuss. *Was the 2004 Presidential Election Stolen? Exit Polls, Election Fraud, and the Official Count.* 2006, New York: Seven Stories.

Fried, R. M. *Nightmare in Red: The McCarthy Era in Perspective.* 1990, New York: Oxford University Press.

Friedrich, C. J. *The Pathology of Politics: Violence, Betrayal, Corruption, Secrecy, and Propaganda.* 1972, New York: Harper and Row.

Fulsom, D. *Nixon's Darkest Secrets: The Inside Story of America's Most Troubled President.* 2012, New York: St. Martin's Press.

Galbraith, J. K. Did the U.S. Military Plan a Nuclear First Strike for 1963? *The American Prospect* 1994 5(19).

Garrison, J. *On the Trail of the Assassins: My Investigation and Prosecution of the Murder of President Kennedy*. 1988, New York: Sheridan Square Press.

Ginsberg, B., and M. Shefter. *Politics by Other Means: Politics, Prosecutors, and the Press from Watergate to Whitewater*. 2002, New York: W. W. Norton.

Gould, J. TV: Truman Capote Defines His Concept of Justice: He Offers Theories on the Assassinations. *New York Times*, 1968.

Graham, H. J. The "Conspiracy Theory" of the Fourteenth Amendment. *Yale Law Journal* 1938 47(3): 371–403.

Gray, L. P. *In Nixon's Web: A Year in the Crosshairs of Watergate*. 2008, New York: Henry Holt.

Greenwald, G. *A Tragic Legacy: How a Good vs. Evil Mentality Destroyed the Bush Presidency*. 2007, New York: Crown.

Griffin, D. R. *The New Pearl Harbor: Disturbing Questions about the Bush Administration and 9/11*. 2004, Northampton, MA: Olive Branch Press.

Groden, R. J. *The Killing of a President: The Complete Photographic Record of the JFK Assassination, the Conspiracy, and the Cover-up*. 1993, New York: Penguin.

Habermas, J. *Legitimation Crisis*. 1973, Boston: Beacon Press.

Hall, M. Ridge Reveals Clashes on Alerts. *USA Today*, 2005.

Harris, W. R. *Tyranny on Trial: The Evidence at Nuremberg*. 1954, Dallas: Southern Methodist University Press.

Heyman, J. M. E., ed. *States and Illegal Practices*. 1999, Oxford: Berg.

Hofstadter, R. The Paranoid Style in American Politics. *Harper's Magazine*, 1964.

Hunt, E. H. *Undercover: Memoirs of an American Secret Agent*. 1974, New York: G. P. Putnam's Sons.

Husting, G., and M. Orr. Dangerous Machinery: "Conspiracy Theorist" as a Transpersonal Strategy of Exclusion. *Symbolic Interaction* 2007 30(2): 127–150.

Isikoff, M., and D. Corn. *Hubris: The Inside Story of Spin, Scandal, and the Selling of the Iraq War*. 2006, New York: Crown.

Janson, D. The Dallas Mystery: The Events in Dallas: Large Questions Remain Unanswered about Oswald and Ruby. *New York Times*, 1963.

Johnson, H. *The Age of Anxiety: McCarthyism to Terrorism*. 2005, New York: Harcourt.

Johnson, L. K. Covert Action and Accountability: Decision-Making for America's Secret Foreign Policy. *International Studies Quarterly* 1989 33(1): 81–109.

Jones, S. E. Why Indeed Did the Buildings at the World Trade Center Collapse. In *9/11 and American Empire: Intellectuals Speak Out*, D. R. Griffin and P. D. Scott, Editors. 2007, Northampton, MA: Olive Branch Press. 33–62.

Kay, J. *Among the Truthers: A Journey through America's Growing Conspiracist Underground*. 2011, New York: Harper's.

Knebel, F., and C. I. Bailey. *Seven Days in May*. 1962, New York: Harper and Row.

Kornbluh, P., and M. Byrne, eds. *The Iran-Contra Scandal: The Classified History*. 1993, New York: New Press.

Kuhn, T. S. *The Structure of Scientific Revolutions*. 1962, Chicago: University of Chicago Press.

Kutler, S. I. *The Wars of Watergate: The Last Crisis of Richard Nixon*. 1990, New York: W. W. Norton.

Lane, M. *Rush to Judgment: A Critique of the Warren Commission's Inquiry into the Murders of President John F. Kennedy, Officer J. D. Tippit, and Lee Harvey Oswald*. 1966, New York: Holt, Rinehart and Winston.

Langguth, A. J. Twelve Perplexing Questions about Kennedy Assassination Examined. *New York Times*, 1964.

Lawyer Disputes Warren Findings: Article Says at Least Two Persons Fired at Kennedy. *New York Times*, 1965.

Levy, L. W. *Freedom of Speech and Press in Early American History: Legacy of Suppression*. 1963, New York: Harper and Row.

Liddy, G. G. *Will: The Autobiography of G. Gordon Liddy*. 1980, New York: St. Martin's Press.

Loftus, J. A. Johnson Promised Place on a '64 Kennedy Ticket. *New York Times*, 1963.

Lowi, T. *The End of Liberalism*. 1969, New York: W. W. Norton.

Madison, James, Alexander Hamilton, and John Jay. *The Federalist Papers*. Classic Original Edition. 2012, Lindenhurst, NY: Tribeca Books.

Maraniss, D. First Lady Launches Counterattack. *Washington Post*, 1998.

Mann, J. *The Rise of the Vulcans: The History of Bush's War Cabinet*. 2004, New York: Viking.

Marrs, J. *Inside Job: Unmasking the 9/11 Conspiracies*. 2004, San Rafael, CA: Origin Press.

Marrus, M. R. *The Nuremberg War Crimes Trial, 1945–46: A Documentary History*. 1997, Boston: Bedford/St. Martin's.

Martin, A. *The Conspirators: Secrets of an Iran-Contra Insider*. 2001, Pray, MT: National Liberty Press.

McCool, D. The Subsystem Family of Concepts: A Critique and a Proposal. *Political Research Quarterly* 1998 51(2): 551–570.

McCullough, D. *Truman*. 1992, New York: Simon and Schuster.

Miller, A. *What Went Wrong in Ohio: The Conyers Report on the 2004 Presidential Election*. 2005, Chicago: Academy Publishers.

Miller, M. C. *The Bush Dyslexicon: Observations on a National Disorder*. 2001, New York: W. W. Norton.

Mills, C. W. *The Power Elite*. 1959, New York: Oxford University Press.

Morris, E. *The Fog of War*. 2004, Sony Pictures Home Entertainment.

Munson, R. *From Edison to Enron: The Business of Power and What It Means for the Future of Electricity*. 2005, Westport, CT: Praeger.

Nelson, P. F. *LBJ: Mastermind of JFK's Assassination*. 2010, Bloomington, IN: Xlibris.

Nixon, R. M. *Six Crises*. 1962, New York: Doubleday.

Noelle-Neumann, E. *The Spiral of Silence*. 1993, Chicago: University of Chicago Press.

Norton, A. *Leo Strauss and the Politics of American Empire*. 2004, New Haven: Yale University Press.

Olmsted, K. S. *Real Enemies: Conspiracy Theories and American Democracy*. 2009, Oxford: Oxford University Press.

Parry, R. *Lost History: Contras, Cocaine, the Press and Project Truth*. 1999, Arlington, VA: The Media Consortium.

Parry, R. *Trick or Treason: The October Surprise Mystery*. 1993, New York: Sheridan Square Press.

Pease, L. The RFK Plot Part I: The Grand Illusion. In *The Assassinations: Probe Magazine on JFK, MLK, RFK, and Malcolm X*, J. P. DiEugenio and L. Pease, Editors. 2003, Los Angeles: Feral House. 536–570.

Pease, L. The RFK Plot Part II: The Rubik's Cube. In *The Assassinations: Probe Magazine on JFK, MLK, RFK, and Malcolm X*, J. P. DiEugenio and L. Pease, Editors. 2003, Los Angeles: Feral House. 571–610.

Pentagon Papers: The Defense Department History of United States Decisionmaking on Vietnam. 4 vols. Senator Gravel Edition. 1971, Boston: Beacon Press.

Persico, J. E. *Nuremberg: Infamy on Trial*. 1994, New York: Penguin.

Phillips, C. Major Political Scandal Looming in the Bobby Baker Case. *New York Times*, 1964.

Pigden, C. Popper Revisited, or What Is Wrong with Conspiracy Theories? *Philosophy of the Social Sciences* 1995 25(1): 3–34.

Pipes, D. *Conspiracy: How the Paranoid Style Flourishes and Where It Comes From*. 1997, New York: Simon and Schuster.

Polk, W. R. *The Birth of America: From before Columbus to the Revolution*. 2006, New York: HarperCollins.

Polk, W. R. *Violent Politics: A History of Insurgency, Terrorism and Guerrilla War, from the American Revolution to Iraq*. 2007, New York: Harper Perennial.

Popper, K. R. *The Open Society and Its Enemies, Volume I: The Spell of Plato*. 1962, Princeton, NJ: Princeton University Press.

Popper, K. R. *The Open Society and Its Enemies, Volume II: The High Tide of Prophecy*. 1962, Princeton, NJ: Princeton University Press.

Raskin, M. G. Democracy versus the National Security State. *Law and Contemporary Problems* 1976 40(3): 189–220.

Rich, F. *The Greatest Story Ever Sold*. 2006, New York: Penguin.

Rogow, A. A., and H. D. Lasswell. *Power, Corruption, and Lies*. 1963, Englewood Cliffs, NJ: Prentice Hall.

Rohter, L. Havana Journal: Remember the *Maine*? Cubans See an American Plot to This Day. *New York Times*, 1998.

Russell, J. F. S. The Railroads in the "Conspiracy Theory" of the Fourteenth Amendment. *Mississippi Valley Historical Review* 1955 41(4): 601–622.

Savage, C. Obama Reluctant to Look into Bush Programs. *New York Times*, 2009.

Schmitt, C. *The Concept of the Political*. 1996, Chicago: University of Chicago Press.

Scott, P. D. *Deep Politics and the Death of JFK*. 1993, Berkeley: University of California Press.

Shenon, P. *The Commission: The Uncensored History of the 9/11 Investigation*. 2008, New York: Twelve.

Shirer, W. L. *The Rise and Fall of the Third Reich: A History of Nazi Germany*. 1959, New York: Simon and Schuster.

Shofner, J. H. *Nor Is It Over Yet: Florida in the Era of Reconstruction, 1863–1877*. 1974, Gainesville: University Press of Florida.

Sick, G. *October Surprise: America's Hostages in Iran and the Election of Ronald Reagan*. 1991, New York: Random House.

Sobieraj, S. White House Mail Machine Has Anthrax. *Washington Post*, 2001.

Spertzel, R. Bruce Ivins Wasn't the Anthrax Culprit. *Wall Street Journal*, 2008.

Strauss, L. *An Introduction to Political Philosophy*. 1989, Detroit: Wayne State University Press.

Strauss, L. *Liberalism Ancient and Modern*. 1989/1968, Chicago: University of Chicago Press.

Strauss, L. *Natural Right and History*. 1950, Chicago: University of Chicago Press.

Strauss, L. *On Tyranny*. 1963, Ithaca, NY: Cornell University Press.

Strauss, L. *Persecution and the Art of Writing*. 1952, Chicago: University of Chicago Press.

Strauss, L. *The Rebirth of Classical Political Rationalism: An Introduction to the Thought of Leo Strauss*. 1989, Chicago: University of Chicago Press.

Strauss, L. *Studies in Platonic Political Philosophy*. 1983, Chicago: University of Chicago Press.

Summers, A. *The Arrogance of Power: The Secret World of Richard Nixon*. 2000, New York: Viking.

Sunstein, C. R. *Going to Extremes: How Like Minds Unite and Divide*. 2009, New York: Oxford.

Sunstein, C. R., and A. Vermeule. Conspiracy Theories: Causes and Cures. *Journal of Political Philosophy* 2009 17(2): 202–227.

Tackett, T. Conspiracy Obsession in a Time of Revolution: French Elites and the Origins of the Terror, 1789–1792. *American Historical Review* 2000 105(3): 691–713.

Talbot, D. *Brothers: The Hidden History of the Kennedy Years*. 2007, New York: Free Press.

Tanner, H. Nixon, Back in Moscow, Debates Again. *New York Times*, 1965.

Tarpley, W. G. *9/11 Synthetic Terror*. 2005, Joshua Tree, CA: Progressive Press.

Toulmin, S. *Foresight and Understanding: An Enquiry into the Aims of Science*. 1961, New York: Harper and Row.

Tusa, A., and J. Tusa. *The Nuremberg Trial*. 1983, New York: McGraw-Hill.

Upton, L. Nixon's Reply to Russian Criticized. *New York Times*, 1965.

Waldron, M. FBI Chiefs Linked to Oswald File Loss. *New York Times*, 1975.

Walsh, L. E. *Firewall: The Iran-Contra Conspiracy and Cover-up.* 1997, New York: W. W. Norton.

Warren Commission. *Report of the President's Commission on the Assassination of President Kennedy.* 1964, New York: St. Martin's Press.

Webb, G. *Dark Alliance: The CIA, the Contras, and the Crack Cocaine Explosion.* 1998, New York: Seven Stories Press.

Weldon, D. The Kennedy Limousine: Dallas 1963. In *Murder in Dealey Plaza: What We Know Now That We Didn't Know Then about the Death of JFK,* J. H. Fetzer, Editor. 2000, Chicago: Catfeet Press. 129–158.

White, R. F. Apologists and Critics of the Lone Gunman Theory: Assassination Science and Experts in Post-Modern America. In *Assassination Science: Experts Speak out on the Death of JFK,* J. H. Fetzer, Editor. 1998, Chicago: Catfeet Press. 377–413.

Wiese, A., and M. Downing. Bush's Son Was to Dine with Suspect's Brother. *Houston Post,* 1981.

Wilford, H. *The Mighty Wurlitzer: How the CIA Played America.* 2008, Cambridge: Harvard University Press.

Wilson, J. *The Politics of Truth: Inside the Lies That Led to War and Betrayed My Wife's CIA Identity.* 2004, New York: Carroll and Graf.

Winkler, H. D. *Lincoln and Booth: More Light on the Conspiracy.* 2003, Nashville, TN: Cumberland House.

Wise, D. *The American Police State: The Government against the People.* 1976, New York: Vintage Books.

Witt, M. T., and L. deHaven-Smith. Conjuring the Holographic State: Scripting Security Doctrine for a (New) World of Disorder. *Administration and Society,* 2008 40(6): 547–585.

Wolin, S. *Democracy Incorporated: Managed Democracy and the Specter of Inverted Totalitarianism.* 2008, Princeton: Princeton University Press.

Wright, A., and S. Dixon. *Dissent: Voices of Conscience.* 2008, Kihei, HI: Koa Books.

≡ INDEX ≡

Printed in the USA
CPSIA information can be obtained
at www.ICGtesting.com
LVHW090248310124
770278LV00003B/4